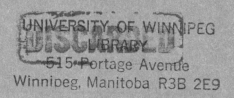

Savior, Savior, Hold My Hand

BOOKS BY PIRI THOMAS

Savior, Savior, Hold My Hand

Down These Mean Streets

T.

SAVIOR, SAVIOR, HOLD MY HAND

PIRI THOMAS

Doubleday & Company, Inc.

Garden City, New York

1972

ISBN: 0-385-00518-0.
Library of Congress Catalog Card Number 77-175401
Copyright © 1972 by Piri Thomas
All Rights Reserved
Printed in the United States of America
First Edition

DEDICATION

Thought about mucho kinds of dedications—and
like my corazón just settled peaceful-like to a dedi-
cation to all the people, past-present-and-future that
were-are-and-will-be willing to lay their lives down
for human dignity so that all can walk tall no matter
what their color may be.

CONTENTS

Born Anew at Each A.M

The street got its kicks, man—like a bargain shelf,
In fact, cool breeze, it's got more of a kick than
    anything else.
It's got sewers, man, like an eating mouth that swallows
    all the street can pour down its throat.
It's got windows, man, like eyeballs with glasses on
    and hope wearing an old overcoat.
It's got lights that shine up the dark parts and make
    the scene like new—
It's got stores, man, that sell what you don't need and
    never let you forget what you blew.
It's got shape, man, like a broad on her first put out—
It's got high powered salesmen who push pot and junk,
It's got mucho hustlers, man, who can swallow you up
    in a chunk.
Man, like we know what it's all about.

It's got class, man, that rings out like Barrio bells,
It's got brains, man, made up of a billion gray cells—
It's got heart, man, and shows it in its flung out shout,
It's got our most beautiful children playing make-believe games
    in terrible ghetto hells—
Hoping to survive until tomorrow, while ignoring the filth of
    garbage's most horrible smells,
Swinging together in misty darkness with love for everyone
    to share,

Smiling their Christ-like forgiveness that only a ghetto cross
*   can bear.*

The streets got life, baby, like a young tender sun,
And gentleness like a long awaited dream to come.
It's got beauty and dignity, man, that others have looked at
*   with scorn.*
Though sometimes it dies at night,
It's born anew at each A.M.
Diggit, man, like we know what it's all about!

Cara palo thoughts

Dark old streets and mucho things going.
Dig my stick, man, I'm made whole, I feel great.
Look into my big brown eyes and tell me I don't belong.
"I dare you punks," just say I don't belong.
Between my fingers, I'll break your dick string and
     become a man, superman, that is.

I'm gonna fling my elbows straight up and down,
I'm gonna walk tippytoes like I ain't got no wants,
I'm gonna stay half high always, so I can change my mind
     either way.
And I'm gonna make all the mañanas bend to my way of
     eating up my mind.

I got all the reason for being—
I'm no nothing that's gotta disappear—
I'm not just another square on a sidewalk street—
I'm not just another light bulb that'll soon go out.

I'm a voice who digs his scene, who makes his way.
I can shed tears with the best of them and smile also,
     like a champ.
I can flex all my muscles, baby, and can crack ten
     knuckles at a clip.
I can pick my nose and pare my toe nails with fingers
     so strong.

I can scratch my back to the thirteenth bone of my spine,
I can yawn like crazy, mundo, and I can swell with pride
    and lust.
I can hang my head with shame and like the sun, shine
    with dignity.
I can rub my balls and chase off some crummy fly.
I can pucker in disgust at a tenement's lousy rats
    and with coolness supreme, crush a muy grande roach.

I can drink sweet water or down a pint of wine.
I can inhale a morning air or a night that's truly mine.
I can laugh at a muchacha's joke or crush her loud lips down.
I can hear a cool old rumba or dig a crazy clown.

I can hate with the best of them or make love to the worst.
I can hold hands with anyone who friend wants to be,
Or spit in pure chiste in anybody's teeth.
I'm not just a lonely cat, for company I've got,
Just look anywhere around you or think of anyone
    you've forgot—
AND DIG ALL THEM PLACES THE SUN COULDN'T LIGHT UP.

1

God's gotta know I'm trying

I cut down Lexington Avenue. I couldn't help bouncing
Carlito inside my head. I kept seeing a moving picture of him
sitting up on that roof landing and shooting out his brains
and veins with doogie drugs—and how I had been like him.
And when I had been on drugs, he hadn't been like me.

My mind did a fast take backwards into tiempo-time, remembering he was Trina's cousin and his introducing us
made our falling in love come to be for real. It was a chevere
love while it lasted. Like real. But like going to prison does
a lot to break up the promises of swearing to love and waiting
for each other for ever and mucho ever.

I dug a kid running across the street. His face was fulla
hope. It almost blew my mind thinking how much the kid
reminded me of Carlito when he was all of twelve years
old and mucho happy, content to be our bat boy in our street
stickball games, wearing a dirty handkerchief apache style
around his forehead, copying us big guys three, four, five,
ten years older.

I couldn't help wondering, *dammit to hell, had he copied
using drugs from me? My God, I hoped to hell it wasn't
from me.*

I got some kind of strong urge to turn around and run

back up to the roof landing and to ask him point blank, "Hey, Carlito, diggit, lil brother. It wasn't me that put you on that shit kick drug? I mean, you didn't copy getting strung out from me, uh?"

I cooled my role, half-ass comforting myself by thinking, *hell, if he didn't learn it from this Piri, there were mucho other Piri's to git it from. Wow, Carlito, I feel so bad inside for you. Christ Almighty. What can I do? Gotta fight it somehow. Like fighting beats a blank. It's better than copping out.*

Gee, beat it, Carlito, por favor.

I hoped my prayer would reach his muy lonely-sick self sitting on that rooftop landing.

"Por favor, Carlito, get that drug not only out of your body, but out of your most chevere alma."

I stopped on 106th Street and Lexington Avenue to catch the bus to 118th Street, but then changed my breath and decided to shoe-leather it all the way.

I let my eyes cut into the poolroom on 108th and heard the rapping of pool balls as they made unfriendly contact. I walked in and dug the dinginess of lights and cigarette smoke, entwined with body sweat and quiet-like mumblings of, "Bet a man you can't sink that shot," and the light reply of a sure winner's arrogance, "Make that two bucks instead of one, and you're on, amigo." I eased my way down the side of the wall and sat on the long bench holding it up. I looked around for a face I knew. Seeing none, I settled for remembering the pale peeling yellow paint of the walls.

"Wanna shoot some eight ball?" someone called out to me. I looked up to see standing before me a young killer-diller, his hat coolly pushed back on his head. Surely this cat assumed that the world inside this poolroom was his. I remembered him as the "make that two bucks instead of one, and you're on, amigo."

"Why not, Bris?" I smiled.

I took off my coat, hung it on a wall hook and started to check on a pool stick, but with a quick afterthought, I reached into my coat pocket and copped my wallet, slipping it into the side pocket of my pants. I matched Bris's smile with a knowing one. The way I figured it there was enough temptation in this poolroom without my wallet adding to it.

Being last winner, Bris had the right of first break, but with his young blood's arrogance, he gently—kinglike—offered me the right to break first. I shook an equally arrogant "no" at him.

I walked out an hour or so later thinking how *chevere* it had been to play pool again and how much better King Bris had been at it. I felt about five bucks lighter and made a mental note to play for nothing from now on, at least until I got my pool stick back.

It was still kinda early to go home to Tia, so I let my shoes pull me back to 104th Street, cause diggit, even though me and my familia had lived all over El Barrio, 104th was the Queen Bee block for me.

What had been happening to my sweet land of dirty streets. Could I ever feel the kicks again? Had I outgrown them even if I tried to do them again? Was my sense of being a kid almost gone? It would be impossible to be the same Piri or Johnny Gringo in my heart.

I dug the kiddies playing tag, the cats with their dap vines making dance steps I never had seen, the chippies making cuerpos bonitos at their cool studs. I measured them against the cats and chippies from my time, and, man, we were out. We had grown up and it wasn't our world any longer.

Jesus, I thought, *my world done passed me by. During the six years I had spent in prison, the street never changed in my mind. Everything was the same. Nothing grew older. Nothing grew up—and here it is before my eyes, all changed.*

I looked at my face in the reflection of the bodega's window-panes and I realized I had changed also.

"Hey, Piri, is that you?" someone called out to me.

I turned and saw Crazy Horse, one of my old day amigos. He's changed, like mucho, I thought.

"Hey, Piri, you sure changed."

"Yeah, I guess I have," I said quietly. "We all have, huh?"

"You been out long?"

"Yeah." Six years, I thought. "I mean, no. Just a little while. What's been happening?"

"Lots of things. Mostly dope. Man, practically all the fellers are hooked. It's been hell. A lot of the fellers have gotten the big one, the fatal O.D."

As we talked, I spotted a familiar-looking face sitting on a stoop, nodding away.

"Ain't that Dynamite over there?" I asked. My God, the cat really looked wasted.

"Yeah, man, he's on it, too," Crazy Horse said.

"Hey, Piri," somebody else called.

I turned. It was Joe. I dug his haggard look, the "I'm hooked too" look, but we threw our arms around each other.

"Hey, baby," I said. "How's things going for you?" I added, "Looks like Junk has taken over 104th Street."

"Yeah," Joe nodded. "It's like all over plus bopping."

"People still rumbling?" I asked, like as if I didn't know.

"Lotta cats been busted, wasted, or burned," Joe informed me.

We walked over to the stoop of 115th Street right across

from one of the old tenement buildings I had once lived in. I noticed the condemned sign on it. All the windows were broken or boarded up. *You too*, I thought. *I left you in rotten shape with all kinds of memories and now I find you wasted, too. They took your heart out, and now they're gonna waste you brick by brick. It's about time. You wasn't nada anyway. Nada but a rent-collecting slumhouse run by that lousy landlord Mr. G.*

"Yeah, so like I was about to tell you," Joe added. For a minute I had forgotten he was even there. "A lot of the cats are dead."

"From bopping?" I asked, all the time still digging the wasted building, wondering how many people had lived in her before she died.

"No. Mostly from drugs."

"What's happened to The Happy Knights?" I asked, wondering what had become of our club.

"Well, man, you know how things change. The Happy Knights became the PRKs—Puerto Rican Knights. Then they were the Mystic Toppers, and now they're the Dragons and they're plenty big. Got Dragons all over Bronx, Brooklyn, all over."

"Yeah, everything changes, mostly from bad to worst. I wonder what happened to Fat Josie, eh?"

"Still fat," says Joe. "Yeah, she was not too bad-looking as a kid. Remember the story that got around when we were kids? An old man got to her and gave her a Coke with some knockout pills. He had her up his apartment and after she fell out, he took all her clothes off and busted her cherry."

"Yeah, I remember. She was about twelve years old. He really hurt her bad I heard. Blood and scum. All of that crap."

"A lot of guys have gotten to her since. Once I was copping from her in the backyard standing up and some m.f. threw some piss out the window at us."

"What cats O.D.ed?" I asked.

"Well, some of the guys you may not remember so good, cause they were only kids when you got busted."

Yeah, I thought, *I've been gone 600 years.*

"Wally was the first to go."

"Naw," says Crazy Horse, "Fifty was the first."

"Oh, yeah," says Joe, "that's right as a bomba." And the naming of the O.D.s began, and in my mind as they called off the names, I made the list of street war victims and the headings on the tombstones were like so:

"Twenty"—nickname
Italian cat
Age 19 years old—lived like a thousand other overdosers in a cellar basement on 104th Street, next to Police Station 23d. Super found him dead—summertime
Heroin

"Billy"—overdose
Age 18
Rooftop shooting gallery—on 107th Street
Away from home—Johnny Sweater was with him
Tried to save him—got warm water and salt and shot him up with the hope of speeding up circulation and pull him through—tried to give him warm milk
Slapping him hard—making him walk-slip-blip-too late
He died—O.D.
Heroin

"Tano"—a weight lifter's brother. A real hot shot—
On overdose kick—Stuff much too pure—
In a cellar—died
Heroin

Bobby Cruz—22 years
Overdose with Billie and Ropita on a roof
There was Bobby, Billie, and Ropita
Only Billie and Ropita came down
Bobby died—too much at one time
Heroin

"Next."

"Wait a minute," says one voice. "I've got something to say on Bobby Cruz and it's a damn shame. This is the way it happened. I don't give a hell who knows it, but when guys shoot up, together, they're suppose to take care of each other."

"Aw, cool yourself," says Crazy Horse.

"No, man. I remember before, when all us guys used stuff. If one didn't have, another would share and everybody would look out for everybody else. If a cat copped an O.D., well, everybody would try and pull him out, like with Tano. But with Bobby, it wasn't like that."

I looked up at the dark sky and heard the voice full of anger and despair at the lack of humanity and what had happened.

"Dig, Piri, Bobby got out of Riverside, where he went to kick the habit. I mean this was his first hook and he was gonna try to go right. So he made it to North Brother Island, to the 'kick factory.' So after he got the stuff out of his system, they let him come home on a pass. He didn't have no kind of habit. Some of the guys, Billie and Ropita, met him and joy-talked him into coming with them. Bobby had some bread, and they conned him into buying some stuff. It was good stuff cause I copped from the same pusher. Well, anyway, they make it up to the roof and there was some other cat they met on the way there and the four of them make it up to the roof. The first cat shoots up. Then Billie. Then Ropita. Well, damn man, these guys had a habit and could stand more. But Bobby was shooting off clean. Them bastards should have known better than to give Bobby the same dose they took. Well, my boy, Bobby O.D.s and falls out. The first guy and Ropita start slapping him around and dragging him all over the rooftop, but no dice. He won't come out of it.

"Well, instead of calling for help, them mothers take his watch, his gold chain, and about eighteen or twenty bolos. That damn Billie took everything from his dying body. Then they went downstairs and after a while called from the Park Avenue police call box. You know, the one on the corner there."

I looked and nodded yeah.

"The cops came up and brought him down, but it was too late. He was dead. I ain't never gonna forget that. Nunca. Nunca."

"Me either," Crazy Horse said.

"Not me either," say me . . .

"Many guys been busted since I've been gone?"

"Have they!" says Crazy Horse. "Plenty, Piri. Most of us been in one time or another, for the cure or for some jive bust, but not no long time like when you pulled them six. I just got back. I took a rap for my brother. Some broad got busted, or says she did and said my brother copped her cherry. But I got to her and told her to tell the Cop I was the one, and told her I could also find guys she was giving it up to for the longest time."

Crazy Horse laughed low and said, "I can see the D.A. trying to get me to cop out to statutory rape. Later for that. I told him, I ain't copping out to that. 'I can get mucho time for that.' I got word to that heba again and told her if she didn't get her story straight and I only pulled ninety days on Riker's and then nine months I owed at Coxsackie."

"Yeah, world sure got all kinds of breaks, diggit. I not only gotta report to my parole officer, but to a probation officer. Like I got two of them, one for a three-year probation, one for a nine-year parole."

"Whew, they sure got you up real tight."

"Yeah, but it beats a blank, better than being locked up. Cool it, amigos."

"Say, Piri, when you coming back?"

"I ain't never left."

"Yeah, that's right."

And all heads shook up and down in yes time.

I walked up Lexington Avenue, heading towards Tia's house. I went past the familiar local movie house. It was still there. Still old. Still called THE STAR.

I half chuckled, thinking of the long-ago days when as kids, we'd make out innocent-kiddie style with wet kisses and fumbling hands. There was nothing bad about that. Like how corrupt can little boys and girls be. The images on that wide-wild screen were doing their cosa thing to a much stronger degree, and like we were only copying.

I almost laughed aloud at a past memory. Some kid was mushing it up with his girl when somebody snatched him out of his seat. It must have been the girl's mother and she was screaming something angry.

"You dirty little son of a pig. If I ever catch your dirty hands on her again I'll—" and I could almost see the kid trying to defend himself while yelling out his justified cry of innocence.

Where was that mother at? Didn't she see that it was her little girl that had been climbing all over him? Oh well.

I found myself on 112th Street. I dug the bodega, and it brought back mucho bad memories of Jimmy, amigo panita Ramon, and me. I sat on the stoop across from the bodega, lit a cigarette, and soon a nightmare experience came back to me. There I was fighting to get out of some kind of hell. I was some kind of Puerto Rican Jesse James. I was getting shot and I was shooting. There was much blood and pain on both sides, and then I was getting my life saved at St. Vincent's Hospital and then, later on, there was a fast transfer to the Bellevue Hospital Prison Ward . . .

Time went by in the prison ward and like it had nada meaning for me except that I was getting stronger.

I was even making it to the toilet under my own power. But, man, did it shake me up the first time I dug myself in the mirror. Wow!!! I looked like one of the people who came out of some kind of concentration camp. *Man, do I need some arroz y habichuelas.* I smiled at myself in the mirror. Man!! I looked horrible. I walked slow-like out of the bathroom and sat in a chair and watched what was going on around me, and it looked like everybody in that ward was in mucho trouble, even the doctors and nurses looked like they were gonna do time and were nervous about going up before the judge.

"Hey, panin?" Someone had called out to me. I looked up. The voice was cracked.

"Hey man, no me conoce? Don't you know me?" My God, his hair was long and his eyes were wild, but cunning wild. It was Ramon.

"How you doing, Ramon?" I really didn't give a damn.

"Good, man, good. Hey, I read about you and some cats sticking up that joint and you getting burned and burning some cops."

I looked at him kind of shitty, like he didn't have to remind me that this was no nightmare. I knew it was for real.

"I got my little bit of troubles, Ramon, but like you got yours, too. I heard you and Jimmy held up that bodega on 112th Street and offed the bodeguero in the bargain. Like he's dead."

"Yeah . . . yeah, but no chair for me. I got it worked out. Like if you listen to me you can beat the chair too."

My blood went down to mucho below zero.

"What the hell do you mean I can beat the chair! You only get that shit if you kill somebody like. . . . ."

Ramon looked around suspiciously. Man, he looked around as if the whole damn world was watching.

"I thought you knew. I heard the cop died and that means the chair and . . . ."

"You're fulla shit," I yelled at him. My chest hurt with the effort, especially with my frozen blood. But I kept my face cara palo.

"Go screw yourself, Ramon. If you ain't got good news, shove the other kind up your culo."

"Hombre man, I'm sorry. Maybe I got it wrong, but just in case. Hey, got a smoke?"

I shook my head. He disappeared and came back with two tailor-mades, handed me one, and lit it ever so careful.

"Look, man," he went on. "Just in case the cop doesn't make it . . . . . ." I wished he'd stop looking all around him.

"You can beat the chair by going into a crazy act. Just like I'm doing, like all this looking around and acting crazy is just an act. Diggit, I got everybody so damn convinced that if I ask a dude for smoke or candy or some other shit, like I got it. Man, you don't refuse a nut, not unless you're crazy yourself, diggit."

And Ramon laughed just like some nut in a horror movie. *Concho,* I thought, *either he's a good actor or he really is stoned out of his natural head.*

"Look, panin."

I looked down at him. He was squatting by my chair.

"I'm looking, Ramon."

"Just act crazy. They can't kill a crazy person. It's against the law. They can only kill sane people. Diggit. Flip your wig, panin, it's your only hope."

"Hey, Ramon," a voice boomed at us. It was a seven foot two attendant, at least he looked that big to me from my dried-up height.

"What are you doing out of your cell?"

"I was to the head doctor."

"And where's the attendant who was in charge of you?"

"Damn if I know." Ramon laughed weird-like. "Maybe he got out on bail."

"Let's go, Ramon."

"Yeah, yeah." Ramon scuffled away, doing fighter's steps, jabbing lefts and rights, ducking hard lefts and roundhouse rights from some heavyweight challenger in his mind.

"Don't forget, panin, flip."

Wow, I thought, *he's gotta be a nut, nobody can be that good an actor.* And that thought went out the window with the thought, *You damn sure can be that good an actor if your life depends on it.*

The giant attendant came back and started to pass me, stopped and said, curious-like, "I read about your big splash!"

I just nodded.

"Ramon a friend of yours?"

I nodded a yeah.

"He got cucaraches up there." He smiled, pointing to his head.

I smiled at his brave translation of cockroaches into Spanish.

"You think so?" I wished that cat would go about his business.

"I know so. From time to time he shouts out at everybody that he's gonna eat his dinner and he keeps shouting till somebody comes and then do you know what that crazy guy does?"

I looked out the window, wishing Bellevue Hospital Prison Ward didn't have bars on its windows.

"Well, he's saved all his crap, you know, his shit."

"Yeah, I know, like what he defecates." I almost felt proud at one of my few big words.

"Yeah . . . yeah, well, he starts to eat . . . ."

"Hey, man, spare me the shitty details, uh?"

"Wow, I can tell you things," he continued. "Like doing masturbation in front of the nurses and—" I felt anger steaming up inside me.

"Hey, attendant, I wonder who's more crazy, him for doing them numbers, or you for getting your jollies outta repeating. His excuse is he's crazy. What's yours?"

The attendant's expression changed. He wasn't getting his kicks any more. Now he was angry.

"Just trying to be friendly," he said brusquely. "Hope you get it handed to you good. Hope they throw the whole damn book at you, wise guy," he snarled, then walked bad away.

"I might get lucky, they might throw the Good Book at me."

I stared out the window. *Sorry, Ramon,* I thought. *I'm not nuts, no how, no way . . . I think?*

Soon I had forgotten the incident and was back in now time. Back on the streets. I lit another cigarette and stared at the bodega. I thought about making it up to see Tia. Like she might be worrying. But somehow having thought about Ramon really beating the chair by being crazy and then being sent for mucho years to a nut house only brought Jimmy to mind. Jimmy was sent to Sing Sing ahead of me. That was the last time I saw him. He got the electric chair. But I had seen somebody who was mucho close to him when I was in Sing Sing.

I watched some people buying groceries, while at the same time debating if I should try to stop re-creating baddo memories. But my mind was on a "let-it-all-hang-out" kick. I went on thinking.

I remembered one of my first jobs in Sing Sing was in the Jobbing Shop. I was handed a mop. The mopping was painful because of my butterfly stitches. I did my besto.

I noticed some stacked-up green wooden boxes, and I mopped toward them. They reminded me of coffins. As it turned out they were coffins and they had names on them, like Martha Beck, Fernandez and some others. But the one that shook me up was the one that read: Jimmy Soto. Another con had seen me staring at it and he had said, "That's for them that's gonna fry."

I stood silent.

"You know," the con went on, "the ones that gonna get the electric chairs. Will ya look at the size of the one for

Martha. Man, she's a big woman. They say she weighs about three hundred pounds. That's a lotta beef to fry."

I didn't answer. I just pushed my twenty-pound mop so hard that even the pain from my stitches didn't hurt.

The months in prison had gone by quickly and we were lined up by the greenhouse, which was right next to the low-long red brick building known as the Death House.

I was hungry and wondering when the prison band would start playing a la John Philip Sousa, so we could begin the long march up the hill to the mess hall. Then I saw this little thin old-looking brown Puerto Rican woman come out of the Death House with some other people.

My God, I cried to myself, it's Dona Soto, Jimmy's mom. Her eyes caught mine, and mine caught hers. She stared at me and her expression when she saw me there dressed in prison gray at the head of the line was like a scream.

"Bendito, Dios-ssssss, you're here too, Piri. I'm so glad your madre is in heaven and cannot see you."

I lowered my eyes and looked into the greenhouse and saw different colored flowers. I looked up at the guards in their towers and then back at the Death House and at Dona Soto's eyes, who were still looking at me.

I smiled gently, as if to say, *How do you do, Señora Soto. How is the familia? Fine I hope*. Then John Philip Sousa's march began, and I marched past Dona Soto, and my hand waved to her un adios from waist high. I didn't look back. What was the use? Jimmy would die in the chair very soon, this week—and who knew how long I would be marching to John Philip Sousa's stirring music?

I got up off the stoop and, out of habit, dusted the dirt from my pants.

I know where Jimmy's at, I said to myself, but I wonder how Ramon is doing. I hear say if you ain't crazy when you get committed to them prison nut houses, you're sure to go crazy there. It's hard enough to keep your wig cool in the regular jail house.

I made my way to Tia's house and dug the dingy hallway lights, and as I climbed the long stairs, I had a passing thought like the night Jimmy and some others died in the electric chair. It wasn't like in the movies where when the switch is thrown and all the cell light bulbs grow dim and the convicts know exactly that it's happening. It ain't like that. The Death House got its own generator and our cell lights didn't even blink while Jimmy's and the others' lights grew dim.

Once I had put the past momentarily behind me and had made my way to Tia's, I felt sort of good and like secure. When Tia opened the door, she was smiling and telling me to come on in. As I walked into a kitchen, I could smell the rice and beans and frying chuletas (pork chops). I took my coat off, flung it on the sofa and sat down at the table.

"No te vas a lavar tus manos?" (Aren't you going to wash your hands?) Tia asked.

I looked at my blue pool-chalked fingers and smiling walked into the toilet and took care of business. I came back and ate like there were no more mananas. Tia waited for me to finish gritting and when I had drunk my good Cafe Bustelo, she started talking and I dug some kind of concern in her voice.

"Piri?"

"Yeah?" I didn't look up. The chow was like out of sight.

"Hijo, you've been in the poolroom, no?"

"You saw the blue chalk on my fingers, Tia. So you know it."

"But you know, hijo, that in places like that you get into trouble. It is places like that where you find all kinds of garbage, and you are not for that basura any more. You should go to church a little more. It is the best kind of life for you. You cannot forget all that El Buen Dios has done for you. He has—"

"Tia," I gently cut in. "I was just playing a few games of pool—like it was something I missed doing for a long time. I ain't got no kind of mente for doing what I done before."

"I know, hijo, but it always starts like that when one goes backways—a little thing at one time and before one knows it, he is back en un mundo de pecado, in a world of sin. Is your memory so bad, Piri? Have you forgotten all the infierno you have been through. None of those amigos of yours gave you so much as one little pensamiento when you were in the presidio."

I kept hearing her talk. I wanted to tell her to knock it off, that who better than I should know all the shit I had been through? But I didn't. Like she was right. I got up without saying a word and let myself drop heavy and lazy on the living room sofa.

She walked by me into her bedroom. I heard her rummaging around in her closet and then walk into the living room. I didn't look up—I made believe that the Spanish *Reader's Digest* I was reading was the most important thing in the world.

"Hijo, hijo, escuchame. I am speaking to you. Mira."

I looked up and my eyes grew mucho open. Like I didn't believe what I was digging.

"Si—I know you remember." She was holding a blue doe-skin suit on a hanger in one hand and a pair of blue suede shoes in the other. In the crook of her arm was a shirt.

I sat up and my face got up tight as I dug the clothes. They were caked with blood. I took the shoes from her hand and stared at them. They still were blood-crusted inside and out. I looked at Tia. She was holding the jacket and shirt. I saw the bullet holes. . . . . . I got a funny feeling in my stomach like ants running all around inside. . . . . . I felt like a long time ago.

"Why did you save those clothes all these years, Tia?" I screamed. I was angry yet somehow hurt, too. "Why didn't you burn them when I sent them back to you from Sing Sing? I don't like looking at them. Dammit, Tia."

I slammed my anger at the wall and heard the blue suede shoes bounce off the wall, watching each shoe going its own damn way in slow motion, one out the open window, the other behind a chair. I walked over to the window and watched some kids in the backyard looking up to see where one blue suede shoe had come from.

"Hijo, don't be angry. But I know Dios put it into my heart to save these clothes all this time for this one purpose."

"What kind of purpose, Tia? I mean it only brings up a lotta baddo memories."

"Exacto, this is the reason I save the clothes. So you can remember it all as clearly as it was happening now. It is easy for a man to forget, and to forget something as malo as this, will cause you not to have learned nada, and you will be in danger of falling into the basura again."

I thought a long time and when I turned around again, Tia was sitting on the couch sort of gently holding those stiff clothes to her bosom. I knelt before her and took her face softly between the outstretched fingers of my two hands. I dug her face. My mouth began to make sounds and I fought to make them come out as soft and gentle as her eyes.

"Tia," I said, "burn those clothes. I won't forget ever. I'm going to fight the garbage, like somehow for all of us. It's gonna be hard, but I'm gonna try." Tia interrupted, her hand was caressing my face.

"Piri, why you no come to my church?" I didn't answer and like got lost in some kind of thought.

Tia must have dug my thinking face, cause she just sat there cool and tried not to appear up tight.

Wow, I could understand her not wanting to see me blow the jewels again and find myself busted and once again long gone behind some malo gray walls called prison.

I wished badly that I could reassure her that I was with her a hundred per cent on staying free-side, whatever that meant.

Tia's fingers were busy fishing out long needles and some kinda thick thread, and her fingers were soon like with a mind of their own, taking care of creative business, knitting out some delicate doilies to decorate the backs of living room chairs.

"It is not too much to ask for you to visit my iglesia, is eet?" Her voice was madre warm.

I didn't answer. I just smiled, thinking about Tia's Pentecostal church and the visits I had made to it when I was a hundred years younger.

The most beautiful thing about the Pentecostals was their ability to pour themselves into the power of the Holy Spirit. They could blend—like nobody's business—into the words of the Holy Scriptures and do their best to uphold their conception of Christianity. It was a miracle how they could shut out the hot and cold running cockroaches and king-size rats and all the added horrors of decaying rotten tenement houses and garbage-littered streets, with drugs running through the veins of our ghetto kids. It was a miracle that they could endure the indignities poured upon our Barrios. I knew that every one of them didn't get weaker. They got stronger. Their prayers didn't get shorter. They got longer. Those who looked for God to come closer were blessed with El Bautismo del Espirito Santo, and they spoke a language that I could not understand. Tia had said it was the tongue of the angels, and only a few could interpret it.

Wow, I thought to myself. *If ever there were an escape this has got to be it. Is God gonna make it up to us in heaven?*

Caramba, I smiled, *maybe it ain't an escape, maybe like a sombre Pentecostal guy had once told me. Maybe, like he had said, they aren't interested in material wealth. God's Kingdom will provide enough for all in the sweet bye and bye. God's work and God's will be done. But shit. "How about starting here on earth, brother, with the nitty-gritty reality?" I had asked this Pentecostal guy. He had looked at me funny and had said, "God's Kingdom is not of this earth." "But we are," I had insisted. He just shook his head and walked away.*

"Tia?"

"Si, hijo." Her fingers never stopped knitting. But her eyes reached out to me.

"What does being a Pentecostal mean to you? I mean, like I'm asking without disrespect."

Tia smiled like always, sure and secure in her iglesia.

"It's what binds much of us poor Puertorriquenos together. It gives us strength to live in these conditions. It's like being part of a familia that is together in Christo and we help each other with the little materials we may possess." She talked on about us not having silver and gold but having instead peace in our corazóns and salvation as our goal.

Wouldn't it be better to have all four, I thought, not quite able to accept her religious jive. But for some strange reason I wanted to hear more.

I smiled gently, "Okay, Tia, I'll go to your iglesia and, Tia . . ." She looked straight into my eyes. "God's gotta know I'm trying, and trying beats a blank."

Tia kissed my hands and whispered in the most tender way, "Dios es amor."

God is Love, I thought. *Wonder why the hell we're such bad learners.*

"Piri, I will take these clothes down to the cellar in the morning and burn them to ashes in the boiler."

"Si, Tia, buenas noches."

I went to my room, laid down, and spent what seemed like a week just falling asleep, thinking about things like God is love and hate is garbage and a first night in Sing Sing.

Caramba, I thought, *I hope when I wake up in the morning I'm in Tia's house.* Soon I fell asleep, sadly dreaming of Sing Sing.

A first night in El Sing Sing prison

I stand on the hill, on top of the rocks,
I stand and I look and stare inside,
And remember, the whole, the mass, the past . . . .
I see the gray figures, like walking alone,
The blast of the then, the walking alive,
I look and remember . . . I was there with you once . . .

I was with you, I search into the building,
Many years ago break through the walls,
I see my cell block, my cell, my bunk, my wash bowl, my ca-ca
    bowl,
I see my grim bars, around and around,
The long march upward to the dining room mess.

I do not see them playing, I hear only the marching,
The long line, upward climb, a gray . . . a sea gray,
A mass of thousands of identities, thousands of locks, thousands
    of keys.
Look, I cry, the cells are open—
Wake up . . . I can't, I'm not asleep, I'm dreaming, Piri.
Can you hear the clicks of thousands of keys being turned?
The soft pad-pad of the back, the man, the turn of your back
    so he'll not see your face.

The gripping of the wash bowl—the dizziness will pass
Sit on your bowl . . . crap . . . move your bowels. . . .
Defecate . . . oh, man, do something, don't just sit there.
Make them shadow bars go away,
Count the bolts on your cell, how big is it?
$6 \times 9 \times 8$ . . . who cares?
It could be Grand Central Station, it's too small for me.

Smoke a smoke, read a book, plug your ear phones . . .
Shut out, drown out, don't listen, don't hear, don't look,
Don't let it get to you.
Forget the green dark pressure that pulls you in a short while
    back.
Forget the last hard-flung look before your back was trapped
    by a hard-flung gate,
Forget your loss of clothes, identity, forget your bug killing shaves,
And the spread your cheeks inspection, or lift your feet, puleese.

Forget the damp filled hell, no room in reception.
Forget the two matches left in the book,
And three tailor-made smokes.
Forget your splitting these in half
And now four matches and still three tailor-made smokes.

Forget laying on the dingy mattress . . . . . .
And inhaling time and no space.
Forget the damned feeling, the hammering damned feeling.
As === time roars in on you . . . .
Smashing the thought into your mind.
You drag your burning cigarette.
Oh, God, here it comes.
Fifteen fuckin' years . . . . of this.
      Gee whiz . . . Hope I make it . . .
       Got too . . .
        Got too . . .
         Got too . . .

2

Ain't there no way we can talk, pops?

When I called my sister Miriam, her voice sounded funny over the telephone. It was squeaky and full of static noises.

I laughed and made some kind of joke about like she sounded two years old.

"Give me your number and hang up, dopey—we got a bad connection. I'll call you right back."

"Okay, Sis." I hung up and looked out through the greasy glass of the phone booth and dug the street outside. Like the candy store I was standing in sure was some kinds of mucho years old. It smelled musty and sweaty and yet there was something about it, too, what with the memories of jillions of candies and ice cream sold or stolen. I scratched my nose and puzzled over the way a strong ray of sunshine burst through the aged window pane of the candy store and broke up into three parts to make room for the name, DANDY'S CANDY STORE.

The phone rang back at me. I snatched it up.

"Hello, Dandy's Candy Store. Who do you wish to speak to?"

"Who's this?" Miriam's voice asked. "Piri?"

"Yes, what can I do for you?"

"What are you out of your mind! I was suppose to call you back and . . . ."

"Ha Ha," I laughed. "Down, Hermanita. I was kidding."

Sis began to make talk. She wanted to know when I was coming over.

I tried explaining why I hadn't been there sooner. "I'm looking hard for work, and I wanted to wait till I got some things together, like clothes. But, anyway, I'm straight now and I'd like to visit . . . like when is it convenient?"

"Convenient!" Sis exploded. "What is it with this convenient! Now! Tomorrow! Anytime is convenient!"

"Okay. Chevere. How about mañana? It's Saturday."

"Sure. What time are you coming, Piri?"

"Does it make a difference?"

"Si, I wanted to know whether to cook breakfast, lunch, or supper."

"How about all three, Sis? How about me getting there around eight A.M.?"

"Bueno. We'll see you then."

"Uh, Sis?" I hesitated a minute, not sure how to ask the next question.

"Ahuh."

"Er," I hesitated. "How's Poppa?"

Sis was silent for a minute or so.

"Okay, I guess."

Her voice had begun to crack.

"Does Poppa know I'm outta prison?"

"Yes," she answered. Then she said nothing.

"What did he say?" I asked.

"You know Poppa," she explained. "He just shook his head up and down and said something like, 'no kidding' and something like, 'hope he learned his . . .'"

"Lesson . . ." I broke in.

Sis laughed. "If you don't show up tomorrow I'll . . . ."

"Damn, Sis. I'll be there."

I hung up the phone and dug a dusty reflection of my face. Like it revealed my mind was thinking up a storm. *Christ Almighty, Pops,* I thought, *is that all you had to say? "No kidding" and "hope he's learned his lesson." Wow, Pops. Don't you know I learned a whole lot of lessons in those six years of prison hell?*

A little fat Puerto Rican woman broke into my thoughts by rapping her dime on the plate glass of the telephone booth with much impatience.

"You got idea of living in there?" she smiled, kind of sarcastically but yet in a good-natured manner too. I opened the phone booth's rusty door, returned her smile, and stepped out. I dug how the three rays of sunlight had become one. Like the sun had descended and it no longer split up by the window's sign, DANDY'S CANDY STORE.

I side-stepped a kid whose funky street-dirt fingers were tearing the hell out of a dusty wrapper that hid a Milky Way Bar.

His eyes gave me a dirty look while his mouth and teeth were grinning as the dandy bar made a fast chopped-up exit down his big mouth.

I started to bad look him back, but changed my mind. That nine-year-old kid probably thought I was gonna cop his dulce (candy).

I satisfied myself with buying a Milky Way.

I walked over to the stoop and leaned against the railing and gently removed the wrapper. The candy was sweet like the kind that could be found in DANDY'S CANDY STORE.

As I stood there, I watched the street scenes going by and swallowed the last of the sweet candy that somehow had copped a bittersweet taste.

I rolled the candy wrapper between my palms into a tiny round ball. Then I made a mock basketball from it and threw it towards an overflowing garbage can. It landed on an edge, teetered for a second and fell, to become part of the garbage on that already littered sidewalk and the street. I picked it up, in part because I didn't want to add to the garbage-covered streets and in part because I didn't dig missing an easy basket. I tried my throw again . . . and smiled with mucho satisfaction. Like this time it scored, making itself snug inside a smelly sardine can. I felt some minor sense of triumph—but only for the minute, because as I walked away my mind kept mumbling to itself, *"Dammit—ain't there no way we can talk, Pops? Ain't it about time we became tight-ass buddies instead of just father and son?"*

The Saturday morning sun shone brightly as I walked up to Sis's house. The door to the kitchen was opened and I heard the noise of laughter, plastic dishes, and the boiling of Cafe Bustelo.

Sis's kids Cherry, Alice, and Donny jumped up and made all kinds of hugs and "Hi, Uncle Piri."

"Kick off your coat and sit down," Sis told me. Her husband, Don, shook my hand and by the time I threw my coat on the sofa, eggs, coffee, and the whole bit were waiting for me.

After breakfast we watched some television and I kept looking out the window.

Don made some light conversation. The two of us had yet to feel fully at ease with one another. I couldn't forget that the cat was, after all, white.

"So how's it going?" he asked.

"Like Chevere." I smiled.

"Working?"

"A-hum. Not yet." I smiled.

"I see. Hey, you took up brickmasonry, didn't you? In—"

"Yeah. In prison." I finished the question that was embarrassing Don.

"I'm sorry, Piri." He looked even more embarrassed.

You shouldn't, I thought. *You wasn't the one to do the time.*

"Hell, Don, what's there to be sorry about? Tell ya what. Don't let it get to you and it won't get to me." We both smiled.

"Yeah," I went on, "but I can't seem to get work as a mason because of the union and other things."

"What other things?" he asked.

I looked out the window and felt some kind of rising resentimiento make its hot way out from behind my belly button.

How in the hell was I gonna say it nice and easy to my white brother-in-law that I couldn't get into the Bricklayers Union because it was a closed union? Closed to non-whites, like to dark-skinned Puerto Ricans like myself. How was I gonna run it to him that that made it almost impossible? How was I gonna explain it to him that the last of the locks being turned against me was that my brickmason's certificate had come from Comstock State Prison.

I couldn't explain and so I settled for a smile.

"Well," I said, "things like . . . well, like a father gotta belong to the union and his kids can get into it on account of that. You know, the father and son to the father and son shit."

The little word "SHIT" made Don's eyes look funny. I guess it was because it came out hot and heavy in capitals.

I looked out the window for a while, half talking to myself. "Union sometimes can be full of shit," I said.

Don soon eased the tension that was building up in our conversation. "Say, Piri," he said, "I've been wanting to make a brick front in the kitchen for a built-in oven and an arch. How about giving me a hand?"

"Like when?" I was eager already.

Don was good at whatever he tackled. He probably needed my help like a hole in the cabeza.

"Like next Saturday."

"Chevere," I laughed.

"And we can fix up a price between us . . ."

"Nunca," I grinned. "This is like a como con amor for all of you. You can't pay for that."

"It's a deal." Don's handshake closed around my own.

Strangely, as we shook hands I couldn't help digging out the whiteness of his skin. It accentuated the darkness of my own. I tried to make my eyes noncommittal as they searched his face for even the smallest amount of insincerity or prejudice on his part, like white skin being always such a burden on my back. It was hard to fully trust him, brother-in-law or not. I tried to ease my own inner tension by reminding myself that my enemy didn't have to be just white. He could be any color. But that thought came to mind weakly. Ah hell, I finally punched the thought in the mouth. *Everybody's got the right to prove where he's at.*

"Deal?" I smiled and squeezed a handshake like for real, yet tacking on a question mark just in case.

Some coffee came. Morning became afternoon and evening cut in after that.

"Bueno, Sis, gotta be moving." I moved into my coat and said a beau-coup adios. They wanted to drive to the station.

But I wanted to walk. Like it had been a long time since I walked through that part of Babylon.

I felt Sis's eyes on my back. I got to the road and turned and dug Sis looking at me.

Funny, I thought, she reminds me a lot of Mommie.

I made a sign with my finger and she walked to where I was.

We stood quiet for a while. Sort of looking at each other and around each other. I looked over her head and quietly asked, "Why wasn't Pops here, Sis?"

"I don't know, Piri."

"Did you tell him I'd be here? Does he still live at the same place?"

"Yes, I told him. He knows where you're living, too."

Sis wasn't looking at me any more. I noticed her finger brushing away a noisy nosy mosquito.

"I guess he was busy or something," she said.

"Yeah, I guess so."

"Piri, maybe it's as hard for him to get to you as it is for you to get to him or . . . something. I've had my own problems with Pops."

I smiled at her. Then I gently pinched her nose.

"See you este Sabado, this Saturday." I said good-by again.

While I waited for the train at the station, my eyes focused on a maroon-colored house two blocks away.

I was still watching Sis's house as the train moved off. I knew that of the two or three moving figures in the yard at the maroon house, one of them was my father.

I ran a thought to him. Ain't there no way we can talk, Pops?

3

All-around man

Gotta get me a job. Gotta get me a job. Like any job. I fell
flat asleep with that chant running thru my mind. Mingled
with my chant was that of my parole officer: "Did you get
a job yet . . . did you get a job yet? You gotta have a job.
You're on parole . . . you're on parole . . . you're on
parole."

When I woke up the next morning and as I dressed quietly,
the chant was still ringing in my ears. I looked at the clock.
It was smiling a 7:30 A.M. I made a strong cup of Cafe
Bustelo. I sipped it, made a face on account it was too hot
and I had forgotten to brush my teeth. While the coffee
cooled, I brushed my teeth with care, digging myself in the
mirror.

I did all kinds of numbers, like gargling, letting the gargle
go down as far into my throat as I dared without throwing
up. I stopped being a daredevil when I began to gag. I looked
at myself in the mirror and smiled as tears forced out of my
eyes on account of my stupid gargle game.

I walked out into the kitchen and swallowed my good-o
Bustelo coffee and then gargled again, but this time without
living dangerously.

I hit the candy store and bought the New York *Times* and
El Diario. Went back to my stoop and like many other

mornings since I had gotten out of prison, I turned to the want ads and looked immediately under CONSTRUCTION. Like my eyes were looking for one of the ads to say: BRICK MASONS WANTED, but most of it read, *Construction Engineers Wanted* . . .

ELECTRICIANS	UNION
PLUMBERS	UNION
CARPENTERS	UNION

My eyes caught a *Brick Mason Wanted, Tall-Build Construction Co Union.*

"Aw shit," I said out loud. "Hey, here's something. *Construction Work Overseas.*" Fat chance, I thought. Like I gotta almost get permission to cross the street.

People were coming out of the building on their way to work. I scrunched my behind to the corner of the stoop.

"Ah, buenos dias, Piri."

I looked up. It was Mrs. Lopez, middle-aged, short, chubby, and, like always, very cheerful. She taught Sunday School at Tia's church. As I watched her eyeing me, I braced myself for a short sermon on how come I wasn't visiting the church.

"Er, Piri," she started in her good-natured way. But I cut her off mucho fast in self-defense.

"Como esta, Señora Lopez? Going to work?"

"Si. You don't haf job yet, Piri?"

"Uh-hu," I shook my head.

"Lessen, where I work, they are looking for a . . . how you say . . . all-around man."

"All-around, Mrs. Lopez?" I smiled.

"Si. You know. Delivery, giving out material to the sewing machine operadoras, cleaning, going out for lunches and coffee."

"I don't know, Mrs. Lopez. I'm trying to find work as a bricklayer."

"Bricklayer?" She didn't understand.

"Albañil," I said, helping her out in Spanish.

"Oh si, oye. That is good monee . . . Bueno. Bueno suerte. I have to go now. Give my love to your Tia. Oh," she smiled, "when you coming to visit church?"

"Pronto, Señora Lopez. Hasta luego." I smiled.

I watched her slowly making her way towards Lexington Avenue, and I mulled over her words, All-Around Man . . . All-Around Man. My mind was quick thinking about the mucho past mornings of getting up, buying the New York *Times*, going to construction sites, asking for a job as a brickmason or as a brickmason's helper or a brickmason's apprentice. Hell, even brickmason's water boy. I had even gotten close a few times to copping a job.

I remembered the closest.

A construction company was putting up low-income projects right in my Barrio. I had walked up to an Italian-looking heavyset guy.

"Say," I smiled. "You the foreman?"

"Yeah." He looked straight at me.

"I'm looking for a job."

"Doing what?"

"Bricklaying."

"Got any experience?"

I went for broke.

"Lemme show you." Before he had a chance to say anything, I picked up a trowel and laid six bricks without touching the line, cut the mortar off as pretty as a Madison Avenue barber, jointed with a conductor's stroke, and smiled at the foreman . . .

"Didn't even smear the bricks." I laid the level on the side and then let it lay on the top, the bubble was dead on level.

"Not bad, kid . . . Union?"

The tight look around my mouth told him.

"Not in. You trying?"

My head nodded up and down. You better believe it.

"Try for apprentice?"

"Yeah, Mac." I spread my hands out to him. "You must know how it is with the union."

"Yeah, I know, but there's ways of getting around that. I might be able to help, but you probably hafta start off like an apprentice. But you shouldn't have no trouble. You lay bricks like an old-timer. Where did'cha work before? There ain't much non-union bricklaying going on, not if the union can help it."

"Around. I worked different places."

"Where? Cause they'll wanna know, you know, like for reference."

"Uh, upstate, near Syracuse."

"Non-union?"

"Yeah," I smiled, "non-union."

"You work on different construction gangs?"

"Naw, just one." I was trying hard not to lie to this hombre, like I had a really chevere feeling he wanted to help me.

"How long?"

"Does it make a difference?" My eyes looked at the trowel and at the bricks and mortar and they seemed to be getting further and further away.

"Hell, yes, son, the more time you've put in bricklaying, the better it is, specially when it was steady with one construction company. It shows you're steady and dependable when they keep you on, and like especially if they're non-union."

I wanted to laugh. Like this was a not-for-real scene. My

mind thought up mucho fictitious construction companies, so that I could shoot out a lie.

I looked at the bricks. I stole a couple of seconds lighting up a smoke, took a deep breath, and let it out Gung Ho, with some kind of intermingled thoughts of, "AND THE TRUTH SHALL MAKE YOU FREE." I looked him dead in his Italian eyes and, trying not to feel ashamed of it or proud either, I told him soft—but clear like, "Look, I'm not gonna con you. I worked with bricks for about four years or so. Like steady. But it wasn't with no construction company. I learned brickmasonry at Comstock State Prison during a six years outta fifteen year bit. I gotta certificate of Brickmasonry with thousands of hours of practical and theory experience. In fact, I became a bricklayer instructor. I can do damn near any type of construction, brickwork and . . ."

The foreman's head nodded and like his mouth started to say something but I cut in . . .

"And I got about eight more years to do on parole. And like if I could get in, even as an apprentice, my parole officer could vouch for me as well as other people that know me and . . ."

"What were you in for?"

I laid it out natural-like.

"Armed Robbery, Attempted Armed Robbery. Felonious Assault with intent to kill . . ."

"Jesus Christ, kid." His eyes were looking dead into mine. "The union is tough to get into. I won't go into the crap involved. It was gonna be hard to get you in, being straight, but having been in the can, that blows it, kid. There's guys trying to get in that could be priests and aren't making it and . . ."

"Damn, damn, damn." I could feel crushing disappointment spreading over my face. I pulled a grin from out of my guts and gave the foreman a half-salute in a way of saying, thanks anyway, and started to walk away.

"Hey, kid," he called.

I looked back at him, casually checking out his heavily lined face. He stood stiffly, almost rigid as a board. He seemed strangely ill at ease, a bit out of place standing there in his cement-plastered coveralls.

"Why doncha try something else? There's udder things. You can make it. I'm sorry, I don't wanna fool ya, but you got as much chance as a snowball in hell. Someday things'll change." He rubbed his nose with a hand that had a hundred pounds of calluses on it.

"Thanks anyway, mister. I appreciate you're being straight with me."

"Hey, kid, like I got experience with jails. I don't mean I was in but my brother-in-law did time."

"OK, mister." I smiled. "I know ya understand."

I walked off the construction site and looked back at all the building going on. I barely heard the foreman yelling at me.

"Hey, kid, keep batting."

I waved back and walked off thinking, *I will, paisan,* but like I got a baddo feeling my bat got mucho holes in it.

I came back to now time and dug Mrs. Lopez making the right turn at the corner heading for the Lexington Avenue IRT. I jumped off the stoop, stuffed the New York *Times* into the garbage can, shoved *El Diario* into my back pocket and ran like hell after Mrs. Lopez, laughing and thinking, "Look out, mundo, here comes the all-around man."

I caught up with Mrs. Lopez.

"Señora, oye, señora." I puffed my way up to her.

"Que pasa, Piri?" She looked a little alarmed.

"Is it all right if I go with you for that all-around job?" I asked. "Think it's taken?"

"I don't theenk so, Piri. They don't stay too long on that job."

Holy Mother of the Lord, I thought. Must be some kind of work in some kind of salt mines.

We got to a raunchy-looking ten-story building and a tired, jerking elevator jerked us up floor by floor to number ten. The elevator man, as on every floor, missed his stop, like stopping two feet below or two feet above the floor.

"Cat really needs a level," I said, but the elevator man had a chevere sense of humor. I remembered his Puerto Rican accent as he stopped on every floor . . .

Theese is Ponce. . . .
     next floor
Theese is San Juan. . . .
     next floor
Theese is Mayagüez. . . .
     next floor
Theese is Fajardo. . . .
     next floor
Theese is Aguadilla. . . .
     next floor
Theese is Carolina. . . .
     next floor
Theese is Jayuya. . . .
     next floor
Theese is Caguas. . . .
     next floor
Theese is Santurce. . . .
     next floor
Theese is San Germán.

We got off at San Germán and I smiled at him and said, "Oye, how come you didn't mention Bayamón. Like that's where my people are from?"

He smiled and said, "Don't worree, thas the next floor."

"Caramba, man, like that's el rufo . . ."

The elevator man grinned. "Si, don't complain, Bayamón is close to heaven."

"Chevere." I tapped his shoulder with love.

Mrs. Lopez led me through the most chaotic scrambled-up skirt-making factory I had ever dug. All the women, about fifty of them, were roaring away at their sewing machines like their lives depended on it and, como, like it did. Cause I found out they were doing piece work and that's like if you don't produce, you get no juice. I felt my face put on a disgusted look, like legalized slavery. The pay for each skirt was so low the operators had to tear the heart out of their sewing machine motors to come out an inch above defeat. Memories came back to me of mucho, but mucho times when I saw Mommie coming home bent and weary after long hours of hassling packed subways and roaring heartless sewing machines.

I noticed one thing though. The women, most of whom were Puertorriquenos, damn near drowned out the deafening noises of the motors with their yakking. Caramba, it was a joy (almost) to listen to about fifty women trade gossip like it was going out of style. Talk about put-ups and put-downs. Their tongues were mucho sharp, and dirty linen was being pulled out of all kinds of closets. Yet it was friendly talk and I had the feeling they yakked to take their minds off aching backs and fingers that had been run through by mucho sewing machine needles, not to mention the screaming yelling boss-o, who I dug was making his way toward Mrs. Lopez and me.

He was digging his watch and como like his eyes fastened on pobre Mrs. Lopez with a . . . you are late again and ought to be shot at dawn.

Mrs. Lopez smiled at him and offered me as a sacrificial sign of peace.

"Mr. Greenstein, I breeng you an all-around man."

I had been feeling so damn angry and frustrated that I was determined not to lose my sense of humor, so I smiled an all-around smile at Mr. Greenstein, who was built like a tough, little ornery bull and had practically not a hair on his cabeza. In the meantime he looked me up and down and grunted, "You is speaking English?"

"Yes, sir, Mr. Greenstein. I am quite proficient in its usage."

My mind did a quick flash back into prison time, when all my English was mixed in with street talk and when the first big words I had learned had come from a college kid who was doing time for murder. He and his girl had killed her mother and put her in a bathtub with a cover of plaster of paris. I mouthed the words over in my brain, *manifestation and conglomeration,* and how I had walked around the prison yard socking my newfound knowledge by telling my prison amigos, "Hey, diggit, I am a conglomeration of a manifestation of myself."

"And you can maybe talk Spanish also?"

"Pure Spanish no, but I can handle Puerto Rican."

God, but my face was straight. I wanted to burst out laughing.

"You are not being afraid of hard vork?"

"No, I'm not, Mr. Greenstein. If the pay is fair."

Mr. Greenstein must have had eyes in the back of his head cause he turned around like grease lighting and his roaring voice grabbed two women by the throat who had stopped sewing and were involved in something important, like a little friendly yakking session.

"Vot am I goink to do?" he yelled to them. "Maybe I should pay you joust to speak." The two women dove for their machines and roared away in a dead heat and Mr. Greenstein's voice unwrapped itself from around their throats.

"The pay is forty dollars a week. You vork forty hours. Time and a half for doing overtime. You ever vork as all-around man?"

Probably have, I thought, just ain't recognized it.

"Sur have. What do I have to do?"

"You vanting job?"

"Yes, sir, Mr. Greenstein."

Mr. Greenstein was about to say something to me when suddenly he stopped, his eye dead fixed on Mrs. Lopez. All this time she had been standing beside us like one of the gang, smiling and nodding in agreement at everything said. Mr. Greenstein's eyes looked like they couldn't believe that they were looking at fat little Mrs. Lopez, who was feeling that she was in like Flynn with Mr. Greenstein for having brought him an all-around man.

"Mein Gott, since ven you becomink mine partner? You vorking here yet or maybe you got plans for retirement?"

Mrs. Lopez's bubble of democratic comradeship blew up and she moved away so fast that by the time Mr. Greenstein gave me his warm attention again, she had socked six skirts through the sewing machine.

Mr. Greenstein nodded warmly and with mucho approval. Then in a very friendly manner, he told me, "She is von of our best vorkers. I am loving them all, but got to keep on top or no producing. Hokay, you start now."

I nodded a "Si, señor. What do I do?"

"Goot, this is nice place to vork in. You vork, nobody bod-
der you. You sweep place out at closing time. That's a half
hour or maybe one hour overtime if you're slow."

My eyebrow did a pick up at the warning sound of "one
hour overtime if you're slow."

"In the morning," he continued, "you put the garbage out,
store material, and you keep the goils busy with bundles. You
learn sizes. You hang skirts. You make delivery. You get
lunch for anybody who vants. You know anything about
sewing machine motors?"

"Er, not too much," I answered, unsure whether or not
he would hold my ignorance of machine motors against me.

"Don't vorry, I'll teach you."

God, I thought, I'm gonna be a machine mechanic, too.

"And you help my partner to stretch cloth for cutting.
That's him."

My eyes followed his pointed finger to a cutting table,
where a thin man with a beard and a skullcap on his head
was sadly stretching cloth by himself.

"He's my partner. He also is a rabbi and my brother-in-
law."

God, I thought, *you sure got this cat sewed up.*

"Go and tell him you is helping him."

I spent the rest of the day running around and stretching
cloth. El Bosso, Mr. Greenstein, spared no one, not even the
partner-rabbi and brother-in-law combination, the blessing
of his roaring mouth. But it was always in his own language.
The partner must have gotten bawled out a couple hundred
times. Towards the end of the day he was completely insult-
whipped.

I stood on the other side of the table smoothing my side
of the cloth while he took care of his with a quiet, patient-

like dignity, when all of a sudden he caught a blast in his
ears from Mr. Greenstein about having laid out a layer of
green material instead of blue.

The poor combination in front of me took it like a champ.
When Mr. Greenstein cut out, I looked up from the cloth
at the way-out sound of a pent-up expelling sigh. It was
the combination. He murmured, sad-like, "Svear tsuzien a
Yid."

"What does that mean?" I asked muy friendly.

He nodded his head sadly and with a dying smile answered, "It's hard to be a Jew."

I let out a deep sigh and smiling compassionately said,
"Sveare tsuzien a Puerto Rican too."

The combination laughed.

There was some kind of strong instantaneous friendship
established between us for a moment. Perhaps it was because
we both knew the feeling of insults. I checked myself out
at getting to like him. Man, he was making mucho dinero
while getting insulted, while the rest of us workers were
getting mucho exploited. I stopped laughing and he turned
off likewise. I stared at his intense, thinly bearded face. He
adjusted his skullcap and grunted.

"Vell, let's get to vorking. Much to do . . . much to do."

"Yeah!! Ain't there?" I thought and went on spreading
red cloth on top of different colored cloths.

Caramba! Mrs. Lopez wasn't kidding when she said all-
around man. I think it would have been more chevere for
her to have said, all-around superman.

My parole officer was pleased I was taking care of business
with my newfound slavery. He even nodded approval when
I told him I was thinking of getting a part-time job three
nights a week at Macy's, cause like after taxes, social se-

curity, living benefit, death benefits, subway, lunch, my share
to Tia, the forty-eight bucks (with overtime) got so chewed
up, I kept feeling I owed somebody money. So the months
rolled by and at the night job I was spotless, dressed up like
a general, pushing an elevator up and down and shouting
out things like:

First Floor . . . . . . Women's Underthings
Second Floor . . . . . Men's Underthings
Third Floor . . . . . Anything at all

As a matter of fact, I felt a little superior every time I
stepped in the elevator at Mr. Greenstein's factory.

"Hey, Panchito."

"Si, Hermano." The Puerto Rican elevator man would
smile.

"My elevator at Macy's is like a Cadillac compared to your
Ford-thing-go," I would say.

"Perhaps," he would grin, "but mine goes all over Puerto
Rico, where does yours go?"

"Mine goes to women's underthings . . . men's underthings . . . and anything at all."

We played the game mucho times, but like it wasn't a
funny thing inside. At least not for me. The factory and the
elevator job both kept me dead tired, and I could hardly
save up any bread.

Wow, Mr. Combination Partner-Rabbi and Brother-in-Law,
sveare tsuzien . . . dammit to hell, why can't I lay bricks?

Anybody can hang up a skirt or push an elevator, but not
everybody can lay down a leveled brick.

How about that for an all-around man?

4

Gee, pops, glad to see you again

One Saturday I was working on the brickwork at Sis's. It was looking good, like almost finished.

Don, Sis, and the kids had gone out on some errands, and I quietly went about my work.

I laid bricks on carefully. I cut them with mucho precision for the arch, and troweled and lost myself in mortar, bricks, and level. I was using my level more than needed, but I wanted to make sure all would be perfecto when finished.

"Looks pretty good," a voice hit at my back.

I turned my head and looked over my shoulder. I dug Pops standing in the kitchen doorway. Jesus Christ. Like I couldn't quite believe it at first. I looked at him. Poppa's hair was nearly stone white. He was still lean and wiry-muscled, but he seemed a little shrunken. It was as if the years had absorbed some of his body moisture. His face was still like smooth brown leather and there was not a wrinkle in sight. But, like time's got a way of whipping on the young until they're finally old. I got up almost instantly. "Yeah, it's coming along pretty good," I mumbled, looking at my brickwork.

I wiped my hands, and we moved toward each other to shake hands. I dug he still walked lightly and with ease, like a much younger man. We took each other's hand, even made some kind of brave attempt to put our arms around each other.

"Glad to see you out, Piri."

"Glad to be out, Pops."

Poppa smiled, "It's been a long time, boy, since we've seen each other."

I picked some drying cement off my bare arms. "Yeah, Poppa. Except a few years back. I think, when you came with the family to visit me in prison . . . We both were quiet for a while.

"But like we didn't have too much to say then," I went on. "I guess it's been about fifteen years since we really have said much to each other. . . . . Uh . . . Jesus," I finally blurted out, "you're looking *good*, Poppa."

Pops ran his fingers through his hair. "I feel pretty good," he laughed, "except for a few gray hairs."

I laughed. "You gave up pulling them out, eh? Hey, remember when I was a kid how you use to give me a coupla pennies to pluck your gray ones out?"

"Yeah, but there weren't that many then, feller. I couldn't do that now. I'd be bald as a cucumber."

We laughed and then got hung up in some kind of what-to-say-next silence.

"Hey, I see you learned a trade, uh?" Pops suddenly said, pointing to the brickwork.

"Yeah, Poppa!"

"It's a great trade, a whole lot of construction going up and it pays good, too."

"Sure does, Poppa."

"I guess you're set now."

"Yeah, Poppa. Now all I've got to do is break into that goddamn union."

Poppa looked at me and said, "Yeah, they are kind of hard to get into."

"God damn it, Pops. What are we bullshitting about? You know damn well we're shut out."

Pop sat down at the kitchen table. I sat across from him and stared at the brickwork.

"Pop, before I even got out of prison, I was planning to go into brickmasonry. I even wrote my brother James in the Army to save his money and we'd go into a partnership. Like he knows construction."

"He's a pretty good carpenter," Poppa broke in. "I hope he's okay."

"Pops, when I got out of jail, I busted my ass going from construction company to construction work. God, like all kinds of buildings are going up and all they said was, are you in the union? When I told them no, they shot me down with their ready-made sorry but . . . Pops," I said, looking at the brickwork. "When I finally got a job with a construction company, I told them what I could do. They put me to work—guess at what, Poppa? digging, just digging. I dug in that hole like a mole, Poppa, grinning all the time my back was breaking up with knots of pain, cause I figured I was on my way. Como, like from shit laying to bricklaying and diggit, Pops, at the end of the week, the hole was finished and so was I. The blanco-hombre handed me a brown envelope with ninety-three bucks worth of green money in it and said, 'You're a pretty good worker.'

"I smiled a back-broken smile and told him, 'I'm better at laying bricks.'

"Poppa, like his eyebrows raised a little and he handed me

the brown envelope along with 'Are you in the union?' And when I told him no, the usual came out, 'Sorry, gotta be in the union.'"

Poppa got up and casually inspected a piece of mortar I had forgotten to trowel off. He picked up the trowel and cut it clean from the bricks and then tapped the brick even. Like he must have at one time done his thing with brick and construction. He looked at me, and I saw a sad, melancholic smile on his face.

"I've been through that route, *son.*"

My ears perked up. Caramba, it had been a long time since he had called me *son.* I silently looked at him.

"God damn, I wish you could really know just how God damn hard it was, Piri." Poppa picked up the jointer and finished the bonds like an expert.

"Did you try the union?" he asked. His voice was soft.

"One time."

"And . . ."

"And the guy there said like the books were closed and they weren't accepting any more members. But I got it straight from a Puerto Rican that the books were closed to certain people and them people were us. The only thing open was pick and pala. Pick and shovel . . . and that was only if they couldn't get their own kind to take care of that business."

"Son, do you remember when you was a little kid and I'd come in from work all torn up and damn near frozen to death?"

I nodded, thinking about the mucho times I had dug Poppa putting on double pants, double shirts and sweaters and double heart to make a freezing cold scene at 4 A.M. in wintertime, sometimes softly cursing or sometimes maybe softly praying.

"Well, just to get even that job, I had to damn near beg. And the God damn truth was that even then I refused to admit it, I did beg, son. I Did Beg. Not on my hands and knees, but with a smile that wasn't there. I felt like a dog wagging his God damn tail in gratitude for some kind of bone. I knew, though, that if I didn't, there were a hundred men with hungry families behind me willing to outdo me just to get the job. For God-sakes, son."

Poppa's voice was angry and for the first time I really sensed his embitterment.

"Them foremen would play us one against the other. Like it was the rule to get as much work out of you as possible. There's others that are willing to work if you're not. Son, in those days the unions were formed for the working men to keep them from being exploited by the companies. But us that weren't white were not only being screwed by the companies, but were forced into a certain work mold by the unions. With all its talk of equality and better working conditions for the working class, the union really meant for whites first. The rest got the short end of the stick, and because of hungry families, we were forced to feel grateful for that. Son, many of us bullshitted ourselves to believe that in being part of the union we had it made."

I looked at Poppa's face. Funny how come me and Poppa never got to talking like this until now.

"And the truth was, that when getting a job got tougher, we were the first to find the going rougher. Talk about prejudice . . .

Poppa shook his head from side to side. "We must of been nuts. We should have fought harder, but we didn't. I think in those days people like us were living scared. They ate up our brains into just being grateful in being allowed just to exist.

Poppa was smiling, but the smile was vacant.

"We must have been nuts." Poppa began to chuckle.

I watched him closely.

"What's the joke?" I asked.

"Ah, just talking about being nuts, in the kind of jobs we had to take. No matter how good we could handle the better jobs."

I lit a cigarette.

"It reminded me of something funny that happened in 1937."

1937, I thought. *I was only nine years old then.*

"We were working on a construction job in an insane asylum somewhere and the hospital had lent us some of the better patients to help wheeling dirt up a ramp."

I smiled. Poppa had forgotten he'd told Mommie and all of us that same story for the last hundred years, but I listened.

"And that ramp was set up at a high degree. Between the ramp and the wheelbarrow whatever sweat you had left in that hot July sun was turned into steam.

"Well, we noticed one patient that kept going up and down the ramp with his wheelbarrow always empty. One of the workmen asked him what the hell he was doing. The patient just smiled and said, 'Look, I may be crazy, but not as crazy as all of you. This is work for a jackass and I'm not about to let my ass be jacked. It's easier this way.'"

I laughed now as I always had at hearing the story.

Si, I thought. *If one can do something else better, why get forced into doing what nobody else wanted to do?*

"Poppa?"

"Yeah, son?"

"This may sound stupid, but why didn't you talk to me about your going through all them bad-ass times? I mean, okay, I was a little kid, but I would have understood. The only times I ever knew of anything happening with you was when I overheard it and then it was all mixed up with screaming and a lot of anger. Pops, like I was your first born. I'd a been mucho proud if you had let me share part of . . ."

"Proud of what, son?" he said solemnly. "Of hearing me pour out frustration, of trying to make it and never even getting close?"

Poppa's face was lost in remembering.

"But, Poppa, at least I would've known where you was at. God, Poppa, I was always thinking I was a pus-pocket on your nerves and you kept me around on account it was against the law to dump unwanted kids outta windows. You could have talked to me, Pops, instead of clamming up. I would've understood, Poppa. I ran into that kinda shit in the streets. I would've understood. But you not talking to me gave my mind different ideas."

Poppa smiled and said, "Well, we all make mistakes, son. Maybe my pride was a fault. But it may not be too late, son. We're talking now."

I nodded. Then I patted him on the shoulder and walked over to the stove. "Want some coffee, Poppa?"

"Fine, but easy on the sugar."

I handed him his cup and Poppa and I went outside the house.

We sat outside where it was warm. I stared at the green grass and the green trees and the different colored houses, and I wondered if Babylon was friendlier than it had been years ago. Looking at Sis's house, I felt happy for her. Why not? It was a beautiful ranch-style house, practically brand new and everything in it was like expensive and in mucho good taste. I dug the grounds and I estimated it was almost close to half an acre with neatly trimmed grass and some fruit trees and different kinds of flower beds. About time she lived in a decent pad. Sure beats them hot and cold cockroach holes-in-the-ground we had grown up in. Compared to them, it really seemed like a mansion.

I eyed Poppa, who was staring into his coffee cup. I shifted uncomfortably, maybe because of not being use to the rich-looking surroundings in this foreign land. Or because of just not being use to sitting there with my father. Poppa cleared his throat and gave me a half-smile. I figured he felt something like me. I looked at him for a couple of seconds.

"Poppa?" I asked suddenly, "did you ever feel ashamed of what you were? I mean, like not being white. So you could make it. I mean . . ." I couldn't finish the sentence. I was floundering because I knew I was hitting at something Poppa might not want to talk about.

Poppa swallowed a gulp of coffee.

"Might as well be truthful," he said with a casual shrug of the shoulders. I can't count the times I wish I had been born white. My God, as a kid my whole world was baseball and goddammit to hell, I was good. Damn good, and I wanted to break into the majors."

"Yeah, Poppa, I use to hear you pour out your anger at Momma."

Poppa went on. "And like it was nothing. I took second place. Hell, I didn't take it . . . it was all there was to take. I played semi pro with the Black Stars, Cuban Stars, and the Puerto Rican Stars."

Yeah, I thought, *I remember, caramba, Poppa*. But I had never realized it was so important to him.

"Poppa!"

"Ahuh . . ." his voice answered across the warm sunshine.

"Poppa, remember the time I was bat boy for your team and we went to play a white team in Mt. Vernon?"

"Jesus Christ, do you remember that?"

"Sure do, Poppa. We beat the Hell outta them . . . didn't we, Pops?"

"Yeah, it was a slaughter. But like my batting was kind of off that day. God, you really remember."

"Shit yes, Poppa. I'm always gonna have a memory. Wow, did you take care of business in right field."

"Left field, Piri."

Poppa talked on about only hitting a double and a long fly that brought in some kind of run and while he was talking, I remembered the time years ago when Poppa had taken me to Central Park to see his team, the Puerto Rican Stars, play the Cuban Stars.

God, I had felt so damn proud. Poppa was holding my hand. His uniform was gray and the stockings were blue.

I watched Poppa as he changed into his spikes and then he took my hand again. I had tried to imitate his walk and I wanted my sneakers to make the same sound his did as he walked on the tar walkway.

Like I felt as if I was back in Central Park and Poppa was giving some kind of advice.

"Don't run across the field when the game is on."

I could see the whole scene.

I think the game was somewhere in the middle innings. Poppa's team was now up. I was sitting in the Puerto Rican

Stars bullpen (which was only a long bench). I asked Poppa if I could go for a drink of water. I found myself running across the field to the water fountain, being careful to go the long way around. I heard cheering and jeering.

I gulped my water down, keeping my eye on the game. I saw a Puerto Rican Star get up to bat and I thought, Poppa's going to bat next.

Like always, I wanted to cheer Poppa on. I ran like hell across the field. Like forgetting Poppa's warning. Like forgetting everything except that I hadda be there to cheer Poppa on. I heard some kind of yelling and looked out, and then something hard and angry hit me on the side of my head and the sunshine vanished, and I couldn't run and I was falling down.

My eyes opened and I saw a lot of baseball players and people around me. I saw my father's face and it was scared. And I was trying to tell him not to hit me for not listening to him, and then I heard somebody telling somebody else that Poppa's kid had been hit by a line drive. Then everything went dark.

I came back to now time and Poppa was still in the sixth inning. I smiled.

"Hey, Pop," I gently broke in. "Do you remember the time I got hit by a line drive in Central Park?"

"Do I remember! God, son, it took some kind of stitches to close your head up, and your mother was so . . ." Poppa broke it off. It still hurt him to even think about Mom.

Poppa adjusted his lean body out on the lounge chair in some sort of attempt to let his body relax, resting his arm on his forehead to shut out some kind of sunlight. There was a mucho quietness between us. I kinda felt we both missed my mother in the same way.

I stretched out on my chair thinking how much Poppa and I looked alike. I felt some kind of not fully understood pride at being a younger version of him. I closed my eyes and through the red sunlight coming in behind my eyelids, I dug myself thinking that all I needed was stone white hair, and we could almost be twins.

I checked Poppa out through one eye. His eyes were closed, like maybe copping a nap or thinking mucho things just like me. I closed my eyes again.

Hey, Poppa, I wonder, I thought, *if you remember the time I went out and got my hair straightened on a* KONKOLEEN KICK *just so as I could have the first time feeling of my hair being able to fall down over my forehead just like my brothers. You should have seen Momma's face when she dug what I had done. Man, Poppa, I can hear her now. "Aye bendito, negrito, what have you done to your beautiful hair?"* I smiled to myself. *I can even remember the look on your face when you saw me with a stone baldy. Pops, did you know I had made my mind up never to be ashamed of my curly hair again? And how about the time I was playing the dozens with Ralphie El Loco? You didn't know he sounded Momma bad with something like,*

Yellow is yellow and green is green . . .

I put it to your mother like a submarine . . .

and I shot him down in Momma's defense with

A car is a car

A bike is a bike

Your father's a faggot

And your momma's a dyke . . .

and Ralphie El Loco got up tight and him and his father sicked that cop on me and I got my culo wasted from a shot of his macana (nightstick) while he called me all kinds of spics. Remember how he dragged me upstairs and ran all kinds of lies to you. I felt so mucho brave at your being there. I cursed him out for being a fuckin liar. He was gonna do me up, but you got in between us and didn't let him and after he was gone you beat the living ca-ca outta me for cursing in front of Momma. But you shouldn't have, Pops. Didn't you know I was in the right? You still don't know this, Pops, but I gave the cop back some of his own shit by smearing some chevere mixture of cat and dog ca-kee all over his call box phone. Some kind of shitty victory, eh, Poppa?

I shifted my weight and went on thinking. You know, Poppa, I do remember you working your corazón out with pick and shovel. I remember you being mucho out of work and Momma going to her slavery over a red-hot sewing machine in some greasy sweatshop, while you burned up inside and outside taking her place cleaning house and bending over an emasculating estufa cooking our comida. Poppa, I wasn't asleep when you blew up and punched the shit outta the living room walls and Momma screaming that you were gonna break your hands and you coming back with something like, "So what . . . what good are they to me if I can't use them to do a man's work?"

I remember you slamming the door as you went out to clear your head of some bad anger and how quiet it was for a while and then Momma breaking up the silence with the roar of her sewing machine as she went back to all that work she brought home from the factory.

Diggit, Poppa, I remember when war broke out and you got a chevere job and that Christmas we got a tree so big that we couldn't get it up the stairs without messing it up so we hoisted it up the side of the building by rope. Wow . . . when we got it all fixed up, it looked better than the *one at Rockefeller Plaza. Jesus, Poppa, you blew all kinds of dinero getting us chevere presents. I guess you were trying to make up for all the other Christmases that had been a blank.*

I got up and dug Poppa was lost in sleep. I went into the house, washed the tools, and cleaned up the little mess here and there and then washed and changed. I brushed my hair and digging my face color I thought, *I guess you couldn't see my hurts on account of you hurting so. I'm glad as hell we talked, Poppa.* I went back outside and sat down and quietly dug Poppa for a while.

"Poppa?"

He stirred a little.

"Poppa?"

"Yeah, son." He raised his head and sleep dropped from his eyes.

"I gotta be splitting back to El Barrio."

We got up and went into the house. I cut into the bedroom to get my jacket. When I came out Poppa was looking at the brickwork. "Damn good work, son," he told me.

"Thanks, Poppa." I felt pleased. "Well, I guess I better check out. It was chevere to see you again, Poppa."

Poppa just nodded a smile, letting me know he felt the same, and said, "Let me take you to the station."

"Chevere."

I snapped the latch and closed the door behind us. There wasn't too much said on the way to the station.

I got out of the car and looked at Poppa.

"Poppa?"

"Ahuh. . . ."

"Can we get us a chance to talk again? I mean like we did today. I mean . . ."

"I know what you mean, son. Can't make it all up at one time."

Poppa started to say something and perhaps because he couldn't find the words at that moment, he instead raced his car's motor.

"Son, I'm not ashamed . . ." he started, but his voice soon gave out.

I stood there, leaning into the car, waiting to hear more.

"Piri, remember when we moved to Babylon?"

I nodded, recalling all the prejudice and the humiliations.

"I moved us out here just to prove we got a right to live where we want to and not where they want us to. I hadda do a lot of things I didn't like, and I had to prove I . . . ah . . .

"I understand, Poppa. Como, like we'll talk again." *I mean, my God, I told myself, we still both feel uncomfortable.*

"See you, son . . . uh . . . say, do you want to come over to my house?"

"Some other time, Poppa. See you and take care." We shook hands and hugged each other, but this time like it was more for real.

I watched his car cut up two blocks, make a left, and then make its way into the driveway of a maroon-colored house.

The train pulled me into Penn Station. I caught the IRT and headed towards Tia's house. My eyes checked out different subway stops, but my mind was still talking to Poppa.

Diggit, Poppa, I sure wish we could start all over again from scratch, but, wishing like this ain't no way of looking at a reality. All we gotta do is just keep getting together and we'll get to know each other mucho better. Poppa, I'm sorry as hell you didn't make the Major League. . . . Gee, Popi, glad to see you again. . . .

5

See, moms, I didn't forget how to pray

Wow, man! I climbed the five flights up to Tia's all the
while thinking on how Mr. Greenstein had taken all the
juice out of me. Damn, in mucho language, tote that barge
and lift that bale, all on $42.50 a week.

I smiled, because I knew that even with all that heavy
sweat, that cat was teaching me how to lay out cloth and
who knows, maybe I could even become a cutter. Had to
admit, though, that I sure felt cut up. But thoughts jumped
into my mind, on how he took special time to show me the
way the cloth was cut and how sharp the blade was, and
that with one slip I could blow the jewels on one pattern
and como he was working on marginal contracts and could
go out of business overnight and mucho problems involving
unions and contractors and competition and prices.

I smiled, thinking about how I looked at him, telling him
with my eyes, "Hey, amigo, I'm gonna cut this cloth and you
got me all shook up with your problems. Cool your cosa,
cause I'm liable to make your problems come true sooner
than you think."

"Are you ready for cuttink?" he had asked.

I turned the blade on and cut so pretty and with mucho
care that he smiled approval and I smiled back, content that

I was helping him from going bankrupt all on $42.50 a week.

Screw that barge and off that bale.

When I finally had climbed to Tia's floor I slapped my secret knock. Poom . . . pu-pu . . . tum . . . tum . . . tum. She had supper waiting. I ate slow and kept shaking my head no in between mouthfuls of food. Like always Tia stood by my side with a serving spoon as big as a shovel, ready to sock some more comida on my plate as I ate.

Wow, like for every forkful I took out, she laid twenty more. The food was cutting smooth into my estomago. My eyes whipped across *El Diario* laying next to the kitchen sink.

I reached over and brought Barrio news underneath my nose and digging mucho bad news, settled on the "Consultorio Sentimental"—advice to the lovelorn—and gave up on that after digging "Dear Sentimental, My husband left me on account I liked other men. Do you think that's fair?"

I changed to the funnies. They were just as bad. Caramba, now they got frogs talking to flies.

"Hijo?"

"Si, Tia?" I made a perfect basket of *El Diario* right back next to the kitchen sink.

"I'm going to church. Did you have enough to eat?"

"Thank you, Tia. It was good food."

"Do you want to go to church with me?"

"No, Tia. I have eaten well and I am in my glory now."

When I saw Tia frowning, I quickly excused my lack of reverence.

I could tell she was hurt.

"Tia."

"Si, hijo."

"I'll see you there."

Her voice changed behind my back to a happy song.

"Aye si, hijito, aye si."

"Tia?"

"Si?"

"Yo te amo."

"Que Dios tu bendiga, negrito," she said, and I watched her walk out the door.

I checked myself out in the mirror and made it to la iglesia. As I approached the church, the doors were opened and a fast chorus was pouring out. I sat in the last bench next to the door, in case I'd change my mind. I began to feel self-conscious as heads began to turn towards me with friendly smiles of "we know who you are."

A young husky Puerto Rican sitting next to me extended his hand and whispered, "You're Piri, verdad? La Hermana Angelita's nephew, right?"

That's right, I nodded.

"My name is Victor Cruz. I'm pleased to know you. We have been hearing about you for years. You have been part of the church's prayers. It's funny to pray for somebody for years and finally get to see him."

I smiled. Now I was even more self-conscious. With a great deal of embarrassment, I asked myself how one thanks a stranger for praying for him for six years.

"Thanks uh . . . a lot, Victor. I appreciate your prayers."

I saw Tia sitting near the front pew and her head was turned toward me with a pleased smile. Next to her was a pretty girl, who was also smiling. But her eyes looked at me with what I thought was a mixture of awe and fascination. Or perhaps it was just mucho curiosity on what an ex-bandido fresh out of the jail looked like.

I stared at her and my face copied her expression right down to her half-opened mouth. I turned that expression into

a real Humphrey Bogart cold-eyed mean sneer. She blushed
at my deliberate comic play, and I smiled her a sincere apology
for my lack of manners.

Tia had been watching my fooling around and I saw her
eyebrows raise as if to say even in church he has to make
like a clown. She whispered something to the girl, who
nodded and a few seconds later turned and smiled.

Tia was one heck of a chevere defense lawyer. All the
smiling faces turned back towards the sermon and I looked
at Reverend Hernandez, who interrupted his Christ on Calvary message to acknowledge my sitting there by waving a
friendly welcome to me and then went on about how they
had hung Christo on a cross.

I only half listened. My ears split between the sounds
of the street and his voice.

After his sermon, somebody, perhaps a deacon, stood and
laid out all the ground rules for an oncoming church picnic.

My eyes read Bible verses painted on the walls and I noticed Tia make her way to Reverend Hernandez' side. She
whispered something to him and looked towards me. His
head nodded up and down in some kind of mutual agreement
and I sensed that something that included me had just gone
down between the two.

Pastor Hernandez stood, smiling at the picnic organizer's
concluding remarks. The organizer warned the boys and girls
of the Young People's Society not to wander into the woods
and fool around.

The girls who sat on benches that separated them from
the boys giggled and the young men looked solemnly at each
other, as if trying to outdo each other's saintly expressions.

Pastor Hernandez gave a stern look. The giggles ceased.

And the saintly expressions must have returned to normal. He spread his arms out and his deep voice boomed down.

"Hermanos y Hermanas, you, of course, remember years of prayers for a young man named Piri, who was languishing in prison. Well"—and here Pastor Hernandez gave a long pause—"tonight, praise God, that young man is free, liberated from prison like Paul, and tonight he is here sitting in the back."

Oh wow, I thought, as all heads turned around looking for me. Out of the corner of my eye I saw Victor Cruz's finger pointing at my head and he seemed to be saying, "This is him. This is him."

I turned my head toward the street sounds but they was drowned out.

"Piri, will you please come to the front?" Reverend Hernandez gently asked.

I wondered if I couldn't just raise my clenched hands together like a boxer and be done with it.

Victor dug my hesitations and apparently with friendliness, he damn near broke my arm as he wrestled me up from the seat and hustled me down to the front.

I stood there muy awkward. I hadn't even time to think that my prison-issued yellow horn-rimmed glasses had Scotch tape on a broken frame.

Tia's face was blurred before me because of my nervous embarrassment. Sweat rolled down my face. Tia's head was bobbing up and down in some strange sign language.

I cleared my throat and croaked out ass-fast.

"Thank you all for your affection and prayers. Uh . . . uh . . . they helped me out a lot . . . uh . . . uh . . . and I'll pay you all back as soon as I can."

I smiled fast and damn near ran back to my seat, wondering

how I could have said something so stupid. How can you pay people back for their prayers? *OK*, I thought, *I'll pray for them too.*

When the service was finally over and all the church members were milling around on the sidewalk, Tia came up to me. With her was the young girl I had made faces at.

"Hi." I smiled at both. But really I looked at the girl only. Seeing her close-up was twenty times better than having dug her mucho miles across the church aisle. *Caramba*, my mind ran it to me, *she's beau-tee-ful!* My eyes clicked all kinds of photographs. She was about five foot high with a chevere build. Her dark hair covered her shoulders like velvet softness, framing her face and making her fair skin glow. Her nose was small and delicate and those large dark eyes must of had a hell of a time seeing out from under those long thickly curled eyelashes. *Diggit*, I told myself, *like she can't weigh no more than a hundred pounds of orchids, and she can't be no older than eighteen warm summertimes. Wow, just digging her makes me feel like a stone poet.*

"Piri," Tia panted, "we were muy contento to see you een church. And everybody was so happy to see you."

"I was glad to see them too." I said it to Tia. But I was still checking out the girl. I looked at Tia and then back at the girl. Tia caught on and smiled.

"Oh, Nita, may I present my nephew Piri to you. Piri, theese ees Nita Rivera."

I extended my hand. Hers was so ding-dong small it got swallowed up in mine. I opened my hand to check out if it was still there and before I could squeeze it again she took her property back.

"Er, my name is really Anita Luz Rivera, but everyone calls me Nita for short." She smiled.

"Really glad to know you, Anita."

"I'm very happy to know you. We have heard of you for a long time."

I looked at the skyline and wished she hadn't heard of me under those circumstances. Like who wants to be heard about on account of having gotten busted? I couldn't explain to her that I wished it could have been some other way. Finally I settled for some great silly line.

"Really was a chevere service. That cat in charge of the picnic is kind of up tight."

"Up tight?" she asked.

Before I could answer her question, Tia said something about walking home, and I started to say good night to Anita.

"Oh, I live right next door to you," she said. "With my sister Carmela, who is married."

"Great." We started to walk.

"Uhm, what is up tight?"

"Si," I smiled. "Like jumping frustrated and neurotic."

"Oh, I see," she smiled. "I don't think he is up tight. He's just a stupid . . . how do you say? Oh yes, a stupid jerk. He really wants to walk on the water."

I laughed, "What do you mean, walk on the water?"

She lowered her voice so Tia, who was really socking a sermon to a newly converted Christian walking next to her, couldn't hear her.

"It means, he wants to be so pure and heavenly so as to walk on the water like Christ. Oh, my God," she suddenly shouted out, "please forgive me, Lord. I didn't mean to make a blasphemy against you."

"Hey, don't worry, Nita. I'm pretty sure He will." I smiled warmly. It felt kind of nice walking with a girl by my side.

"How come they call you Piri?" she suddenly asked.

"It's a name of affection. When I was a kid I guess I was too skinny to be called Pedro or to be called Pedrito, I wouldn't let them call me Pirolin, and so it settled on Piri."

She stopped walking and I realized we were in front of her stoop and next to mine.

"Good night, Nita," I said gently. I shook her hand.

I watched her lightly climb her stoop and I smiled to myself at the way her dress bounced all over the place.

I followed Tia up to our stoop and waved to Nita once again before the hallway swallowed her up. I managed to see her tiny hand wave back.

"Tia, what kind of dress is that?"

"I no understand what you talking about."

"The one Nita is wearing. What do they call it?"

Tia smiled. "It's a can-can. Porque?"

"Nothing, Tia, just curious."

"Uhmmmmmmmmm," Tia teased smiling.

"Uhmmmmmwhat?" I smiled.

Later that night in bed I began talking to myself inside my head.

"Diggit, Piri, like she's fine. Really fine. And she's a lady. So don't go getting no bad-ass ideas. Man, like she's from the same kind of flowers that Trina came from."

Trina, I thought. Like WOW!!! What made me bring Trina into this conversation? Perhaps it was because Trina was no quick jump in the bed like so many of the others . . . like in my eyes, she made her being a woman count for something chevere. I mean, she had *feelings* just like me, but like in some kind of fairy tale, we wanted to dig each other for the first time on our wedding night. Oh Shit.

. . . I laughed almost out loud. All that saving I did, and then some other cat cashes in.

I shrugged, "Well, the idea was beautiful. Just didn't work out. But still. Diggit!!" I told myself. Like Nita's from the same kind of mold.

"How do you know?" the other side of me asked.

"I just know. I got a feeling," me answered.

"Yeah . . . . yeah . . . . yeah," the rotten me comes back.

"You better keep your mouth shut, you evil-thinking mother-jumper." Me was sure jumping stink with me.

I grinned in the dark, enjoying my little game and kinda glad nobody could dig what was happening. I'd probably be trying to rip myself out of some strait jacket. My mind got serious, and dug myself being out of jail after six long years. Been almost ten months I've been out on free-side.

"Hey, me," I thought. "I went in in 1950 and like it's 1957."

"Yeah, I know."

"Remember when I first went to report to the parole officer —and had to read that paper with all them seventeen RULES OF MUST NOT DO'S? Like break one and you're back doing time for violation. Remember?" I asked my other self.

"Yep," he solemnly answered.

". . . and like one of the outstanding ones was Number Seven."

"Yeah, Number Seven," the other me remembered. "It goes something like 'I will not marry without consulting with and obtaining the written permission of my parole officer. Nor will I live as man and wife with, nor have sex relations with, any woman not my lawful wife.'"

"Kind of stupid rule isn't it?" me grinned.

"Mucho stupid, man," me answered.

"Let's see now, according to Rule Seven, I should have gone back about seventy times for violating it."

"Closer to a hundred," the rotten me grinned.

"Whatta ya bragging or something? You didn't get it all free."

"Most of it, turkey . . . most of it. Don't think I didn't try to cop free all the time, but like with some of these women business is business and love is bullshit, but what's the difference, stupid? We split fifty-fifty all the time, didn't we? Anyway, I took care of business through a loophole."

"Whatta ya mean, loophole?"

"Check it out, dopey."

Rule Number Seventeen, like it just reads SPECIAL CONDITIONS—_____. With a blank space after it. So I just filled it in mentally like. *Broke this rule on account of that the special condition is that I was horny after six years in prison and like it ain't natural to expect a man to be freeside and not cop a warm woman's love, like with any woman who's willing if you ain't got a wife.*

"Good thinking, man," me praised me.

"Hey, me."

"Yeah."

"I know Nita's no cheap throw. So no more downing her."

"I was only kidding, man, like I know it too."

"Okay, then. Now we got things straight."

"Chevere. Good night."

"Good night, ace."

I went to sleep thinking how many funny games one can play inside yourself where nobody can see.

In the days and months that followed, I'd see Nita on those rare occasions when I went to church. Or sometimes I'd be sitting on the stoop and she'd come from seemingly nowhere. We'd talk and smile, como, light stuff, and she'd invite me to a young people's get-together and I'd say maybe.

I usually walked away wishing I didn't have such a hell of a record. How could I hang all my past crap on her by asking her to get serious.

One night I shook Tia up by getting dressed up and sort of hanging around.

"Are you going out, hijo?" She took a kind of gentle pause. "I don't mean for to run your life, Pero. . . . I hope you're not hanging in the poolroom."

"No hanging in, Tia, it's hanging out. Nope, Tia, I'm waiting for you to get some change of clothes on that Mae West figure of yours. Ain't it church time tonight?"

Tia started to say something, but didn't want to push a good thing too far. She cut into her room and about fifteen minutes later we were in front of the Spanish Mission Pentecostal Church.

I looked at it. Years ago its congregation held its service in a little storefront makeshift church and after a whole lot of saving, holding clothes and food bazaars, they were able to build a regular church. I remembered Tia telling me in a letter all about their opening day ceremony. I checked my eyes towards the store where the church use to be, it was now a liquor store. I smiled at the irony.

But this new church was really something. It was made of concrete blocks with a cream-colored brick front. It had an iron fence and a cross above the doorway. It was a hollow cross with a lightbulb inside. When it was lit, the name of the church showed through the stenciled openings. It was big enough inside to seat a couple hundred people. The long row of benches on both sides were made to order. On one wall, there was a painting of a cross and a Bible inside a crown of thorns. On another wall, a painting of a white dove that represented the Holy Ghost. Carefully lettered verses from the Bible were written on all the walls.

"It's a beautiful church, verdad?" Tia said as we entered the church.

"You betcha, Tia, but like you all worked hard. You deserve to have your own church."

"It's ours and also the banco. We still owe about seventy thousand dollars." I just nodded like it was nada.

Tia made her way to the front bench. I sat on the last bench. As usual everybody smiled at me. It was one of the things I liked about this church. Everybody smiled at each other and called each other Hermano o Hermana. I dug the Pentecostal music and the way everybody really swung in the worship of God.

My eyes began digging the members of the church. Most of the members were either very young or much older. Surprisingly, the teen-agers were in the minority. I dug the faces of the older members. Some looked peaceful and serene but the most curious expression on practically all the faces was a kind of great self-awareness, the kind that one can only get after having gone through one kind of hell or another out there in the world and then finally discovering some sort of refuge by becoming a part of the church. And this is where it was at, cause everyone that would at one time or another give a personal testimony would talk of living in their own personal hell until they were liberated from it by giving their hearts to Jesus Christ, the one and only Savior. The plate offering was passed and like diggit, every one of these people, poorer than a ghetto mouse, came up with some kind of coins, like from a penny way up to a quarter. I dug their clothes and a couple said, *Big Department Store*. The rest were screaming clear, we're straight from La Marketa. Diggit, I thought, like they're giving to God with a good heart.

What did Tia say one time? "Yeah, like bread cast upon the waters . . ."

I couldn't help thinking that God wouldn't mind if they kept their coins sometimes and copped themselves a little better living outta Harlem once in a while. But there was nothing except for real in a lot of the church members, like they were singing for real . . . praying for real . . . loving for real . . . and well . . . just asking God to give them courage, strength, love, and mucho faith so as to be able to walk the rocky roads of the harsh reality of the living hell out in them streets.

I dug an old wrinkled hermanita bent on knees, who was at least eighty years old and like one look at the intensity of her face as she prayed let me know that for her God was the only reality. All else was an illusion.

I heard a voice up front and looked fast towards it. It was Tia. She was praying out loud, something about not wanting to be rich in silver and gold if it meant the danger of losing her soul. I caught some more of . . . she would rather be a servant in the House of the Lord than a Princess in a Palace.

I just looked down and picked at my fingernails. Tia finished and I heard another familiar voice talking. I looked up. It was Nita taking care of business by directing a part of the service and after calling on different people to pray, she asked if there was anyone who would like to give his testimony on what the Lord Jesus Christ had done for him. I watched an elderly cat whom I knew to be Brother Rivera walk quietly to the front of the church and turn to us all. He had a big smile on his face. Someone said, "Amen." Someone else added, "Hallelujah." Then still another cried, "Look how beautiful his face is. It is the joy and love of Christ in his heart."

I closed my eyes, determined not to look at the beautiful cara. I only heard his voice.

"Hermanos y Hermanas. It brings me great honor to thank my Lord Jesus for the wonderful mercy and love He has shown towards me."

"Gloria a Dios. Amen. Amen," all the church members intoned. All except me. I didn't think I had a right yet.

"First of all," the beautiful face went on, "I salute you too in the name of my Christo, and then in my love for all my Christian hermanos y hermanas."

"Hallelujah, praise be the name of Jesus," a woman called out. I knew it was Tia.

"I once was lost in sin, but Jesus took me in. First, he saved me and then he healed me. I was un borrachon. I couldn't live without my Ron. I would rather drink rum than eat. It was my love, my children, my wife, my friends, my family. I lost my job, I couldn't hold another—I didn't care—all I wanted was rum and more rum."

Just like doogie drugs, I thought. I listened closely to confession to God.

". . . And one night, I was passing this iglesia and I heard the message of God pouring out through those same doors."

When I looked up, the beautiful cara was pointing toward the back of the church, and half the congregation turned around to the direction where his finger pointed.

". . . and I walked through them and ran down this same aisle." He pointed to the aisle and those nearest the aisle looked down at it.

"I threw myself at the feet of God's pulpit and asked Christ to come into my life, to forgive my sins, that I would accept Him as my personal savior, that I believed He died for my sins, that He could truly save me and make a new creature out of me, y, Hermanas en Christo, I felt God's love and mercy flow over and through me. I felt Christ's sweet hand of salvation break the stones in my heart and light up the darkness of my soul, and, queridos Hermanos . . ." The beautiful face took a long breath amidst the growing Amen, Praise God and Sweet Jesus, We love you . . . and then went on . . .

"All the time, I had a full bottle of rum in my pocket. Praise God, from that day I haven't tasted a drop of rum. I have my family back, my friends, my home. I've got a good job, my health, and most of all, I've got salvation and grace. I got Jesus's love in my soul. I've got my chance to eternal life and, Hermanos, praise Jesus, that's been over five years ago. Hallelujah."

I heard someone break out into a funny kind of speaking and knew what it was. It is called speaking in lenguas, or tongues. It is said to be the language of the angels. It comes only from the Holy Ghost. Tia had told me about it, but I wasn't too hipped on what it was all about yet. The whole church was singing and praying. I cut my eyes to the door and wondered if I should split.

Finally, the church was quiet. I heard Reverend Hernandez' voice from the pulpit. One could tell from the voice alone that he was a big man, at least six foot two. Tia told me he had been a former heavyweight boxer. That merely added to my respect for him. Yet strong as he was, his words were soft and pastor-like.

"Dios es amor, God is Love. He can help where no one else can, by Faith, then understanding. Christ, the only Son of God, died on Calvary . . .

For God so loved the world he gave His only begotten

Son, that whosoever believeth on Him should not perish
but have everlasting life.
For God sent not his Son into the world to condemn the
world, but that the world through Him might be saved.
Salvation is the Gift of God.
God gives peace, contentment, serenity, confidence, assurance, hope, joy, a feeling of belonging."

That's it, I thought. I want to belong to something, too.
I already know how to be a bad stud. But if I belong to God,
maybe I can do *something* right. But, man, I told myself,
I've thought of this before.

"Those of you who are in need of peace, who walk in
darkness and despair, who want to find your way out . . ."

That's it, I thought, to find a way out. I wanna get out
of the basura. Can you help me, God? Do I gotta be ashamed
to believe in you? Do I gotta worry about my boys knowing
I'm on a "God kick"?

And some kind of war started breaking out inside of me as
my mind started throwing thoughts at my corazón. You're
gonna find yourself hung up in the middle again, Piri, trying
to keep your down rep on the street while trying to be a down
Christian. You're gonna have to put up with a whole lotta
ca-ca. Your boys gonna start seeing you going to church
regular-like and walking them streets with a Bible under your
arm instead of a pistola. The word's gonna go out that you
lost heart for the street, Piri, and religion's gonna be your
excuse for punking out, and don't think you're not gonna
hear words in your defense, like—"Piri's got a good reason
for making the church scene, like probably Piri's trying to
make some chippie in that church or trying to get in real

cool so he can cop some good bread like some of them rack-
eteering phony preachers."

I almost said aloud, "Well, to hell with them streets and
the stuff they put down. I made a deal and I'm making it all
the way. I don't see no changing in the street from the way
I was, so the change maybe is in here."

The reverend's voice continued. "If there is someone here
who has not accepted Jesus as his personal savior, now is the
time. The door to heaven is now open. Accept a new life in
Christ. He can take away your sins. He can create a new man
with joy, tranquility, and inner peace. Who will come to
Jesus? Raise your hand and we will pray for you."

I didn't look right or left. I just got up and started walking
down that aisle. I dimly heard the "Praise God, Hallelujah.
Piri's gonna accept Christ as his personal savior." I swear my
Tia was yelling the loudest, but my heart talking to my mind,
was drowning them all out.

This walk was nothing like I ever took. It was different.
There wasn't anybody waiting at the end to hurt me. It
wasn't like the long walk down El Barrio's streets on the
way to a bop, or to pull a job—or holding my bloody side,
stumbling and walking down that long cold street. It wasn't
nothing like the long walks through the echoing Tombs—or
the way to Courts—or the walk before the Big Judge. Oh,
God, it wasn't like the long walk through the long years in
prison through cell hall blocks and green-barred cell tiers—
or the long wait and long walk to see the Wise Men, the
Parole Board, and going back again after two years. It wasn't
like the long walk from one prison to another, from one court
to another—or the long walk to freedom with the long in-
visible rope around my neck held by a probation officer and a
parole officer. It was unlike any of my long walks. This one

hadda be for something better. This one couldn't be a blank—
it hadda be for real. I was gonna be somebody after this long
walk. I was gonna be a positive power—like I said—like the
Big Man said—like on the kick of "Suffer the little children
to come unto me." *Jesus, I don't feel like a punk or nothing.
I don't feel ashamed. I just don't wanna feel like I ain't
going nowhere.*

"Kneel down, mi hijo." The man on the pulpit sounded
as if he was the old man I used to have. I knelt down. My
eyes closed. My head bowed. I heard the murmur of the
church. "Praise, God. Glory Jesus" . . . In my mind, I could
almost see Mom's happy face, smiling like everything that
had happened had been worth it, just for me to make it to
here. *Moms, how did it go?*

"Padre Nuestro, Que estas en los cielos santificado sea tu
nombre, Our Father, Who art in Heaven, hallowed it be
thy name."

See, Moms. I didn't forget how to pray, did I? I kept my
eyes tightly shut. I wondered why I felt embarrassed.

"Do you accept Christ as your personal savior and re-
deemer?"

I nodded yes. Then I cried aloud, "I do." I barely heard
the rest. Neither the pastor nor the church. All I could hear
was the pounding of my heart. I wondered when God's love
and mercy were gonna flow over and through me. I waited
to feel Christ's most sweet hand of salvation break the stones
in my heart and light up the darkness of my soul. But it
didn't happen. I felt good, but not like Brother Rivera had.
Maybe I was a harder rock than he had been . . .

The service was over and everybody was shaking my hand
and hugging me and Tia was crying and smiling and Pastor
Hernandez had his arm around me, and I smiled back and

made like real happy. I even said, "Amen, Hallelujah," and I called everyone Brothers and Sisters.

"Bless you, Brother Piri," said Brother Rivera.

I smiled at him but I felt cheated because I hadn't felt salvation as he had.

That night I tossed in bed and couldn't sleep an inch. Tia heard me tossing and came into my room.

"What is the matter, little son?"

"I ain't happy, Tia. I don't think I made it with Jesus."

"Por Dios, how can you say such a thing? Didn't you accept Christ with truth in your corazón?"

"Of course, Tia. It's just I didn't feel it like Brother Rivera did. I just didn't."

Tia laughed and said, "Dopey, do you not know that the Lord works with each of his children differently? He comes in each of their hearts with a different color of light. He knows his children and walks with each accordingly. He is in your corazón and His light is in your soul, and you will grow and grow in His hands. Wait and see, negrito. Foolish one. Of course, you're saved. Do you believe it?"

"Si, Tia." But my heart was having a hell of a battle with my mind.

"So go to sleep, hijo. Did you pray?"

"Ahuh."

She left and I prayed laying down. I closed my eyes and knew in my heart I really wanted to believe . . . and my mind went back into time . . .

. . . Like nights are not always made for konking out in sleep. For me as a kid, a lotta times, it was just another ringside seat to a dark street scene. All of us kids had a ball digging the kick that was called 2 A.M. All it took for us to be

awake was the little extra noise trouble seems to make. It
could be anything, a cat's lonely meowing, a pair of high
heels clacking, a scared run for the safe shelter of some hallway—and making it—the screeching wheels of a car being
driven beyond endurance by a drunk who was at the end of
his wits, and the arguments and fights that were referred
by hard whiskey. The bravery it produced—and the challenge
of ghetto despair thrown at all for all to hear, and the even-
tual wasting of one another with a blade so sharp or bullet
so dull or a fist so full of flesh and bone. I hear something
and the sound is coming from Madison Avenue. I wonder if
they are Puerto Rican voices. It's an angry sound, full of
bitter words and anguished replies, and they are in English
terms with black accents—"What's the fuzz, brother." And I
make out the figures of a lurching man and a woman-wife,
I suppose—followed by another lurching man, who has only
one arm. The duel of voices is about grapes fermented, a
lousy fifty-nine cents a pint. Prune juice it really is, at least
until you drink it, and the effect is the same as if you gulped
down castor oil, Epsom salts.

"Damn you, nigger, where's my bottle of whiskey?"

"Wha' you mean, whiskey, it was nuthin but plain ole
Sneaky Pete Mus-cat-tell and you drank that all up. You jus
done forgots."

"Ah ain't forgets anythin', and I'll break your ass from here
till sun up—don't run, you bleary-eyed nigger—ah sho' be
back, jus wait thar . . ."

Caramba, I thought, *he's only got one hand.*

"Come on, honey, let's go," urges the woman patiently.
"He ain't worth all that there mouthing. Come on, honey,
les go on home."

Ringside seats—caramba, ringside seats and this good all-patient woman is muffing it for me. Oh great, he didn't run away—here he comes. Caramba, he got his hand in his pocket, got him a good blade I bet.

"Wait up, you black-bellied yellow-face son of a bitch," shouts the man with one hand.

"Please, honey, don't lissen to that mother. He's stone drunk outta his damn mind."

"Don't be scared, I only got one hand. . . ."

Hot dawg, this cat got heart, with only one hand. Woe-ie, he sure got himself a bitchin' big blade in that one hand.

"You can't do nuthin' to me," says the man with the patient woman.

"Come on back, you cotton-pickin' punk, I gots only one hand. . . ."

"Yeah, and that's why I won't fight you, cause you only got one hand an you need it to wipe youh ass."

Dawg, man, why don't they get closer to each other instead of throwing palabras from half a block away?

"Don't let that stop you, don't make no difference. I can use it to whip your ass."

Oh, yeah, what a big one hand he got.

"Get up, James." I shook my brother. "It's gonna be a big rumble."

"Come on, honey. Let's go."

"Yeah, baby."

One-hand sounds out and sticks out his middle finger on his one hand. "Go on, bitch, take that faa-git home."

"Woman, I can't stands it no damn longer, one hand or no hand, I'm gonna knock that mother out."

Oh, great. "James, get up, little brother, it's gonna be a lulu."

"Puleeze, honey——don't fight."

"I'm waiting, nigger, and I got only one hand. . . ."

"If I went there, you'd run, you slow bluffing son of a bitch."

"Try me . . . jus try me . . . I'm standing here, just try me."

"Go on home, cripple." said the man with the patient woman.

One hand froze, kind of stiff-like.

"Oh, he did it, James, he hurt him with that. Damn, wake up, James."

And the dang man with the one hand just stands there at 2 A.M. in the light of the street on the corner about a half a block from the man with the patient woman and cries—

"Why didn't you fights me? You didn't hafta call me that. I ruther you hit me, you son of a bitch. Damn you, I'm glad I drunk your half'ass bottle of wine. . . ." And turns slow-like and walks away.

I heard the going-away steps of the dang man with the one hand and the man with the patient woman.

"Hey, Piri." Good ole James, sleepy little brother. "What's happening out there, huh?"

"Ah, nuthing, just a cat and his old lady having the shit called on by a damn man with one hand."

"Anythin' happen?"

"Naw, move over and gimme some space, will ya?"

. . . I turned over and came back to now time and thought about what had gone down in church tonight and wondered how my brother James was doing and where he was. Finally, I fell asleep, like konked out, and the silence was like a welfare blanket, the kind that covered us ghetto people with warmth, but no sense of pride.

6

Trying beats a blank

I began diggin' the Bible in earnest. As the months rolled by, I was made a member of the Young People's Society in church. I got a membership card and I began to direct services. I had so much feeling busting out inside of me, I even copped a second-hand guitar in a pawn shop on 125th Street and began making up spirituals. The first was called, "Savior, Savior, Hold My Hand." Others were like, "None but the Mighty Hand of Jesus," "None My Lord but Thee," and "Heaven Bound All the Way."

I even got to testifying at the street corner meetings.

Man, that was the hardest, cause I could witness for the Lord all day and all night as long as it was in church, but out on that street corner, wow-ee, that was something else. . . .

Like that day I was sitting on a chair on 118th Street for the outdoor service. I looked up just in time to see Reverend Hernandez put out his hand, signaling for me to get up. I did and walked 100 short miles to the mike. I looked out at a sea of faces and I heard a gulping of air that ran through my chest, hit my adam's apple, and exploded, then re-emerged into some kind of words that seemed alien to me. Because I was trying to drown out my nervousness, my voice tuned up high, and I sounded like I had been turned loose in an echo chamber in Grand Canyon.

"Brothers and Sisters, I salute you," I began, gradually easing up. "First in the name of Christ, then in the name of my church, Rehoboth, a little Spanish Mission, and then in my name."

Gee, Brother Rivera, I learned well from you. You really did make it turning yourself over to God, while all the time you had a bottle of Ron Rico in your pocket. . . . Man, like I really sound like you.

"There are many things I learned in my life, but none so full of beauty as the power of God, the love of Christ, and the joy of the Holy Spirit. Oh yes, I was lost, born, bred, and grew in sin. But Jesus took my hand and led me to where I now stand. It wasn't many years ago that I was entombed within prison walls. But you remember that Peter, the Fisherman, he was once in prison, too. But because he had faith —Brothers and Sisters—the prison walls came tumbling down, just like when Joshua blew his trumpet."

I could hear "Amens" and "Hallelujahs" all over the place. I cleared my throat and let words pour out.

"One day I was sitting next to the stands in the prison grounds, a place called Great Meadows Correctional Institution, Comstock. There were four young black men dressed in prison clodhoppers, uniforms. All four had git-fiddles.

"I closed my eyes to shut out the prison walls. But I listened intently. Them young cats went from one gospel hymn to another in four-part harmony, words on how Christ had turned water into wine and raising a Lazarus from the dead, and how he had put out some chevere Sermon on the Mount. They ended up with one whose very words I remember."

I stopped my testifying for a minute, like trying to catch

my breath. Then I pointed my finger straight out at the street audience and then lifted my hands above my head and said, "It was a hymn called, 'Just a Closer Walk with Thee.'"

I turned away from the mike. In fact, I paced three or four or was it eight or nine times, hoping with all my heart and soul that God would continue filling my mouth with a sense of beauty, mucho belief. All this time I had been digging some of my boys, who were also digging what I was putting down.

Wow, diggit. Like Carlito fighting to keep from nodding from all that doogie drug inside his veins.

I thought I saw Waneko. I quit looking for faces and pushed my eyes up and beyond the tenement roofs, like straight up into heaven while I let my voice tell the world public-like what Christ had done for me. I had an uneasy feeling that if I let my eyes meet some of my amigos' faces and saw one little bit of a ca-ca grin on their expressions, I'd chuck salvation out the window and bust a couple of jaws.

Yet, when it was all over and my eyes had to come back to earth, I saw my boys' faces. They were still there. Some looked real serious. Others wore proud smiles.

I wondered what I had said? I had been talking so fast and so loud there had been no time for me to remember. I vaguely recalled saying, "No one should have to live under conditions like this . . . poverty, dirt, and injustice."

I wondered if God heard and would understand that I wasn't sure what Christ was supposed to have done for me. Jesus . . . I was trying and didn't that beat a blank?

7

You did right brother

The months rolled on by and as they did, I couldn't help
becoming more caught up in the pain and despair that was
such a baddo part of my Harlem. Even with salvation, I was
no exception. No matter how hard I tried to make myself
believe I didn't belong to the streets any more, I felt the
weight of what was happening. Bopping and drugs were in
full swing time and kids were getting wasted by both; only
difference, bopping could kill quick-dead, while drugs could
make your dying your whole lifetime.

Sometimes I'd get a real bug to join the easy living . . .
like I hadda fight the big bread temptation kick. One night
I was walking up Madison and 110th Street and dug some
cat making motions to me from across the street. I stopped
and tried to make out his cara. I pointed a me-finger at myself
and he yelled, "Yeah, baby." I crossed the street and damn
sam if it wasn't old Oscoot.

"Concho, man, I ain't seen you for many moons. Man,
don't you know me?"

I grabbed his outstretched hand, shook hands and slapped
skin.

"Porque no, baby?" I smiled. "How you been doing?" My
eyes did a pawnbroker's estimate over his total worth and it
came out like a $250.00 suit and $40.00 shoes. I didn't even

bother figuring out the cost of his watch and a ring that had a rock in it like a king-size boil.

"Doing chevere, baby, like bread is all that's inna world. An' you, baby?"

His eyes totaled up my worth. Like I was wearing a cheap store suit, eight-buck shoes, and a Mickey Mouse watch and no ring.

"I'm doing all right."

"Where you at?" He patted me on the shoulder.

"Working." I couldn't help hoping he wouldn't ask where.

"Where, man?"

"Downtown."

"Where?" he insisted.

"Gotta full-time job in the garment center and part-time at Macy's." I made it sound like I was president of both.

"Don't sound like you, baby." He tried hard not to show his disbelief, let alone sympathy at my failure.

"What's happenin with you?" I asked, trying to change the conversation.

"Pulling down some long green bread, man," he whispered.

"Tecata." No sound out of my mouth, only my lips found the word. His wink said, "Si, baby."

"Damn, Piri, you got anything you doing now?"

"Porque?" Anger was growing mucho inside of me.

"I got a snow party going up at my pad and . . ."

I started to shake my head no, and he added, "So if you don't dig hard stuff, I got some fine yerba, pot—that will open your throat and make your adam's apple do all kinds of ups and downs, not to mention your head getting stick tight."

I kept shaking my head like in no-no soft-slow swing time.

"You really ain't on that kick no mas?"

"That's right, baby." I was just about to cut loose when I suddenly turned and asked him, "Hey, man, uh . . . why don't you stop killing our people?"

Then out of habit I slapped skin with him and walked away. I made it about four steps when he called, "Wait, panin."

I stopped. Then we both walked down towards 112th Street.

"I got some time left," he said, digging his slim jim golden watch. "Look, I got a setup for you, amigo." I just listened.

"I know you're straight, baby, with mucho corazón, so dig this stew. You can pull down five yards a week."

"Doing que?" I asked. The night air was coming on like I couldn't breathe it. I knew what was coming.

"Tecata." He breathed it ever so low at me. "I don't mean pushing on street corners," he quickly added. "That ain't a stick for you. I mean, Hermano, like middleman, just making sure the stuff goes to the pushers and like five yards is just to start. What do you say?"

What do I say? I thought. *Bust him in the mouth. Better come in strong, Jesus. Better come in real strong.* Damn if I didn't find myself praying on a corner on 112th Street and Madison. I dug myself. If I said yeah. I could see myself a short time from now, pretty suits, pretty shoes, pretty broads, pretty car, pretty dinero . . .

"Nay, feller. I got a new stick going for me."

We stood there on the corner and I watched a bus miss a kid by a mother's hair.

"What kind, Piri? I mean nada can be as fulla gold as what I'm putting to you."

"I'm a Christian, Oscoot," I said, looking at a cat looking

for a connection and a broad who was trying to turn a trick with an old man who had forgotten what it was like to have a hard-on.

"I'm a Christian too, man." Oscoot almost sounded hurt.

"I mean, Oscoot, baby, I went and joined up with Jesus and . . ."

"Man, you don't mean you're a hallelujah-Pentecostal?" His voice was like shook up. "You mean just like my old man?"

"Ahuh." I smiled, getting stronger all the time. "See you around—uh, maybe." I skipped slapping skin and left him standing there—sort of wondering how long I'd hold out.

From that night on, I found myself mixing in with kids and older guys. No yakking, a whole lot, but little talk, talking over old days, letting them know in roundabout ways what they were doing was wrong stuff.

One night, as I was heading home on Lexington Avenue, I heard somebody call me. It was Johnny Calo. I remembered him from prison. He was a quiet cat, like somehow always nervous. I had been friendly with him although he had not been in my clique.

"Hey, Piri, wait up," he called to me. I waited for him. "Man, I'm in bad trouble, I mean real bad. I'm on a split for violating parole. I owe em a duce, two years and they've been looking for me, and worse, man, I'm strung out but good on tecata, and I gotta girl who wants to marry me and, oh shit, man, I'm hung up all around. I'm going nuts."

Johnny's eyes were all over the place, nervous as always, but now scared, too. I felt myself thinking, *What's it to me? I mean every cat gotta dig his own means?*

"Hey, panin," I said. "I'm only gonna tell you what I would do if I were you. Diggit, man, right now you're pulling a blank, I mean a real blank. You're running all over El

Barrio cause you don't know any other place to go. You're sitting here on this stoop wtih me and you can't keep still. You're probably needing another fix and the man's breathing down your neck—and like a breeze, if the man don't snag you, the Junk will with an O.D."

"Concho, Piri, I know this. What can I do?"

"Be smooth," I told him. "First of all, if this muchacha goes for you, and you dig her, join together like a fast wedding. This is so you got something that's yours and hers. Then, Hermanito, split on down to your P.O. with your wife and turn yourself in. Explain it to your P.O. How you're hung up and don't want to be and you want help. And, Johnny, even if you gotta pull them two years, it's no time compared to running alone."

Johnny Calo didn't say anything. I thought, *Man, what am I saying? Here I am fresh out of six years in the can, and caramba, I'm telling this cat to make it back there like it wasn't nothing. How do you do this? Is there any right in what I'm doing? Is this what I'm asking Him upstairs to help me do? What am I? A Judas goat?*

"Check yourself in, Johnny. Ask them to help you get into a hospital or something. There's gotta be somebody who'll help you get drugs not only outta your system, but like out of your mind."

All the time I talked Johnny Calo still didn't say nada, and I wondered why Tato Ruiz—of all people—kept jumping back into my mind.

I dug myself back in a prison yard sitting on the ground with my back against the concrete prison wall smoking a tailor-made cigarette and Tato Ruiz walking up and sitting next to me.

"Come esta, Piri?" Tato greeted.

"Okay," I mumbled without much feeling.

"What's the matter, kid? Things bugging you?"

"What to bug?" I blew out smoke.

"Come on, man, you can square with me."

"Aw shit. Trina went and got married."

"Conyo, that's bad news," Tato sympathized.

I dug him pull out some Bull Durham.

"Hey," I said. "Don't smoke that dust, here's some tailor-mades." I handed Tato four or five smokes.

"Hey, good looking out. Thanks. But, man. Listen, Piri. Like you got to face that reality. Like you're not the only con this has happened to. You don't wanna be like some of those other cats that get Dear Juanito letters and crack up."

I answered without looking at him. "Yeah, Tato, I see where you're coming from, but what busts me up is that I never touched her. Man, like I saved her for somebody else. Concho, man, like I'm really bugged. I feel like busting up and out."

"Yo se. I know how you feel. It's a shitty feeling, amigo, but you'll get use to it."

"Like hell I will, Tato. Like hell I will." I looked at him wondering how in the hell could he know how I felt.

"Aw, it ain't too bad. Hell, kid, you're still a greenie."

"Man, Tato, three years inside this place don't make me a greenie and as far as the state's concerned, I got twelve more to pull."

"Hey, straighten up." Tato's voice was trying to make some kind of comfort tones. "You'll make it, kid."

"Hey, Tato, when you up for parole?" I asked softly.

"No parole for me, kid. I'll be outta here in a couple of months, and I won't owe them a damn thing."

There was a sound coming over the prison loudspeaker.

"18193 . . . REPORT TO THE CELL DESK."

"Hey, ain't that your number, Piri? They're calling you."

I kinda shook my head sadly and said, "They ain't calling me, Tato. I ain't no number. I got a name."

I came back to now time but the prison memories wouldn't leave. And still I had to tell Johnny what I thought was.

"Johnny, I ain't telling you to do this. I'm telling you what I'd do, and it's a hard bit to do. But you're pulling a no life bit out here now. You ain't gonna get better, only worse."

I looked away from him and watched the lights go by and kids playing and laughing and I dug the warm life in windows and I thought, *Isn't it worth going through hell just to be a part of this? No matter how bad off you are, doesn't it beat the blank of being locked up in jail?*

And I answered myself inside my mind, *Yeah, but you gotta be able to enjoy the scene. You can't have happy times if you're scared day in and day out by a death habit that got you strung out.*

Johnny's voice exploded into my ear. "I'm gonna do it. You're right, baby. It's the only way. I'm tired of being scared. Tired of running. Tired of dying every damn time a short drives past slowly. Or somebody says, 'They're looking for you.' Tired of walking miles for a connection and tired of getting beat out of it. I gotta good girl. I wanna marry her. I wanna enjoy my scenes."

I felt the squeeze of his junkie hand and saw his skinny back make it down the street. And I didn't feel like a Judas goat, but like that old White-Haired Saint up at the Prison. I wondered what that old prison chaplain would have said if he had dug what just went down. I remembered his words to me when I had gotten hit by the parole board. "Now is the time to prove how much heart you got." I thought, *The only thing about proving how much heart you got is that you gotta prove it every day.*

I remember the chaplain asking me if I thought I was going to make it? I had smiled with street coolness and answered back, "You bet your sweet ass, Chaplain, I'll make it." I remember his face digging my lack of respect and breaking out into a smile. "I know you will, feller. I know you will."

I had watched him split down the prison corridor, tall and lean with those bony, pointed shoulders of his drooping a bit. He turned and smiled a don't-cop-out-now at me. Man, like that old dude's face had a whole lot of serenity etched into it. Like he didn't just preach his Christianity. He practiced it. One thing I know for sure. His sincerity helped a lotta cons pull through some long years without losing their humanity.

Wow, I had never seen that cat up tight. Voice always gentle, but with some kind of strong realness. Diggit, that's a kind of hombre to be admired. "Hey, Chaplain, wherever you are, thanks for everything. You never dug a cat for his color. Just as a human being."

The week after seeing Johnny I reported to my parole officer, and like always, it made me nervous just to sit in a place that smelled like prison. The smell reminded me that if I goofed it was a jumping-off place for prison. I knew the Rules of Violations. I had read them enough.

I sat down at my P.O.'s desk. He shuffled through my records.

"Still working?"

"Yeah, I am."

"Got a pay slip?"

"Yes, I have."

"How are things going?"

"Good."

"That's fine. Do you know a Johnny Calo?"

My heart started to come out of my ear.

"Yeah, I do."

Oh hell, oh, Jesus. This guy knows I've been talking with him and the rules say no consorting with known criminals or ex-cons, and Johnny Calo's an ex-con—and up the river we merrily roll along, to pull a bit for violation.

I looked at my P.O. I knew my face was cara palo. Nothing showed. I waited for the P.O. to show a signed warrant that would send me back.

"Johnny Calo is one of my parolees."

Damn, man, what rotten luck. Of all the cats I try to help, just the first one and he's gotta have the same parole officer as me. Johnny, why didn't you keep your mouth shut? You didn't have to mention me. God, you hear me, was I doing wrong?

My P.O.'s voice wailed on.

"And Johnny turned himself in to me and we had a long talk. He said the only reason he turned himself in was that he had a talk with you."

The P.O. smiled.

"You did right, Piri."

His hand reached out. I extended my hand, and the two of us shook hands just like that.

I couldn't help thinking, *Did I sell Johnny out? Like am I guilty of consorting with the enemy? UH? . . .*

"Hey, Piri," the P.O. said, interrupting my thoughts.

I looked into his black face, and he smiled, "You did right, Brother."

I just smiled. Inside my mind there went a crashing thought. *Caramba, hope to God I did.*

8

Mucho walking and mucho reminiscing

The next day was a hot Saturday, so I decided to cop a walk. I found myself next to Central Park on 103d Street and Fifth Avenue and I dug that museum on Fifth Avenue, right next to my old school, Patrick Henry. I stared up at the museum. It looked like a little White House stuck right there dead in the middle of El Barrio.

I imagined hard within my cool and saw myself as a kid, playing follow-the-leader. Sometimes I led and sometimes I followed . . . but when I led, mother, I had really led. . . . I turned and looked at the statue on Fifth Avenue and 103d Street and remembered one long-ago day when I had climbed up its old side and sat dab smack dead on the middle of its head. I think I almost saw the statue wink as it remembered, just like me, when I had slipped and crashed a mighty long mile down to a concrete wall called sidewalk. All I could think about then was . . . where the hell are my glasses? *Oh man, Moms, at least we don't have to go through this whole damn routine again of Home Relief to get that welfare investigator to sign her name down so I could get a pair of glasses from Dr. Cohen. You sleep in peace, vieja.* My eyes gave a last look-see at the statue, which since I had last seen it, had copped a cover of about two or three tons of bird shit.

I looked at one of the tall rich buildings in time to see a doorman open the door for some mink-covered broads, who, in spite of the damn heat, were grandstanding their lack of being pobre, and my mind went into another back-into-time trip . . .

. . . Like the time I went to Jack's house. A kid who lived good, ate good, smiled good. I had met him at the YMHA on Ninety-second Street, where I was invited to join the Boy Scouts. We became tight friends and he invited me to his house. My eyes bugged out, but I cooled my expression and acted as if I were use to being taken to big beautiful apartment buildings in the lower East Sixties, where the bread is. A guy that looked like a Mexican general opens the big door downstairs. Jackie says thanks or something. I mumble something that may have been thanks, but probably was "This ain't for me." Scared, like being on another planet, this place was too big and too clean. There were no bad smells, no homelike atmosphere. This block was not my territory. But curious, I stepped into this different kind of pad. Somebody opens the door to the apartment. It's a young broad. His mother, I guess.

"How are you, Mrs. Freckles?"

I strive to do my best. But how does one act? Hands behind you or in front of you? Do you stand at attention, smile, or be serious, look down or up? The hell with it. I'll be me, me with my lopsided grin, with my grubby dirty hand extended.

"Oh, this is the maid, not my mother."

I think I must have blushed. It wasn't too noticeable. My complexion is dark. I sick-grin and follow Jackie through a jungle of carpets that looked to be a foot deep into the presence of the real Moms. I feel lost, out of place, but my block pride comes through.

"Hiya, Mrs. Freckles. I'm Piri."

"Piri," she says.

"Yes, it's Spanish, means little Peter. I'm kinda skinny and small and . . ."

"Piri," she says again, like it was something the cats on 104th Street would leave lying around. I look at Jackie, who is trying to act normal.

I could see he done something his old lady didn't like and was tied up with himself.

Then something happened that made me wish to be on my block. Mrs. Freckles' eyes opened wide and she bugged-eyed stared at my chest like she stepped into something nasty. I looked down at my sweat shirt and there, having a ball, was an imported 104th Street cockroach. I mumbled something like, "later" or "see you" and made it, with the feeling that of the maid, Jackie, and Mrs. Freckles, my only amigo at that moment was the cockroach, who made it into one of the many holes in my pants.

I wondered as I made it back to my block, caramba, why'd she get so up tight looking for . . . this was just a new cockroach. Imagine if the old bag saw one of our king-size, not to mention pony rats. I laughed at the thought of mailing her some. Some joke.

How to count millions of hurts and wants? How to put into words the ugliness and beauty of street life and a boy's constant wants?

"Mom, oh, Mom, I was making number two, taking a ca-ca-shit, in the bushes in El Central Park and I was look-ing for something to wipe my culo with and I picked up a piece of paper and . . ."

"Be quiet and come upstairs."

I flew upstairs. The world seemed brighter, even the dimly

lit hall seemed brighter. My head was light, I felt giddy, well, why not? Wasn't I some sort of hero, bringing home the golden fleece, the singing sword of King Arthur, the Hope Diamond? My heart fairly burst. Oh, Momi, the five-dollar bill seemed to burn hotter and get bigger in my hand.

"Shsh, Piri. Now, what's the matter?"

"Momi, I was cleaning myself and picked up a piece of paper and it was a *cinco pesos*, five whole bucks. Did you ever see so much potatoes in your whole life?"

Moms just crinkled her nose and said, "Did you get to clean yourself?"

"Caramba, Momi, come to think of it," I said, as I sniffed the air around me, "I guess in all the excitement I forgot."

"Take a bath. We'll talk later."

I dashed off and took a bath in our rickety bathtub in the kitchen—total time forty-two seconds. I repeated my story to Momi, who asked, "Was someone looking for it?"

I answered no, trying hard to hide my lie. But as far as I was concerned, we needed it more and whoever lost it, it was their tough shit.

She took the money and said, "We'll spend it for the whole familia; here is fifty centavos, fifty cents para ti."

Still thinking of Momi, I walked toward 102d Street, climbing down that long hill to watch the bus drivers at Madison Avenue. I looked up at the Spanish marquee. Ain't it great, here in Harlem we got Spanish-speaking theaters? No matter that they don't show Puerto Rican films yet. No matter that they come from España, Mexico, or Argentina. Some day, we're gonna be recognized—Puerto Rican actors and Puerto Rican poets, Puerto Rican writers and Puerto Rican politicians, like caramba, man, a Porty Reecan President of my United States of Americanos.

My mind hit on a thought . . . *Inside a man's existence, what is this thing called God? Within the most bottom part of my swinging soul, God, are you for real?*

I guess I must have walked over one hundred miles, all the way from Ninety-sixth Street, clear over the Willis Avenue Bridge. I found myself on Brook Avenue. Concho, man, that's the Bronx.

I heard a screeching way out behind my mind sound. A po-leese siren, and I wished it were a fire engine instead of a cop's car.

I decided to go back to 118th Street and I saw the Spanish Mission was open. I walked in and saw one of the real old sisters cleaning up. She looked up and saw me.

"Dios te bendiga, Hermano." (God bless you, Brother.)

I nodded the same to her and went downstairs to the church basement. I sat down at the piano and casually hit the keys gently, while my mind was thinking up a storm.

9

Identifying with some kinda twig

I kept working at the garment factory job and pushing some extra hours at Macy's, and even pushing away harder at the thought of how little money I had to show for my efforts and the easy tough money to be had by jumping negative.

One day when Reverend Hernandez and I were walking down Lexington Avenue, I told him it was getting harder to be a Christian. Reverend Hernandez put his arm around me and said very softly, "Piri, anybody can talk ugly when he has nothing to say, but if he wants to talk of beauty and doesn't know how, just ask God and He will fill his mouth. You know, once God was walking these streets of El Barrio and He saw a piece of twig on a concrete sidewalk. He picked this little twig up, put his hand in his back pocket, took out a jackknife and began to whittle, cut away. He poked little holes somehow in the middle of the twig and cut little notches into it, and all the time, the little piece of twig was screaming and really carrying on. Finally, old God was finished and snapped the switchblade shut and put it to his lips and it was a flute and God made beautiful music. The little twig said, 'Gee, God, is that me? I'm beautiful!'

"God said, 'Yes, but you sure complained all the time I was trying to make you beautiful.'"

I looked up at Reverend Hernandez. He said casually, "That piece of twig could be you, Hermanito."

Stopping on the corner of 116th Street, I tapped Reverend Hernandez on the side of his arm in a "see you later, Reverend" and walked away wondering if I could identify with some kinda twig that could become some kinda swinging flute.

10

It's bad without a woman's love

Something was missing both inside and outside of me.

It kept churning in my mind and in my heart. I needed a woman. Not just any woman. But my own woman. Being a Pentecostal Puerto Rican-style was a tough bit. God Almighty. I used to sit and hear them shout out fire and hell sermons, and always they would push in, "Thou Shalt Not Commit Adultery," or, in other words, "Thou Shalt Not Sock It to a Woman if You Ain't Married to Her."

I was getting up tight, like my head was telling me that was one of the prices you hadda pay for being a Christian, while my other head was telling me, dang hombre, this ain't natural, but like I didn't let on to nobody on how up tight I was getting. Like after all, if priests can make it without a woman's love, so could I. But forget it, man, none of me could ever buy that. Like it ain't natural.

There was a service one night and some young guy was giving testimony on how he had prayed for some years for the Lord to show him the woman that was to be his wife and that after six years the Lord provided the opportunity. They had met and now were happily married.

Myself, along with the rest of the congregation, strained my neck trying to check out who the Lord had laid on him.

The happy bridegroom asked his wife to stand up and

wow-ee . . . blow-ee . . . The most ugliest, homeliest woman
next to sin got up and smiled her love at the young Christian.

I swear I didn't mean to think blasphemous, but I couldn't
make up my mind if God had blessed him or socked him
with a mucho curse for some deep dark unknown sin of his.
I shuddered and settled on a blessing, cause I was in the
midst of making my request and was hoping (after seeing
this) with all my heart that the Lord would treat me right.
Cause that cat was forty times better looking than me and
look what he got.

As I walked home with Tia after the service, I felt kind
of ashamed for my past thoughts. They loved each other and
their love gave them a special dimension that belonged only
to them.

"Tia?" I said when we got to the stoop.

"Si, hijo."

"I'm going to sit here for a while, it is okay?"

"It's okay, but not too late. You have to work tomorrow."

I listened as she slowly made her way up to the fifth floor.
I kept watching people walking east and west on 117th Street,
between Park and Lexington Avenue. My loneliness for a
woman's love softly stole my thoughts.

I kept scrambling my brains trying to remember all the
past stuff I'd heard from Moms and the rest of the olders on
how to court a girl in the best tradition of Puerto Rican
style.

Later I even got the help of Brother Rivera, but he laid
it on me thick and full of ceremony. He sure was a romantic,
cause by the time he got through trying to put me wise as to
the art of courting, anybody would think I was trying to woo
Nita in a palace in Spain.

"Uh, are you sure, Brother Rivera?"

"Si, it's a very serious business when you are courting a girl with Spanish blood."

"What do you mean, Spanish blood, Brother Rivera. Nita was born in Puerto Rico. She ain't got nothing to do with Spain and fandangos."

I thought of myself underneath her fire escape in the backyard plucking some guitar and howling a love song while trying to keep my balance on top of a ton and a half of garbage.

Brother Rivera looked puzzled. "Er . . . don't you know that practically every Puerto Riquen has the blood of Spaniards in one percentage or another?" he said.

Great shades, my mind went back to mucho time ago, when I was a kid and tried to find out from Moms if we had any noble blood in us. I let go of the flashback, thinking that my percentage was under lock and key.

I checked Brother Rivera's face to see if I could estimate how much of a percentage he had of Spanish sangre. He was copper-colored with Indian features, broad and strong. If his hair had been a little longer, he could have passed for a Geronimo. I smiled at Brother Rivera as he shifted his thin frame as if he were going to show me how to bow a la Spanish Court. He looked at me deeply and said softly, "Anyway, it's a beautiful ceremony. The art of courting." Obviously he must have been reminiscing on his own days of courtship.

I thought of him doing his thing complete from a guitar serenata beneath a balcony, on down to his getting a rose thrown to him. I envisioned him putting the rose between his teeth, when suddenly he spoke and busted the fantasy.

"Ah si, you let your intentions be known as honorable, by smiling courteously and being very gallant, and perhaps, a small gift. Nothing very expensive, for it will be refused, and then write a short letter of your admiration for the lady . . . but nothing too . . . er . . . uh . . . oh yes, passionate. It may tend to frighten the object of your delight and if things go right, maybe a going out together for a Sunday walk in El Central Parque, like the Zoo, or the Jardin Botanicos, or the observatory. This way you can both look at the stars in the daytime. Going out alone with her at night is unthinkable—unless you bring a chaperon—and . . ."

My mind half listening and half seeing me being put through all these changes jerked awake.

"Chaperon?" I asked. "Hey, Brother Rivera. I ain't got any bad intentions, they're, ah . . . honorable."

"Of course, Piri, and that's the sign of your proof of being honorable. By having a chaperon you let everybody know you haven't any interior . . ." Brother Rivera paused with a thinking frown and went on, "or is it ulterior motives?" He laughed. "My English gives me a little trouble from time to time."

It's better than you think, I thought.

"Well, and then having put everything from the beginning in the hands of God and asking our Lord's guidance and blessing, you both take it up from there, asking the Lord's guidance along the way of course."

OF COURSE, I thought. "Amen," I said out loud and meant every letter of the word.

"I'll see you around, Brother Rivera, and thanks."

"Dios tu bendiga, Hermano Piri. God will grant you the one that is to be yours."

"Igual, Brother Rivera." I waved back and left him in front of La Bodega Santurce handing out Christian tracts containing his own personal testimony on how the Lord cut him loose from a bottle of rum and made a man outta a bum.

I finally decided to let Nita know where I was at on February 14, El Dia de los Novios (Sweethearts' Day), St. Valentine's Day.

Heck, man, why was I sweating? I wasn't declaring war. I was declaring love and didn't I come from good hardy chevere stock? Like wasn't I an All-Around-Red-Blooded-All-American-Born-Puerto-Rican Man? Sho-nuff . . . porque no?

I went and bought a five-pound Red Heart-shaped box of chocolates and a dollar "Will You Be My Sweetheart?" card to go with it.

I tried to ease the package past Tia, whose eyes got a kind of shiny look of, oh, how nice, you got a present for me.

When I didn't answer right away, her eyes got a less shiny look of, oh, para somebody else.

"It's a present for Nita." I smiled. "It's Valentine's Day and I figured . . ."

Tia smiled warmly. "You're serio?"

I nodded a si. "I really like her, in fact, like I got a heavy feeling that la amo, I love her."

"She is good muchacha, Piri. She is a good cook and very industrioso and she is spiritual and of a clean mind."

Tia warned on. "So is no fooling around."

"Is eet a nice present?"

"Five pounds of chocolate . . . seven bucks fifty worth," I boasted. My eyes detected a little jealous look on Tia's face. I knew she was wondering why I bought her a five-pound box of candy worth $7.50.

"Tia, this is St. Valentine's Day, not Mother's Day."

"Of course, marizon (bignose). I know it's for Los Novios,

or those who are hoping to be, and those [and she smiled and got even with me] who don't have a fat chance like you."

"Okay . . . okay, if I don't make out." I shrugged my shoulders. "I'll settle for you, beautiful," and socked a ja-lumbo kiss on the side of her face.

I walked into my room, staggering under a five-pound box of honorable intentions.

Tia called out to me. "She is very inteligente also. She is a sewing machine operator, and she makes with piece work sometimes a hundred ten dollars a week."

"A HUNDRED WHAT????? My, you must be kidding," my voice yelped out.

"Si, she is fast and good. It is hard work, but she is strong."

I felt a little depression. *Man, if she's making all that dinero, what she need me for?* I thought. *Even with me holding down a job and a half, I just about tip the needle at eighty-five bucks.* The five pounds of candy seemed to melt before my eyes into a Hershey Bar.

"Hijo, did you know she lived with me?"

"Si, Tia, you told me."

"Si, for about three years and then when you were coming home I needed her room for you so she went to live with her sister."

My eyes left the Hershey Bar, and I slowly looked around the room.

Caramba, I thought, *this was her room for three years.* I got a beautiful feeling of sharing something with her.

I picked up the St. Valentine's card and wrote in my best Spanish, knowing full well it was lousy, but I couldn't find the heart to ask Brother Rivera or anyone on how to do the thing. I wrote with much care:

Dear Nita:

I wish you a whole lot of happiness on St. Valentine's Day. Accept this gift like an honorable intention. It's chevere chocolate.

> Respectfully
> Piri

P.S. *El Señor te bendiga*
P.P.S. *I really dig you and would like to go steady.*
P.P.P.S. *I await your answer.*

The next morning I laid siege to her stoop waiting for the hallway door to open and send her on her way to work. She finally came out and I dropped back into my hallway like the Italian Red Wings had taken a shot at me. I let my right eyeball curl itself around the edge of the door and watched her behind make pretty movements towards Lexington Avenue. I mentally kicked myself for acting like a fag and ran down the street, gung ho after her. She disappeared around the corner. I blasted around the corner and put on air brakes. I walked by her side, she didn't notice me.

"Nita, hi." I smiled.

"Oh, Piri, buenos dias, how are you?"

"I'm fine, uh . . . listen, uh . . . HAPPY VALENTINE'S DAY," I said, shoving the five-pound Hershey Bar into her hands and snapping a fast salute of adios, I split in the opposite direction like as if the last subway train was just leaving. I was moving so fast her "Gracias, Piri" trailed away.

I didn't see Nita until the next night. I tried to act like nothing was happening, but I wasn't very cool. During service she smiled at me across the aisle. I looked at her in search of some reaction to my declaration of Honorable Intentions, but nada—not a hint—just her regular friendly son-risa (smile). In fact, it was the same after the service and I wasn't about to bring it up, but wow, like a whole week passed and nada. I made up my mind to run it to her in verbal palabras.

I came home dizzy from swinging packed people up and down in Macy's elevator and Tia served me arroz con pollo and smiled funny at me.

She gave me cafe after and smiled funny at me. She asked if I wanted postre de flan and smiled funny at me.

I looked at her through squinted eyes and tried looking fierce.

"Enough already. What's with the funny smile bit, eh?"

"Dios mio, was I smiling funny?"

I made my face take on a "I'm running outta patience" mask and pursed my lips.

Tia laughed and reaching up on top of the refrigerator brought back an envelope.

"Theese is for you. I find eet in the buzon theese morning."

I made my hand reach out for it like I was getting a letter from some flower seed company asking me if I wanted to be their all-around man.

"Wise guy." I made a gesture of clipping Tia on the side of her jaw.

"Eet's from Anita Rivera." Tia just about was gurgling.

"No kidding," I said, coolly shoving it into my shirt pocket and picking up *El Diario*.

"You no going to read it?" asked nosy Tia.

"Despues (later). I want to find out the local happenings." Tia roared out laughing.

I peeked at her from the corner of one make-believe bored eye.

"Look at theese bandido, for a whole week hees thinking about Nita so much hees bumping into the walls and doors. Come on, hiprocrita, you're dying to read the letter."

"And you, too, nosy." I laughed and my right hand went faster than a speeding bullet and ripped the envelope open to get at the answer to my declaration of Honorable Intentions.

Esteemed Piri,

I hope you are well at the receiving of this letter and enjoying the blessings of the Lord.

Well, in reference to your letter, I feel very honored and confess that it gave me a bit of trouble to read. I didn't understand what you wished to tell me with "I really dig you" although I understood "would you like to go steady."

I will tell you that I believe it is too early to "would like to go steady." We should get to know each other a little better. If you wish, you may ask permission of my sister, Carmela, so that you can visit me once or twice a week, as a friend, but of this "would like to go steady," I do not believe it can be.

With nothing else.

Your appreciative sister in Christ,

Anita Luz Rivera

I read it over again and again to myself.

Tia stood by patiently as I read it once more, but finally her nose got the best of her.

"What did she say?"

I pushed all the calm valor I could into my voice.

"Nothing too much." I handed her the letter. "She turned

me down like your landlord turns down the heat in winter."

Damn, I thought. *She shot me down.* I picked up the *Diario* and felt almost like turning to the lovelorn column.

Tia read the letter at a glance and began to make Puerto Rican giggles and threw her arm up and then slapped her hips.

"Caramba, for one who thinks hees so smart, eres una cabeza de melon." (Melon head)

"Whatta ya mean, Tia?"

"She is writing you to court her. Of course, she is saying to visit her, with Carmela's permission, only as a friend. Que bobo, Anita cannot just say—how did you say it?—she digs you too. Lees go steady. She is opening the door to get to know each other. Que bobe eres."

Tia's laughter made me smile and then we were both laughing.

"Oh shit, oops pardon me, Lord. I feel great, mucho great." I jumped out of my chair.

"Where are you going?"

"To call up Carmela so I can get permission to visit. Gotta get this honorable intentions gig on the road. What's the numero, Tia?"

"Oye, muchacho, cool yourself, like you say. You have to take it suave. Wait a day or two and then call for . . ."

"Wait, nada. Come on, come on, give me the number." I laughed at Tia. "Man, I've been climbing walls for a week and I'll be a son-na-ba-gun if I bear this cross for a couple of days."

When I saw Tia's frown at my having taken Jesus Christ's sacrifice lightly, I let her know I had only been kidding. But I still insisted on the number.

"Impaciente. To court is a beautiful patient cosa. One does not rush it like a bull."

I winked at Tia and with much romantic feeling in my voice, sexy-like said, "The numero, Tia, por favor." Tia smiled and gave me the number.

I bowed from very low, and said with much love, "Gracias. Thank you, Tia. You are a lady from the most highest."

I dialed. Burr . . . burr . . . burr . . . damn stupid line was busy. Mucho tries later a voice answered.

"Hallo, quien es?"

"Piri, who's this?"

"El Hermano Jose. Dios te bendiga."

"God bless you also. Eh . . . may I talk to la Hermana Carmela?"

"Porque no? Un momento, por favor."

I made a V for victory and thumbs-up signs at Tia, who shushed me away with a put-down gesture of her hands.

"Hello, Dios te bendiga, Piri. Como esta?"

"Bien, er . . . I'd like to ask you something and it's . . . ah . . . very important and I hope you don't take it wrong." I could swear I heard giggling at the other end.

"But I would like to ask permission to . . ."

"Oh, when did you get the letter? . . . ."

"Uh? Oh, yes, a little while ago." I swear some bodies were cracking up on the other end of the line.

"My, my," Carmela interrupted. "What kept you so long in calling?" I rode with the joke now and laughed.

"I hadda read it over a whole lot. My Spanish isn't muy bueno, but, er, listen, would it be all right if . . . ?"

"Thursday evenings, seven to eight-thirty and Sunday afternoons."

"Thank you, Hermana Carmela."

"We shall be most happy to have you visit as Anita's FRIEND. Good night, Dios te bendiga."

"Good night and Dios te . . ." The phone clicked loud and out in my ear. I swore I heard giggling. I turned to Tia, who had a ca-kee grin.

"And wha hoppen?"

I made a grandstand lordly gesture and making like a King Philip of Spain I told Tia, "I've been given the permission to pay court to Her Majesty Princess Anita de la Luz Rivera . . ."

My last thoughts that night were that I better get some more basics from Don Hermano Rivera. Wow, whatever happened to the simple way of doing it? Like, hey, I dig you, want to go steady? Dear Lord, I like this feeling of loving a girl again in this special-like kind of way. Wow, Trina, I wish it could have been you, but como like that's long over and you're a pretty pensamiento from ago. Reality is in front of me now. I got me a novia (sweetheart) named Nita now, even though she's only my FRIEND.

Dios mio, but it really was a pretty way of courting a woman. It was the long way around, but it was pretty groovy in its essence. Sunday was to be my first visit. Nita was teaching Sunday School to the kids down in the basement and I excused myself from my Sunday School teacher, who was Victor. He winked at me. I made my way past a half a dozen young men who all winked at me, others gave me a boxer's salute. Wow, it seems like everybody knew about my Declaration of Honorable Intentions.

Nita was in the second room on the left and I stood by the door, listening to her explain why Jesus had said, "Suffer the little children to come unto me." I could barely hear her though. The little children were yakking away in Spanish

and English about school and baseball and one bright lad
was asking a question on "How come if Christ was Jewish,
why didn't the Jewish people come to our church too instead
of only Puerto Ricans?"

I tapped gently on the open door and Nita with a long-
suffering look turned to me. She smiled almost grimly. I
said, "Can I talk to you for a minute, honey?"

The kids, bless their street instinct, dug the scene and
were unnaturally quiet, except for chevere side glances and
silent kissing sounds making soft winds from their pursed
lips. Two of the youngsters hugged each other in an exaggerated way. One put both little hands over his heart and
rolled big brown eyes in what I took to be a takeoff on Romeo
and Juliet. I jokingly gnashed my teeth at them.

"Que es, Piri?" Nita brushed her hair back with a "like
to give up" attitude.

"Today is Sunday, Nita, uh . . . what's the best time to
come and see you? As a FRIEND of course."

Nita laughed lightly and a lot of kids inside the room
provided a giggling background. I eased her a couple of
steps away. "Nita—I wonder if—"

She cut me off, asking, "Piri—would you like to have lunch
with my familia?"

"If it ain't too much trouble, I'd like that a whole lot."
I smiled.

Nita walked away and I heard her softly telling the kids
that if they didn't shut up, she was gonna slap the beans
out of them. I heard a couple of giggles, one slap, and a
complete reverent silence. Nita walked back satisfied.

"Sometimes Satanas really tries to disrupt, but the Lord
helps me overcome him." She held up a tiny closed fist.

"About one-thirty is okay, Nita?"

"Make it one, because the food will be ready to serve. Okay, friend?"

I nodded my grinning head up and down and said, "Okay, friend."

I started to walk away and Nita whispered, "Don't be late, Piri."

"No te apures. I'll be right on the head, friend."

I heard a chorus of suffering children.

"Don't be late, Piri." *Caramba,* I thought, *these Christian-itos* (little Christians) *must have built-in radar in their ears.*

I won't, kids. I won't. Suddenly the giggles stopped short, like as if Nita was taking care of straight business again.

I walked up the steps of the long stoop. I looked to my left and was 99.9 per cent sure I saw a couple of heads peeking out behind some bright Puerto Rican curtains. My feet made hollow sounds on the wooden stairs. I looked for apartamiento numero 4-B and my knuckles missed the door on account it opened before they made contact.

It was Chisto, Hermana Carmela's twelve-or-so-years-old hijo. He had been the one playing the part of Romeo in Nita's class. He made a magnificent gesture with his arm for me to enter. His head gently rocking from side to side with one of the biggest ca-kee grins in the world. Nita welcomed me in. Carmela and Jose greeted me. The dog smelled my shoes and I stood in the middle of the living room wondering why the hell did I feel like I was in a showcase.

"Sit down," said Jose.

I did. All through the different dinner conversations and even after and until I left, I barely had a chance to say twenty palabras alone with Nita.

I walked home with one consolation. That all through

that heavy period of my first visit as a FRIEND, that damn dog never once stopped sniffing my shoes and trying to make out with my leg. *They ought to marry that mutt off,* I thought, *cause like he's up tight horny. Guess he didn't believe in Hermano Rivera's style of courting.*

Months and the weather went sliding by. The visits to Nita were now more chevere. I was becoming a part of the familia. Nita and I went out together with Chisto, who would stick close by until the magical influence of a half a buck would make him disappear forever for that day.

Nita and I became more serious with each visit to Central Park, the Planetarium, or the Zoo. We liked the flower gardens especially and we'd sit and smell flowers that were for real and I'd tell her how I used swipe them and get chased by the park guards. In fact, I told her almost everything about me. Bopping, drugs, jail, whys and how comes, and she told me about herself, and that she came from a place in Puerto Rico called Carolina, near Luquillo Beach, when she was fifteen years old. And, as we got to dig each other, we were beginning to stop being just *friends.*

One Sunday afternoon we were up on a hill sitting on a bench looking down on Fifth Avenue and 105th Street. My hands played around with the cheap-cheap camera. I pointed it at her and shot the last of the film as she tugged at a turf of grass. She was watching some pigeons pecking away at crumbs. *Funny,* I thought, *me and Trina used to sit here too, a hundred jillion years ago. Wonder how she is? Wonder what she's doing? Wonder if she even remembers me? Holy Christ, what am I doing all this wondering about with Nita sitting by my side?* I reached for a cigarette inside my coat pocket that wasn't there, like Christians aren't supposed to smoke. *Well,* I thought, *a man can do without a cigarette, cause that only goes up in smoke, but a man can't do without the right woman's love, cause that kind of goes on forever.*

My finger kept snapping the button on the camera laying by my side. I watched a young blood and his chamaca close by making sounds of warmth and love, and I let my eyes intrude into their dimension. He was holding her face, kinda tender like, between cinnamon-colored hands and silent words would go to her from his moving lips, only stopping when he would gently kiss her.

I thought of Trina, and it brought a most cracking sense of loneliness upon me, and I felt like most ashamed of my thoughts because Nita was quietly sitting next to me.

I crossed my arms, rested them on my knees, and my forehead followed suit. I closed my eyes tightly and my arms put pressure on her knees. Past thoughts came running out, pinched and gasping. Holy God, the past memories in my head began to ache.

God, I thought, *do you know what it felt like to be in prison and dare think you could one day think, live, and love normal-like once again? Do you really, God? Wow, in prison I dreamed of a day I'd be free from them damn walls. Caramba, God, do you know that in my prison cell I would dream of Trina's warmth? That I could actually smell her natural-like perfume and feel her chevere gentleness? Wow, Jesus, oh, my God, wow. That I fought to create a fantasy of normality among all that inhuman abnormality. Caramba, Dios. I knew I had lost Trina, while I was in prison, even when I saw her again when I was freed. But I knew I'd find another woman that would cause her and me to blend into a most chevere togetherness of one.*

Because of my past love for Trina, I was unable to stop the

memories from flowing. *Golly, Trina, why didn't you wait for me? Damn it.* I roared angry inside at myself. But I was able to break off the sad reverie. *Hey, hombre,* my mind told my heart, *yesterday was yesterday. Today is today and mañana is another day.*

"Nita." My voice sounded very gentle to my ears.

"Si, Piri."

"Yo te amo, Nita. I wish to marry you, I don't know where the future will take me, but I will try to be a good man for you, even though I am not a god."

"Nita, what is your answer?"

"Si, Piri. My answer is si—"

I kissed Nita very gently on her lips with tender care and love and we held each other very tightly and warm.

My mind and its past memories of Trina closed gently to yesterday and 104th Street.

11

Jive smooth-talking salesman

Slam-Bam-Diggit-Man, I was going to get married, hog-tied, balled and chained.

Nita said I'd have to write to her parents in Puerto Rico asking her hand in marriage and that Carmela and Jose would write them also in my favor on how good a catch I was. We planned for an April wedding that would fall on el Dia de Gloria (Day of Glory), around Easter, and the time was spent in getting things ready, like checking our bank accounts and pooling them for furniture and other things, like us shopping for a combination wedding ring and engagement. I hassled like mad to get a set that looked like it cost ten thousand pesos, but really went for $149.99 (cash), like on credit it would end up costing ten thousand bolos. We finally found what we wanted in a jewelry store on Third Avenue in El Barrio.

"You like it, Nita? I mean, like how it's mounted and all?"

"Son hermosa." She smiled. "But a little too big."

"Oh, we can take care of that, Señorita," smooth-talked the salesman. "We can put something on the rings to take up the extra space and the rings will fit perfect."

I looked at the smooth-talking exploiter, who was wearing a diamond ring that could be cut into fifty engagement and wedding rings.

"Later for that, panin. There ain't gonna be no improvising. Measure her finger to fit, and mount the rocks." (I really strained my eyeballs trying to find the diamonds, but I saw they were there when I'd see a faint sparkle of light reflected off them.)

"But you can't even notice the inner band once the rings are worn," Hard-to-die insisted.

"Let's go, Nita." I took her arm and pointed us dead at the door.

"Okay, okay." His give-up smile was something to behold. "The customer is always right. That's our motto since 1927." But his eyes, which looked like diamonds, were saying, but not if we can help it.

I looked cara palo at him and thought, *You probably been stealing all us novios blind since then.* I felt like cutting out, but Nita had put on the rings again and was turning her hand all which ways and the fluorescent lights bounced off them mustard seed diamonds like till they became Hope diamonds. I couldn't bear spoiling her happy scene.

"Okay, we'll take em." I smiled, but my mind for a split instant jumped negative and felt like taking the whole store, including the rock of Gibraltar on his fat pinky.

"Fine, fine, I wish you both many years of success and happiness and healthy children. You're really a fine-looking pair. Ahh . . . to be young again . . . Uh, cash is $199.95. Credit is something else."

I ran my eyes over his thinly framed body, that appeared as if it were being crushed under at least 240 pounds of manteca (lard). If he hadn't been such a hustler, it would have not made him look so maggoty, but being so damn greedy, he looked greasy. *Damn,* I thought, *wonder how this fat crook ever got to live this far. Man, even his half bald head looks greasy.*

"You said it was $149.99." I felt like punching him in

his exploiter's mouth, but getting married and being on parole are a hell of a deterrent.

"I did? Uhm . . . did I make a mistake?" His face should have belonged to an actor. "Let me see them again."

Nita handed them to him, he pulled out a short microscope and shoved it into his diamond eyeball and hemmed and hawed his bull-crap psychology for five seconds or so.

"I don't know how I could have made such a mistake, this is the $199 set."

"Forget it, mister. Come on, Nita, there's other places."

"Wait . . . wait, my word is my word and our motto is, the customer's always right since . . ."

"Yeah," I broke in, "you told us 1927, right?"

I thought, *Caramba, does this guy need an ass whipping?* I looked at Nita and decided to cool my getting up tight. I might have chanced tapping him lightly while being on parole, but I wasn't gonna chance Nita.

"We have nice credit payments that make it a pure pleasure to pay. We give you a payment card and you come in every weekend, make a small payment, and if you don't have time, we even have a special service. One of our representatives can come right to your house and you're spared the trouble of having to come in every week, although we like our customers to visit us after, even if it's not to buy, but just to say hello. A happy customer is a satisfied customer."

Out of respect for Nita and this special-like occasion, I bit my tongue.

"So on credit, making uh . . . say, payments of five dollars a week"—his pencil was working overtime like some computer gone berserk—"plus sales tax, plus federal tax, plus luxury tax, plus credit charge, plus service charge, plus, plus, plus, plus special service of our representative saving you the trouble and time of making payments, there . . . I think that takes care of all the pluses." He looked up smiling, his pencil had seemed to still be vibrating from having plussed its way into Fort Knox, "That comes to $198.99."

"Oh, we're paying cash." I smiled at my weak revenge of letting him cramp his writing hand trying to get up to his original $199.99. That cat could really control his emotions, although I think for a split time he almost clenched his jaw.

"Half down and half when we pick up the set. Fine?"

"Fine, fine."

I handed him the money and asked for a receipt. He added some extra money on it and, catching my eyes boring into his, he quickly said, "I have to say this. It's the law, it's not for me."

Yeah, I thought, *if that's so, you cats should get together.* I added up what he'd written and it was right and we started out.

"Wait a minute, what's wrong with me? I almost forgot." He reached under the counter and brought out a box and opened it. "Here, with our best wishes and compliments, a little gift towards your new apartment."

Nita and I leaned over and dug it was a plaque to hang on the wall. It read: "GOD BLESS OUR HOME."

"Thank you," said Nita graciously.

"Yeah," said I most ungraciously.

On the way to Nita's stoop I asked her again, "Like the set, Nita?"

"Estan linda, bien linda." Her face was happy.

I was happy and that took a little of the anger of having to buy them from that bandito. Nita dug the rings, but, man, it bugged me como mucho that the jive smooth-talking salesman that tried to hype us was a Puerto Rican American born and bred.

12

Brand new apartamiento

Nita and I threw a nice engagement party. Ice cream and engagement cake, triple-layer and much soda—nice and Christian-like—no wild dancing, and no wild drinking. But lots of picture taking. Damn, I felt pretty chevere. The next day we started to check apartments and found one on 117th between Second and Third avenues.

Nita and I walked down the street and stopped in front of the building. I tried to shut my eyes to the garbage-strewn streets, wishing we could have had enough dinero to get our dream, a little house in the country with the white picket fence all around and trees, green grass, and flowers.

My wishing grew dim as we stepped into the dark-damp hallway and climbed up to the fourth floor. I put my arm around Nita and knocked at the door.

"Who is it?" called a voice that was Puerto Rican, but one without too much accent.

"We're here to see about renting the apartment."

The door opened slightly and a young Puerto Rican woman checked us out between the spaces the safety chain allowed.

If I had been by myself, she probably would have said, "Can you come back later when my husband is home?" But seeing Nita, she smiled. "Just a minute." She closed the door, eased the chain away, and cheerfully invited us in. We looked around and the kitchen was nicely decorated.

"My name is Piri and this is my novia Nita."

"My name is Mrs. Rosa Quinones. Glad to know you . . ."

"When do you expect to move?" I got down to business.

She smiled, "Well, as soon as we can sell the apartment."

Oh wow, I thought, *we've been to umpteen places already and the only doggone way it looks like we're going to rent us an apartment is by buying somebody else's furniture.*

Mrs. Quinones must have dug the look on my face because she quickly added, "I know what you're thinking, but all our furniture is in good shape. Take a look at the refrigerator."

We looked and it was a tremendous one.

"The table set is almost brand new."

It did look pretty good. We nodded in agreement.

"Please come into the living room."

We did and the walls were painted forest green, which made the bland living room furniture stand out. My eyes counted the pieces, sofa, two chairs, a console radio and phono, a twelve-inch portable TV, six little pictures on the wall, one big one of a bullfight.

"The carpet is about seven months old, and the ones in the rest of the rooms are about fifteen months old. In fact, exactly fifteen months old. Because that's how long Freddy and I have been married."

"How many rooms are there, Mrs. Quinones?" Nita asked.

"There are four. Two bedrooms, living room, kitchen. Five if you want to count the bathroom."

Nobody counts the toilet, I thought.

"Five rooms is about what we would like, right, Piri?" Nita smiled.

"Right." I smiled back.

Nita then asked what the rent was.

"It's only $63.50 a month, but it will go up a few dollars when you rent it because it's rent controlled."

Nita and I looked at each other. "Not bad," we both agreed.

"Er . . . listen, we were kinda planning on furnishing the apartment ourselves little by little. You know, like with our brand new stuff and if you don't mind . . ."

"I'm sorry, but this is the only way Freddy and I will let it go."

So is everybody else, I thought.

"And it's not junk furniture. Like so many other people try to get rid of. My goodness, I don't know if you know, but there is a racket going on of people getting empty apartments and filling them for a mint. They make a deal with the supers to rent them the empty apartments and then give him a split. We'll have to do the same, but you can see for yourselves, our things are in beautiful condition."

Nita and I both knew Mrs. Quinones was telling it for real.

"How much are you asking for everything?" Nita ventured, and I could see she was holding her breath.

"We're asking $1,200, and the refrigerator, when new, cost $350, the bedroom set cost $655, and the living room set, including the console and TV, was around $600."

Nita looked at me.

"Is there any way you can take your master bedroom set with you?"

"No, I'm sorry, it has to be a package deal. Freddy insists on it. You see, Freddy got a transfer to Puerto Rico. We already got a nice house near Rio Piedras and it's practically furnished, and we don't want to carry anything there except our personal things, and really, Mr. Thomas, the reason we're selling so cheap is that, frankly, we're paying rent here and over there. Otherwise, we could take our time and get a much better price."

"Do you mind if Nita and I talk it over solos?"

"Of course not." Mrs. Quinones went into the kitchen and started to make noises with pots and dishes, like letting us know she wasn't listening in.

"Whatta you think, Nita?" I whispered.

"You're the man, what do you think?"

"I think we ought to take it. We can put their master bedroom set in the smaller room and buy us a new one. Hate to use somebody else's bed."

Nita smiled like embarrassed.

"And if we went out to buy a refrigerator and all the rest, it really would run up a pile of money and it ain't like we're buying junk."

"And," added Nita, "we would have to get most of it on credit and that's like buying it for double."

"Acuerdo." (Agreed.) I smiled, holding out my hand for a handshake.

"Acuerdo." Nita grinned. We quickly sealed our agreement with a kiss.

"We'll take it, Mrs. Quinones," I called out, feeling almost married already.

"Fine, fine," she said as she entered the living room. "Listen, I'm going to leave you some extra things that you can use also, the toaster, an extra iron . . ."

"Thank you," said Nita.

"I hope you don't mind, Mr. Thomas, but can you come back tonight at seven-thirty, because my husband takes care of this kind of business and . . ."

"Sure, I'd be glad to . . . er . . . you won't sell to nobody else?"

"No, no, it's yours."

"Maybe we could leave a deposit," ventured Nita.

"It's not necessary, er . . . Nita. I give you my word."

"Chevere." I grinned. "I'll come see Freddy tonight."

Nita thanked Mrs. Quinones for her cafe.

"Bye, bye, Nita," she said as we left.

"Bye, bye, Rosa." Nita waved as we made it down the stairs. "I wish you both good luck in Puerto Rico."

We picked our way between a multitude of playing kids and hustling people. I put my arms around Nita and said, "Hey, maybe someday we'll cut out to Puerto Rico."

Nita just smiled, her face had a look of being buried up to her armpits in the rearrangement of our Brand New Apartment. *Christ, I hope we can get rid of some of the roaches I saw running up the side of the wall.*

13

Hey, I'm getting married . . .

Dia de Gloria (Day of Glory) was getting close. Nita and I really got together taking care of business. We mailed out delicate-looking invitations. She wrote and wrote and wrote.

I smiled, thinking, *She got more friends than me.* She finally finished and looked up at me.

"Finished, Piri?"

"A-huh."

And her eyes looked up from her pyramid of addressed envelopes to see my piffling five envelopes.

"Is that all, Piri?"

"Si." I smiled. "One for Sis and family. One for James, who's home on leave, one for Poppa, one for Tia Otelia, if she can make it, and, of course, one for Tia Angelita."

"Nobody else?"

"Bueno, you took care of everybody in church, right?"

"I did, but don't you have other friends you'd like to invite?"

I shook my head no and she smiled and went back to addressing a few thousand more she must have forgotten.

I went into the kitchen and her sister Carmela asked, "Want some cafe?"

I nodded a "si" and sat by the chair overlooking the backyard, digging poor people's wealth hung out in a symbolism of worn-worn clothes.

Nita had asked, "Nobody else?" *Sure,* I thought. *I got a whole lot of amigos I know, but they come from another world, from another time and street space,* and my mind went racing back to *Dynamite, Zorro, Pappo, Ace Cruz, Frankie Blue Eyes, Nilda, Brew, Olyie, Pearl, Paco, David, Trina, Red, Lil Louis.* The roll call was busted up by Carmela.

"It's nice and hot. Want some tostada (toast) with it?"

"Gracias, Carmela, golden brown, please."

"Bueno, Piri, uhm . . . nine more dias to go. I bet you suffering from some kind of nervous attack."

I shook my head "no" and thought no more.

Nita and I were in our apartamiento with the forest green-painted living room. She still couldn't understand why I had insisted on painting the living room the same forest green.

"Maybe," I analyzed, "it's because it's a little close to green grass and some kind of picket fences."

We had been to the apartment a lot, working to get it in order. Sometimes it got strained. I mean, if I tried to hold her close, she'd keep it cool. She would smile and I dug that being alone could bring up a sense of impatience and natural-like feelings that wouldn't listen to reason, and why put down a sound of beauty that could be listened to on our Wedding Night?

So, like every time we were there alone, we'd cool our roles. All our clothes were already hung up and the apartment looked like it was a piece of tierra linda (pretty land). We closed the door and we stood looking at the gold lettering I had glued on it: *APT. 4-A.*

I left Nita at her stoop.

"I'll see you tomorrow."

"En la Iglesia." (In the church.)

"Of course, suppose to be mala suerte (bad luck) other-wise." I winked at her.

I walked away thinking how could seeing Nita at any time be anything but buena suerte.

Slam-Bam-Man, Brother Rivera, the art of courting a la Puerto Rican Español really stretches out a rubber band to its enth degree.

Dia de Gloria was here. I walked towards the church making light talk with Victor, who was gonna be my best man. I felt dressed out of place. My tuxedo enhanced by the stiff white collar and black bow tie, somehow didn't jive with the scenery around me, fire escapes, jammed with dangling muchachos, domino games, and Puerto Rican arguments entwined with beer cans, and overburdened garbage cans dimmed into a lesser importance as heads turned and stared at my sweating body encased in a way-out tuxedo. Friendly sound voices called out to me, "Good luck, amigo," or "May your children be healthy" or, not so nice best wishes like, "Have a ball with her."

I just smiled where the best wishes were decent and snarled when they were off-colored.

"Don't pay them attention," smiled Victor. "You should have seen how they laid it on me. I cursed them so much inside of my head that Christ must have turned backwards on the cross."

I looked at Victor and his face did a "Please forgive me, Christ."

We entered the church laughing. It was packed. I knew that Tia had invited members of other storefront churches to my wedding.

I did my best to act cool, with all the best wishes and funny kind of looks from some of the unmarried girls. I could almost read their faces—like as if they were wondering how Nita was looking towards her wedding night. My face was cara palo, but my mind was thinking something like their faces.

Somebody tapped me on my shoulder and I turned my head towards the face of a very, very old hermana. She smiled and added mucho wrinkles on top of her natural ones.

"Que Dios te bendiga, Hermana Diaz."

"Y que Dios te bendiga a ti, Hermano Piri." She barely made her speech understandable. I didn't blame her. Getting old has certain hang ups.

"May I speak to you? Es importante, the Lord, He has directed me to speak with you."

"Okay." I nodded and followed her through well-wishing people down to the basement and into one of the Sunday School classrooms.

I pulled out a handkerchief and wiped the sweat from both my eyebrows.

Caramba, wish I was in mañana instead of today, I thought.

"Buena Hermana, what is it?" I asked, bracing myself for some kind of revelation she had gotten from the Lord concerning me.

"You are a man of mucho experience and Nita she is not. I know Nita when she come from Puerto Rico, I know her familia, she is good, she ees . . ."

I squatted my tuxedoed behind on a Sunday School chair and looked at the mucho brown-wrinkled face of this old Christian woman. I felt my eyes watching her with gentleness.

Quien sabe? If my madre had lived, she would have some

day been wrinkled with the beauty of age and wisdom. Sleep well, Momie.

My impatience gave way to a wish to listen to what she had to say. I wondered as I watched her gnarled hands tremble with mucho anos (many years) and mucho labors, if it was truly a revelation.

"Hermanito Piri, you have seen mucho she has not yet seen."

"What do you want to tell me?"

Her eyes looked into me.

"Piri, treat her gently when you take her to you to make her from señorita to señora. Be tender. To be a man and show proof of it, ees not to crush, but for a unity of love have patience, teach her that physical love is beauty, not pain and terror."

How dare you, vieja, I thought within myself. Do you think I'm some kind of animal? Do you think my mother's gentle love was wiped out because of my life before? Do you think my father's blood was to no avail in my veins? Do you think because I was forced to live in an animalistic hell called ghetto and prison and quien sabe, if they were both the same, I am un animal?

I heard my voice speak. I looked with all the long lost and ever present memories into her wrinkled face.

"Dear Cristo." My voice was very gentle.

"Hermana Diaz, I'm not an animal. I am a person. I'm a human being. Please rest your old heart and mind. I do not wish to rape the woman that is to be my wife. I only wish to make a gentle love as a man should to that which God wishes to add on to his flesh."

I wondered why I didn't feel angry at this old woman, but I couldn't, perhaps because she knew my past and only wished my future muy better, especially where Nita was concerned.

"Vieja?"

"Si, Hermano?"

"God asked you to tell me this?"

"Si."

I rose slowly from my chair—all this time she had not sat down, despite my mucho invitations.

"Tell God I'm not an animal and since he is all-knowing, convince yourself that I am not. Gracias for your concern. If I've offended you, I am . . ."

"No, you have not, hijito."

"Gracias, vieja." My hand touched an age-old wisdomed cheek.

"Que Dios te bendiga." She smiled wrinkled and gentle, and left me alone in the basement room of a Sunday School class wondering if her own wedding night had been such a baddo horrible scene that revelations kept coming to her at every impending wedding . . . including mine.

I went upstairs and stood at the back of the church and saw how crowded it was and listened to coro being sung.

"Hey, Brother?"

I jumped around fast and my voice was forcing words even before I looked in my brother James' face.

"Damn," I yelled, and crushed the damn into a whisper. "James, que chevere Caramba, Hermanito, I am glad you're here."

"Hey, how come I ain't your best man?"

"On account I couldn't get a hold of you, you green-eyed Puerto Rican." We blew our strength hugging each other.

"Hey, where's Poppa?"

James smiled. "Poppa's getting old, he's un poco sick, sends love though."

"Hey, you better pay attention to that body who's making all kinds of hand waves." James smiled, pointing.

I looked and followed his pointed finger. Caramba, it was Sis and Don. I made my way down the aisle. Sis put her arms around me while Don shook my hand. I felt I was getting use to the tuxedo suit. A hand slapped me on the shoulder. It was Victor.

"It's time." He smiled.

I walked down to the front and Tia's hand reached out and grabbed mine. Her face looked like un rayo of sun had placed its warmth all over her. *Damn,* I thought, *like she's contenta.*

I felt all of a 138 pounds inside my tuxedo, and felt muy happy, but scared shitless.

I sat on the front bench and tried to turn the whole nervous scene away. I pushed up the guitar and turned down the amp to a low whisper and my fingers raced a slow blues progression, something that me and Youngblood had practiced some long-ago time in prison, and then my fingers went off into different kinds of progressions and improvisations and my fingers stopped on account the loud mumbling of people went kind of quiet and an organ started to play.

I turned and saw Nita. I dug the maid of honor and the escorts. I watched Nita all dressed in white and wondered on how come I hadn't really noticed how tiny she was. She was barely five feet.

"You have the ring?" James whispered.

And the rest was a beautiful jumble of my getting up and being next to Nita and Reverend Hernandez' words of "togetherness" and ring being given and best man and

"I do" and "I do" and "man and woman" and till death do us in, or something like that, and a raising of a veil and a warm gentle kiss and mucho congratulations and Sis and Don and Tia and La Vieja and her revelations and all made a warmness into a Puerto Rican symphony of getting married sounds.

I made my way cool up the aisle that had all kinds of mickey mouse flashbulbs going off and pictures being taken by the dozens.

There was a studio for more picture taking—
There was a reception—
There was a wedding cake—
There was soda and ice cream—
There was arroz con gandules and lechon asado—
There was many well-wishers, poems and prayers—
There was many presents and promises of them—
There was my Sister Miriam and Don—
There was my brother James and his get-away car—
There was us getting away—and James driving us around—
And finally—there was just us, Nita and I, standing there with mucho presents scattered all over the red and blue linoleum carpet, looking at each other in the middle of a forest green living room on 117th Street between Second and Third avenues in El Barrio.

I felt a funny thing happening to my ears. Some sort of gentle silence had filled our apartment and I couldn't hear the ever present screeching alley cats or the rumbling trucks with their ruptured mufflers making their roaring explosions up Second Avenue.

Nita's face had a half-scared, half-trusting look. I gave her a smile of assurance that had all the tenderness of my love for her. She smiled back. Her eyes were looking the living room over and then making impossible attempts to read the name on a small card attached to a wedding present ten feet away. Caramba, it was almost like a square flick. I mean, like we were glad to be alone with each other and yet were feeling kind of ill at ease with the sense of awkward shyness, yet really digging in all reality that we were married to each other. We were esposo y esposa. And, like it was the first time either of us had ever gotten married.

"Bueno, let me get out of these clothes. Whew, diggit, I really worked up a mucho sweat," I said, trying to make my voice sound matter-of-fact. A wedding sure can be a hassle, running here, running there. I laughed and tried to make Nita feel at ease. I checked myself into the bathroom and jumped out of my clothes so fast it would've made the comic book *FLASH* look like he was standing still.

I turned on the shower and climbed into the tub and soaked, scrubbed, and rinsed about five times in a row. I was most surely determined that not one inch of me was gonna stay FUNKY. I got out of the bathtub and dried off with mucho care and then drowned every Porty Rican pore of my body with sweet-smelling cologne a la galore.

I listened against the door trying to dig if Nita was moving around or something, but it was mucho quiet. I felt my beard and there wasn't much there, but I lathered up anyway and went into much precision shaving with a total commitment to getting my face smoother than a baby's culito.

I went through my thing of singing a couple of beaucoup romantic Puerto Rican songs like "Besame Mucho" and "Amor, Amor, Amor." I dug the songs were as old as a Christmas tree, but they were tried and true. I chuckled a grin and almost shaved half an eyebrow off. I was putting on my face and singing with meaning and feeling, trying to make my voice sound like it was coming through an echo chamber, when I suddenly remembered Pentecostals weren't suppose to sing worldly songs and like mucho probably, Nita wasn't digging my sinner songs. I made cross-eyes at the mirror and whispered, "Estupido," at my reflection for our psychological lack of tact, and respectfully my reflection and I both smoothly eased into a deep bass duet of "NEARER MY GOD TO THEE!" I brushed my teeth twice and gargled with nitric acid Listerine without missing a hummed note, and topped me off with a good hair brushing.

Oh Hell, I mumbled, I forgot to bring in my shorts and undershirt. I moved over to the door, my voice letting "NEARER MY GOD TO THEE" precede me.

"Nita, hey, Nita honey."

"Que es, Piri?"

"Do me a favor, nena, bring me a pair of shorts and an undershirt and . . . uh . . . my dressing gown, its in . . ."

"I know, I know. I hanged all your clothes up. Remember?" she laughed.

"It's hung, not hanged," I corrected her.

"You're so smart, bueno for your information. When you put your clothes away you can hung them, and when I put them away, I hanged them. How do you like that, cabezón? You can eat it or lump it."

We both laughed, but I cut my laughter short cause I wanted to dig her chevere laughter.

She knocked on the bathroom door. I opened but not before I got a mucho tight grip on the towel around my waist, cause the ice was kinda breaking up and I didn't want no sudden shocks making us fall into mucho icy water. Como, like certain appearance at certain times is a muy delicate cosa thing and these kind of first impressions is very important. I flipped the door wide open and wasted a big smile at an arm without a body, whose attached hand was holding the coverings for my body that would make me decently acceptable for other eyes to see.

"Hey." My voice got a little bit loud. "We're married, you know."

I came out of the bathroom after one last look in the mirror. "Man!!" I whispered to my reflection, "Concho, man, you're BEAU-TEE-FUL."

Nita had some soft frilly garment slung over her arm and I felt the breeze as she passed me. I checked the refrigerator out and peeled a mango. I chewed it and began counting the wedding presents. The bathroom door creaked open slow and Nita came out like in one quarter the time I had taken. I put it down to the fact that she hadn't done any singing plus any shaving.

"Want a mango, Nita?"

She nodded a "si." I peeled one for her and she put some salt on it.

"Por Dios, these mangos are so expensive here. Do you know how much they cost?"

"Naw, how much?"

"Fifty cents each." She made a face. "That's a robbery. Do you know that in Puerto Rico, you can buy them twice as big as these and only for a few centavos, except of course in the towns, but up in the mountains, they are cheap. In fact, you can pick them up from the ground."

I didn't answer. I just watched Anita. She kept quiet and demolished her mango.

I got a damp towel and wiped my face and hands.

"Catch, Nita." And Nita cleaned herself.

It got quiet.

"You want to open the presents now, Piri?"

"If you want to." I was yawning for real.

Nita started to open a package and then stopped and looking at me with a chevere smile said, "I think I'm acting un poco foolish, verdad?"

"Well . . . er . . . I don't blame you, honey. It's a natural feeling to get a little funny and up tight, but . . . I want you to know something."

I walked over and sat on the arm of her chair.

"Nita, you know all about me and like what I've lived in the past. Look, Nita, before the wedding, Hermana Diaz approached me and because she loves you very much, hurt me a little bit."

"But como, I don't understand?" Nita's voice got concerned. I softly ran my fingers through Nita's hair.

"Well, she, like the rest of the church members, knows my background and like, honey, most people that hear you been in jail go through all kinds of changes, like they believe everybody that's been to prison is an animal. It ain't like that at all. There's no doubt, corazón, there's people in jail behaving like animals, but you got them outside . . ."

"But, Piri."

"Don't interrupt, Nita. Please, uh? Por favor? I spent about six years going from a lotta months in the Tombs to Sing Sing and finally Comstock Prison, although they call it a Correctional Institution. Nita, look, I can't tell you how bad it is, but the worst thing is you're not allowed to keep your dignity. They tell you that you're there to be corrected, rehabilitated, and, My God, they take away your name and give you a number. Every decision is practically made for you. You get so damn dehumanized that mucho come out twenty times worse than they went in. I don't want to go into a whole lot of crap about the discrimination, but racismo is a bomb in prison. Out here, in so-called free-side, racism is also bad for blacks, yellow, red, and browns, but inside prison it's hell, cause it's racismo in a controlled atmosphere, and recourse is like next to impossible from the racist guard-keepers, and other abnormalities in prison. I've told you much of that in the past, and like it's no time now for this kind of blah-blah. I guess Hermana Diaz really was concerned, like as if she was afraid some kind of animal was ready to spring out of me.

"Diggit, Nita, I went into prison a man and I refused to get institutionalized. That means getting use to prison, getting use to being a number and not a name and like, honey, I came out a man. Not no part of some generalized identity, but as me, not no number 18193, but like Piri Thomas. I won't lie, Nita, corazón, I've come out hurting and with some kind of hate inside me, and part of my going to church is to try to ease my guts from it. I did what I did, whatever got me there or pushed me there.

"Corazón, I used to look out through the bars of my cell. The prison was in a valley, so I could see up into the hills. Aye, por Dios, Nita, this is our wedding night and I'm letting myself go through all these changes."

"It's all right, negrito. It's good for you to get it out and it's good for me to listen."

I kissed her lightly on the temple.

"On one of the sides of a hill, there were many many white boards about six inches wide sticking out of the ground and they each had a number painted in black on it, and like underneath every piece of white wood with a black number was buried a convict. Oh my God, Nita, you can't even begin to count the times I swore that I'd never be one of them. I had a name and was gonna live and die with a name, and it was gonna be afuera (outside)."

"What did they die of?" Nita asked in a quiet tone.

"Caramba, I don't know exactly, but it was made up of a whole lot of cosa things, like getting sick, getting old, getting bent up, getting killed, or maybe just giving up on the whole undignified animalistic inhuman scene, like getting their hearts to stop by hanging themselves or jumping off the top tier. Oh Christ, honey, I swear by Momie I'm a man. I'm not a damn number and I'm not un maldito animal."

"Hermana Diaz had no right to speak to you." Nita came over to my side. "She had no right. She was not marrying you. I . . . me . . . Anita was marrying you."

We put our brazos around each other.

"Jesus, honey, Oh wow. It's the God's truth the majority of us cats that come outta them carcels after any kind of time, come out eaten up."

Nita didn't say anything, but I could feel her heart beating underneath my fingertips, that were soft-like caressing her wrist.

"We use to sit in the prison yard and talk about whether we were considered humans or sub-humans . . . dehumanization, honey, means to be made into an animal, to be considered an animal."

I checked my voice not cause it was loud or angry, but because it started sounding deadly. I stayed quiet for a while and then said,

"Anita?"

"Si, Piri."

"If I'm not an animal, I don't wish to be considered one. Entiende?"

"That is your right, Piri." Nita's hand touched my cheek and it felt warm and for real.

I think she must have sensed what I was thinking, because she said it very clearly.

"I do not love an animal. I love a man named Piri, and do not worry what others think bad about you, as long as you know what you are. They will see that they were wrong in time."

I felt myself growing hot inside from long-ago bad memories. Because I could hardly even talk to break up any tension, I simply asked Nita for some coffee. She nodded and went into the kitchen. I stared out into the backyard and kept bursting apart with a broken record running through my mind.

I am not an animal . . . I'm not an animal . . . and one more time I dug myself in prison time, laying on a strip of grass that grew between the handball courts and thinking up mean storms. Man, can bitterness grow. It sure can make you a filled-up glass of nothing . . . geeze, I wanted to scream, "Let me out of here. Okay, I promise I'm gonna be good. Look, people, just let me out of here, I'll be good. I won't break any more laws. I won't stick up. I won't rumble. Come on, just let me outta here goddammit to hell."

"Como esta, Piri?"

"Uh uh," I mumbled.

Again Tato broke into my wild way-out thoughts. I looked at him, face of my face. Everytime you look at another con, you see yourself, no matter black con, white con, brown con, no matter, it's you all the same.

"What's the matter, kid? Things still bothering you?"

"Whatta you think?" I said tightly.

"Aw, you'll make it, kid. Just pull your bit, then get out, and fly right."

"Tato, why don't you . . . ?" My voice was becoming filled with anger so I stopped talking. But my mind kept on speaking.

Why don't you dig what you're putting down to me? Look at us here in the middle of a country yard, inside a big nothing, swallowed up, hurting like hell inside, wanting to die, wanting to wake up again and find you made a mistake, that you got somebody else's nightmare and you fight your guts out making believe that it doesn't mean anything to be here and togged out like death.

Tato looked mucho thoughtfully at me and for a first time I saw him—I mean I really dug el hombre before me. He was slim-like, about five eight with a fastly receding hairline. His skin was a deep rich Puerto Rican red. He almost always wore sunglasses. Like they were a part of him. He looked like a little quiet schoolteacher. Or an underfed killer. And that's what they said he was. Tato Ruiz. Piece for hire. Tu pagas, yo mato . . . you pay, I kill.

"Piri"—he spoke softly—"let me tell you something. I've been in and out of jailhouses for seventeen years, all kinds —all places—here and in Puerto Rico, and it's too late for me. I ain't got nothing alive inside me except odio, hate."

"I can understand hate, Tato."

"Yeah," he replied. "Guess you do . . . oh shit, I don't even dream good any more. Too many nightmares have messed my mind up."

He stood looking at me silently for a few minutes. I knew then that he really did understand my anguish and depression. Then he put his arm on my shoulder and told part of *his* story.

"All my life I took hard so I just gave it back harder."

I watched him calmly. Tato had already a mucho story—a legend—in the jailhouse. Most cons don't talk too much about themselves, but that doesn't keep them from talking about each other. I heard about Tato. Like he was supposed to be a contract killer. You paid him so much to kill someone and it was done . . . and Tato had principles. My God, yes.

Tato was smoking and looking up and over the walls. I looked at him and thought, *Yeah, Tato, you got principles. I heard that if somebody pays you a thousand bucks to waste somebody and the guy you're gonna hit tried to beg out— even if he offers you five times a thousand bucks to let him live—it's no dice, no gold. You gave your word and you're honor-bound. Wowie, what a man! Killer! What integrity—what's the word?—oh yeah, ethics. Yeah, you got them all. Carajo, I wonder if it could have been different. I wonder if all they're saying about you being a killer is the truth.*

"Nothing else, Tato?" I asked, my finger poking a hole into Comstock prison dirt. "I mean about yourself, about why you can't make it straight up and away?"

Tato's smoke spiraled up—a blue cloud—the words came out, matter-of-fact-like.

"Kid, I got only one way to go, and that's my way. When I get out, I'll live the same, and when they hang me up I'll fight them all down . . . I'll hold court in the streets. If I get away, then I'm innocent. If I get killed, then I got away anyway. But one thing, I'm not coming back to jail any more, I've had it. No more. No time. Nunca mas."

"Tato," my mind said, *"I'm looking at your face. There ain't no mirror of me there, is there? I think I know, Tato. You're that big word—institutionalized—both here and in*

the street, you've lost amor of yourself and living and it makes no difference to you, sort of like you died them times in police stations hanging by your hands or was it your balls? No matter, Tato baby, damage is done. Hell, man, I don't want to get like that. I wanna be alive—in and out. I want to be able to reason and ask why and how. To smell like free smells and have good dreams and, like everybody normal in the world, my few nightmares too. I wanna gulp down air and dust and be kissed by a woman that's mine. I wanna walk down my Barrio's streets again. I wanna live and be able to remember I was a little kid once. Tato, I want to be a cool breeze and make every day a full one, I wanna . . . Dammit to hell, I wanna be free . . . I ain't no God damn animal.*

The bugle blew. Tato and I parted. I watched him walk away.

Nita handed me the coffee and I drank it in three or four hot gulps. I put the empty cup down and soft-like said, "Nita?"

"Si, Piri?"

"I will be gentle with you. Look at me, Nita. Like, I'm not angry with Hermana Diaz. She really is full of mommie-love for you."

Nita pulled my head down and whispered, "Hey, narizon, are we going to stand here forever?"

I clicked all the lights off and I did it like I had seen it done in the flicks. Only this was for real. I picked Nita up in my brazos. I held her close and carried her gently, counting on the outside street lights to keep me from tripping over in the darkness.

And then there was the most beautiful essence of amor, warmth, and gentleness flowing between us until el sol de la mañana poured through the backyard windows and saw a me called Piri, and a her called Nita having become uno. Nita was sleeping mucho deeply.

I laid quiet-like holding her hand in mine, listening to my corazón beating a bongo time to:

Que chevere—Que chevere—Que chevere

Que chevere—Que chevere—Que chevere

Ay Dios Mio—Que amor tan chevere . . . chevere . . . chevere.

I tried to fall asleep con mucho cuidado. And between a waking essence and a dream I had while I was almost awake, trying very hard while I was in prison to reach across to this child that was part mine, I remember telling Nita in one of the moments of truth, "Can we find him, Nita? Will you be willing to raise him if I can find him?" And the finding of Dulcien's aunt and asking her very humbly and most mucho proud, "Could you tell me where my son is?"

I think it was very hard for her and she said it very gently and smiled, "I think that you should ask the Catholic fathers on 105th Street, which is right behind Santa Cecilia's on 106th."

I took the IRT, then ran and walked most of the way and they could not help me to find my son.

One of the fathers, who must have been use to so much asking about lost people and lost children, smiled with compassion and offered a helping hand.

"Have you tried St. Paul's Church," he said, "on 117th Street between Lexington and Park?"

God Almighty, I tried to control my footsteps and tried not to blow my cool as I made my way to St. Paul's, and diggit, St. Paul's was right across the street from Tia's house.

I tried to find a way to get in without disturbing a service that was going on, and finding a side door, I stopped a padre.

"Con permiso," I said.

"Si, hijo?"

And it felt very good that he said it in Puerto Rican. I explained to him and he said to me, "What did Dulcien's Tia tell you?"

"That someone else is raising him. But, Padre, con tu permiso, when I was in prison . . ."

He looked at me but there was no distaste in his face and I did not look for any and I continued, "Padre, when I was in prison I heard that Dulcien use to leave him chained up, you know, tied so she could go to work. Do you think that was true?"

My voice sounded very childlike and very naive.

He said no.

I wondered if he meant to spare me or if he meant that it was not true.

He said, "Hijo, he has a father now and if you go to claim him, you will do him an injustice."

I said gracias and walked out of St. Paul's wondering if the father he now had was a mortal man or the Father in Heaven.

14

Fink Baking

I was sitting in church one day and a Brother Nachin asked me how I was doing work-wise.

I looked up at Brother Nachin, who because he was nearly six feet tall, was a giant among Puerto Ricans. He carried himself like an athlete—gently but with authority. Although he was thirty-four, he moved like a twenty-year-old. What was striking about him were his red hair and green eyes. Like when he spoke, too, there was hardly a trace of a Puerto Rican accent. He had been born in the States like me.

"I'm still working at the same old job." I frowned.

"Good money?" He smiled.

"Good money? I don't ever expect to get rich there."

"Listen, would you like to work in a bakery?"

"I don't know how to bake." I smiled.

"You don't have to. There's other work there. Porter, packer, and you can work yourself up. If you'd like, I'll take you to the union."

Uhm, I thought. *I hope it's not like the Bricklayers Union.* But I just said, "I'm willing. How about next week? I'd have to give notice at my two jobs."

"Next week." He smiled.

"Next week."

Brother Nachin introduced me to a business agent at the union named Cliff Dawson. We talked a while about past working experience.

"No baking experience?"

"Nope."

"God, we're short of experienced bakers. The old ones are dying out. It's a great time for you young ones to learn the art of cake baking, decorating, bread, etc. But no, you young ones ain't got no patience. You got all the time in the world, but no patience. So what do you do, eh?"

I grinned politely, waiting for him to tell me what I did.

"You waste your time. By the time you learn patience, you got no more time. Damn shame."

I nodded in agreement. I hope he didn't mean me all by myself. If he only knew I was an expert on time. I told him a little.

"I can understand, Mr. Dawson, what you mean. I certainly know how to appreciate time and patience."

"Well, maybe there's hope for you." He grunted gently. "Wait a second, will ya?"

He went to a window and the old lady looked at him. He spoke and she read some papers and then wrote out a slip and handed it to Mr. Dawson. Mr. Dawson came towards me with the slip extended to me.

"I don't usually do this." He smiled. "Like union members first, but there's not one here that wants this job. They all want to work the big bakeries, like General Foods, Bond, and so on. So here you are. It's only for a day, but it's a start. Vacations are coming up soon and we can place you more steady. When you get to the bakery, ask for Mr. Gross, okay?"

"Okay and thanks."

I shook his hand and waved to Brother Nachin, who was waiting for a job with General Foods or Bond.

"Where is it, Piri?"

"It says here Fink Baking."

"It's not too bad. What time do you start?"

"In the morning, and it's only about eight steps from home. That's chevere. Bueno, thanks a lot."

"De nada, Brother Piri."

I caught the train home and read the slip of paper. It was a one day only and it paid fifteen dollars a day and it was for a PORTER. That's me, I hummed, keeping time with the rumbling wheels of the train. *That'sa me . . . the all-around American PORTER, and damn glad I thought that holding down two jobs was a played-out thing of the past. Viva la Bakeries. Hell man, how much can a loaf of bread weigh?*

The next morning I was there like on time and asked to see Mr. Gross.

"That's him over there," said a guy who was so covered by flour that I couldn't see how he could've missed being baked in the oven.

"That one?" I pointed from behind my hand.

"Yup, he's Mr. Gross. We call him the Hungarian, and believe me he's so Hungarian he believes this bakery is in Budapest. He's a good man, works hard, but is a slave-driving sonava bitch."

I walked toward Mr. Gross trying to figure out if the guy that looked like an unbaked loaf of bread liked Mr. Gross or not.

"Mr. Gross?" I reached out the work slip to him.

"A-hurp," he grunted, taking the paper and wiping a couple of tons of sweat from his brow. He scrunched a much suffering handkerchief into his back pocket.

He looked me up and down.

I looked him up and down, too. Heavyset man, about six two, with a million wrinkles on his face and a mountain of iron-gray hair on his head, he was so hairy the stuff was even coming out of his nose and ears. I couldn't help thinking he could be put on some kind of display before the Barbers Institute. He'd drive them nuts with all his hair.

"You goot vorker?" he growled at me again.

"Damn good," I quickly replied.

"It's only one day."

"That's okay, try me."

"Follow me."

I followed him across the long room listening to him bellowing all kinds of orders while he stopped to help a five foot two and a half giant of a cat that was being swallowed up by a mountain of hot rolls coming off a conveyor belt.

Man, I thought, *that smells out of this world. Like bueno, like there's all kinds of bread, all different colors and kinds.* I saw a guy pick up a hot roll and bite into it. I did the same, figuring I was an in-guy. I mean with my work slip and all.

"Hey." I heard a roar and thought somebody had got killed.

"You don't just pick up bread and eat. You gotta vork first and at the end of day, you take home one dozen rolls, or a two-pound loaf of bread. You understand?"

I swallowed the piece in my mouth and hoped he didn't notice the rest go into my back pocket.

"Follow me."

I followed and we went down into the basement.

"You got vork clothes?"

"No, I ain't."

Mr. Gross opened a closet and handed me somebody else's soiled, greasy used-to-be-white uniform.

"Vot size pants you vear?"

"Size thirty." I held the uniform, wondering if it had ever been white.

"You got a belt?"

"Yeah, I do."

"Goot, the pants are size forty-four, vith a belt. It will fit you goot." I wrapped the forty-four waist around me and blessed my belt and tried not to look as ridiculous as I felt.

"Well"—I grinned—"Barnum and Bailey's got itself a new clown." Mr. Gross didn't even crack a smile. Not even a faint shadow of humor crossed his Hungarian face.

Man, this cat ain't human, I thought. I knew I looked funny as hell, especially with the huge greasy jacket on. *God*, I thought, *if the people that handle bread all wear uniforms as greasy as this, I ain't gonna eat bread no mo'.*

"Follow me," said the friendly Hungarian.

He led me to one of the greasiest and funkiest bathrooms I'd ever seen.

"Come in, come in."

I stepped in and doggone nearly slipped on all kinds of different mixtures.

"Ve had a stoppage and everything overflowed, but plumbers fix up and drain is fix. You vork goot and make goot job of cleaning."

I was speechless. My lungs were choking on a hundred-year-old urine.

"There's a room vith name on door. Supplies. It's open, plenty soap, mops, disinfectant, toilet paper. Vhatever you need. Let me know vhen you finish, Hokay?"

And for the first time the Hungarian smiled. It must have

been the wide-open drop of my jaws or the pained expression of "one more time oppressed." By the time I could say anything, Mr. Gross had split for someplace that had some kind of fresh air.

My eyes took in six stalls with greenish-brown fungus inside and outside. Six stand up and take care of you know what, and about eight washbowls. My stomach was doing some kinds of push ups and I felt like cutting out after Mr. Gross and snatching my work slip and shoving it down his throat. But I got ahold of myself and did some bad-fast talking to me.

"Well, Ace," I said to myself in the greasy mirror. "You want to work, right?"

"Right," I answered me.

"You said you're a damn good worker. Right? Right." I felt angry at myself for having bragged so much.

"So, git with it. Right?"

"Aw, go screw yourself," I told the mirror. I went over to the supply closet, copped everything I needed, and then dove into Dante's Inferno with no gusto at all, but with a whole lot of corazón.

At last I was finished. The place was sparkling. The walls spotless, the mirrors were out of sight clean, and the toilet bowls, urine stalls, and washbowls were a miracle. They looked like rows of shining white teeth, just like a chevere ad for some kind of toothpaste. I felt like I had been cleaning for a week, but like I done this supreme creation in three and a half hours.

I washed myself up and re-hitched my size forty-four pants and went upstairs to let Mr. Gross know I'd done my thing to the best of my ability for God and country and Fink Bakery.

"You finished?" Mr. Hungarian asked, like not believing.

"Yes, it's clean."

"Uhm, let me see it."

Before he could say it, I jumped the gun. "Sure, Mr. Gross, *Follow me.* . . ."

He went into the bathroom. He noticed the sign:

FINK MEANS GOOD BREAD

IT ALSO MEANS A CLEAN SHIT HOUSE

IT'S YOUR HOME, KEEP IT CLEAN . . . THE SMELL WON'T SPREAD.

Mr. Gross didn't even crack a smile. That cat wasn't human. That sign was a work of art. I dug his face as he looked around and what appeared to be a loosing of flesh around his mouth let me know it was a smile. He shook his head up and down and said:

"Goot, goot, follow me."

I followed and he led me to a large broom, and soon I was sweeping all around the bakery.

When 5 P.M. came, Mr. Gross called me over.

"You're a goot vorker. Vant a job? Vacation time is starting now. Each vorker gets three weeks off. You can replace the ones that go on vacation."

"What do I do?" I asked, and I swear if Mr. Gross had said, "You're captain of the Toilet from here to ever after," I'd have tried to stuff him down one of his bowls.

"Packing, like there." He pointed to a machine.

"What time do you want me here, Mr. Gross?"

"You take different men's places, you have different times. Some day shifts, some night shifts. Hokay?"

"Hokay." I smiled.

"Come seven-thirty A.M., start tomorrow. I call union, fix it up."

"Thanks, I'll be here tomorrow."

"Vhat you name?"

"Piri Thomas."

"Hokay, Tommy, I give you three clean uniform tomorrow."

"Size thirty?" I was still smiling.

"Size thirty. Hokay . . . uh, maybe size thirty-two. Don't make no different. You got a belt."

I did my work well at Fink and got a try out for second foreman, adding up orders, making calls, checking in drivers and handling cash. I felt funny, I mean about my being an ex-con, like I could take it, I thought, if they found out and if they didn't fire me on account of me being a union member, maybe they'd make me stop handling money, but nobody found out.

I had talked with my parole officer and he was chevere.

"Don't worry, Piri. I ain't out to hurt you. They won't know from me. Just do a good job."

"You bet," I told him. "You bet." And better believe things were going so chevere. You know, I forgot I was an ex-con.

Fink Bakery was treating me right. Diggit, like in jail, *Fink* means a rat, a squealer, but this *Fink* is all right. Diggit.

15

What's a tract, chaplain?

I had just finished rehearsing with the kids in the chorus a hymn that I had written called "None My Lord but Thee" and was lost in some kind of good thoughts . . . I heard someone calling.

"Piri, Piri, oye, que te pasa?"

I looked up and dug Reverend Hernandez.

"Yeah, Chaplain, que pasa?"

"*Chaplain?*" He smiled.

"I guess I was thinking about somebody that's as chevere as you. Remember the guy I told you about? Reverend Claude V. Winch, the prison chaplain at Comstock. Anyway, you don't mind, ch?"

"Of course not, Piri. I'm honored."

"Is there anything wrong?" I cut back to his having busted in on my thoughts.

"Si. I mean no. There's nothing wrong. In fact it is something—uh—chevere."

I laughed at his identifying with chevere.

"Bueno, Chaplain, what's great?"

He sat down next to me. While I was waiting for him to tell me something chevere, my eyes dug the paintings on the wall around the pulpit—a Bible entwined with a crown of thorns and a cross—and across from it was a white dove, un pichon blanco, that signified the Holy Ghost.

"Piri," he told me, "the American Bible Society wants to put out a tract about you."

"What's a tract, Chaplain?"

"It's a booklet that's put out to let people know what changes God has made in people. Would you mind doing it? There's a man who wants to talk to you about it."

"I don't mind, Chaplain."

"Bueno, you can meet him tomorrow and you can talk with him. Dios te bendiga."

"The same to you, Chaplain." He got up and walked away. For a big man this ex-heavyweight fighter talked real light.

The next day I met this Christian cat who wanted to turn me into a tract. Together we talked as we rode around in a station wagon full of Bibles and mucho tracts. He had a tape recorder, and he asked questions and I answered him, half of my mind on the golden kingdom of heaven and the other half on the dirty kingdom of El Barrio. I couldn't help asking myself if rats and roaches, garbage and misery, hate and poverty, had to be included in God's overall planning of the universe.

"May I call you Piri?"

"Porque no? That's my name. What's yours again?"

"Philip Walters."

"Glad to know you. You do this kind of work full time, Phil?"

"Yes, I do," he answered.

"Pays good?"

"Well, it doesn't make me rich, but I get by."

"Who's your boss?" I felt I was making nice conversation.

"I work for the American Christian Tract Association."

"You just go around getting information."

"That's about it. If we hear of someone who's really been living a life of sin and then has accepted Christ as their personal savior, we try to get their personal testimony and we put it out in a booklet."

"Who do you sell it to?" I asked.

"Oh, it goes all over the country. Different churches and organizations."

"Cost a lot?"

"No, about two dollars for a year's subscription."

"Do the people who give you the story of their lives get paid for it?"

Phil laughed a little. "No, the people contribute their testimonies to further the Lord's work." When he said that I laughed, too.

"But where does the money go?"

"Like I said, it really goes to further the Lord's work. Printing cost, supplies, salaries, and so on. It's really expensive, but one cannot always judge the Lord's work in terms of money."

"I see," I said, not really seeing.

Phil didn't say anything else. He brushed his crew cut hair with one hand and let his green eyes check out traffic.

At the same time I dug a couple of dogs making out in the middle of the street. There was a ring of kids digging the doggies' sex scene. I copped a look from the corner of my eye at Philip Walters to dig his reaction. He was looking hard at the red light like it wasn't ever gonna turn green. He looked embarrassed. I shrugged my shoulders and mentally chewed back some words to him . . . about . . . what are you so up tight about—ain't that the way most things get started, so things can get born? The cat really looked smug.

"Piri," he said, about four blocks later. "I'm going to interview Captain Donaldson at the local precinct. Want to come along?"

"Porque no?" I smiled. *On my old turf—wowie—I'm going in there without having to be kicked up them steps.*

We walked up them steps and Phil talked to the desk sergeant, who was polite and pointed out the captain's office. I followed Phil in, while my eardrums were catching some cat's outraged screams of, "I'm innocent, you ain't got no right . . ." and as the door closed behind me, "Willya shut up, this is your eighth bust for pushing drugs." My eyes watched a gringo who was about six foot two and yea wide get up and in a hearty-soft voice say, "I'm very pleased to meet you. I'm Captain Donaldson."

"I'm Philip Walters."

My eyes were in the back of my head trying to find the shortest way out, but my mouth said, "I'm Piri Thomas."

Everybody shook hands and sat down, except me. There were a lotta places I could be uncomfortable in—and like this was one of them.

"Take a chair—Piri Thomas, right?"

"Right." I glanced at the seat and my brown eyes turned it into an electric chair and I sat on its edge accordingly.

"Relax."

I relaxed—and then remembered having seen this police-man before. He was a Christian policia. I heard him telling Phil Walters that he was a lay minister.

Captain Donaldson asked me a whole lotta questions. I dug the Bible on his desk and answered them wondering if I were directing my words at his gun or at his Bible. I dug his face and it was sincere.

"Would you two like to look around our precinct?"

"Would love to, Brother Donaldson," smiled Phil. My smile

was so slight that it told its story—like, man—I've been through this way mucho times, like thanks a lot.

"Piri?"

"Sure. Be glad to."

We cut out of that office and ran into a couple of plainclothesmen. Wowie, did I know them! These two cats had earned a whole lot of respect—from bad cats. It was *hating* respect, but respect just the same. Captain Donaldson introduced us to them.

"This is Phil Walters from the American Bible Society and this is Piri Thomas. Do you remember about six or so years ago that big shoot-out with some stick-up men, where some officers got shot. Well, this is one of them." Evidently, the captain had known who I was all along.

I looked cara palo at the dic-te-tives. They looked hard at me. I remembered their nicknames, Smilin' Jack and Bulldog Drummond.

The conversation went back and forth, but my mind returned to prison and once again to Tato Ruiz.

Tato was being released. He had finished up his sentence. I watched him go and wished him luck. But, like every con, I guess I was jealous. It wasn't me going to the free side.

Some months later, Tato was on the lam. According to the papers he was mixed up in a contract killing which involved some judge or other. I don't remember which or what, but it was a big stink in all the newspapers. Most of us were listening in on our earphones in our cells . . . the cops were looking for him, among them Smilin' Jack and Bulldog Drummond, and they were mucho hot after him.

He got trapped in an apartment in one of the projects and somehow or other he got away from them. They found him in an apartment on the East Side and he got away again, after nearly killing them in a running gun battle. Finally, Tato got trapped in an apartment on 112th Street in El Barrio.

The cat on the radio was there on the scene and was playing it up big and bad. His voice had me there with him. I could see it all . . . the police are all over the place, hundreds of policemen are all over the place . . . machine guns . . . riot guns . . . bulletproof vests . . . loudspeakers calling on him to surrender . . . people being evacuated . . . the streets full of living people . . . curious people who would brave a stray bullet in the head rather than miss a ringside show standing room only.

Tato, here you are, there you are, like you said, holding court in the street and damn if you ain't gonna be found guilty. But you'll get away one way or another . . . won't you?

The voice of the announcer was tense. "The streets are crowded. It constitutes a danger. The police are trying to clear the area." The blaring loudspeaker pushed forth an ultimatum, "Ruiz . . . Ruiz . . . come on out with your hands behind your head, you're surrounded, you haven't a chance . . . come on out . . . N . . . O . . . W . . . !!!"

Here and there from different cells come the words of encouragement. "Don't give up, Tato. Waste them mother fuckin' cops!"

Yeah, Tato, hold court right there on 112th Street, baby.

The news announcer wailed on as if he knew what was gonna be the bad-ass end result.

"It looks like he's not going to surrender and has opened fire. The police are retaliating with machine gun fire."

What are you thinking about now, Tato, buddy? Still feel

you can't dream like ordinary people? Still think this is just a part of your last nightmare? My mind kept on working thoughts . . .

The announcer's voice was soon even more high-pitched. *Tato, little baby man, it looks like this fight ain't going fifteen rounds.*

"The fugitive has been pouring out a steady stream of gunfire. He must still have the police pistols he reportedly took from the two detectives and enough ammunition to . . ."

Announcer, caramba, you sound tense, like you're scared.

I wonder how Tato feels . . . the hours went by and like all of a sudden it was over . . . mucho bullets had ripped the dingy flat apart, tear gas and cops with guts crashed into the apartment and they found Tato barricaded behind furniture and under a bed, with his head and arms out, still shooting— and then they killed him.

Not guilty, eh, Tato? Or guilty with a way out, the back door parole, eh, Tato?

I heard cats yelling, "Boo . . . boo . . . boo-ooooooooooo." Like cons are funny people and ain't gonna give credit to no cops.

"Aw, they didn't kill Tato," someone cried out. "He shot it out and kept one slug for himself."

"Where did they shoot him? In the head, right? Well, he shot himself, there's where you usually plug yourself when it's time to go, ain't it?"

Tato, I ain't gonna go your way. At least, I'm gonna try not to go. Jesus, Tato, you had a lot of corazón, but some damn thing else got to go along with that so a cat can make it. You had a whole lot, Tato-killer—integrity, ethics, morals.

But you stopped having dreams, and all you had left was nightmares.

Adios, panin. I promise one thing though, I'm thinking over what you said, and, Tato, I think there was a reflection of me in your face that day in the yard. Like maybe I just didn't want to see. Sleep well, Hermano.

Now, I hear Captain Donaldson saying, "And Piri's doing a good job around here," and Smilin' Jack is saying flat things like, "Well, people can change."

Yeah, I thought, *like people gotta have something to change for and from.* There was some kind of a handshaking and some see-you-arounds and after looking about some more, we were back in Captain Donaldson's office.

I stared at him.

"Say, Piri, I've got an idea." He smiled. "I'd like you to meet somebody. He did some time, too."

Some thoughts jumped into my mind. *Diggit, something's gotta be wrong. This policia wants me to meet somebody that's done time and like off the bat, that's a violation. Wonder if it's some kind of setup. Or maybe this cat he wants me to meet is some kind of rat-squealer.*

The captain must of dug the funny look on my face.

"What's the matter, Piri?"

"It's a violation, ain't it? And like you know I'm on parole, and if it's for being an informer or like in nice words an undercover agent, *NO GOOD.*"

"Nothing like that." He laughed. Philip Walters smiled. I just stared dead-panned.

"His name is John Clause." The captain's finger was dialing a phone number. He explained what a fine Christian and reverend this Clause was. "Hallo, John," he said, once his call had gone through, "can you come over to the station for a while . . . okay . . . okay, fine, see you."

"You said he did time." I made some kind of half-smile.

"That's right." Captain Donaldson had hung up the phone. "Er . . . you heard Clause's testimony, didn't you, Phil?"

"Sure did, Captain. He came from a good, upright Christian family. Got the best education money could buy and still went sour. He started getting into one trouble after another. Small robberies. Then burglaries. Finally committed armed robberies. He was caught and sent to prison."

"Did much time?" I asked.

"Not much," answered Captain Donaldson. "But even after he was out and got into the Navy, he was caught stealing equipment. He served some more time, but through some pull or other, got out with a 'dishonorable discharge' and went on to better—or worse—things, depending on whose viewpoint you're looking at it from."

"He got mixed up with some big-time gangs," Phil interrupted. "And tried some kind of double cross."

I smiled. Like somehow the word double cross seemed strange coming from Philip Walters. He continued. "But you don't do that with those organized gangs and get away with it."

"You talking about the Mafia?" I asked.

"Who knows? Maybe, if there's such a thing."

"There's such a thing," I said. "But how did he double-cross them?" I pumped for information.

"It's quite involved. But he was beating them on different kinds of bets being placed all over the country on all kinds of races and he had a system that let him know the winner of the dog or horse race or whatever. Like five or ten minutes before the bookies. So imagine the money he cleaned up.

Anyway, when they found out, he had to run. In the city he was heading for, they were waiting there for him to kill him."

"And then the Lord put his hand on John Clause," Phil gently broke in. "John's wife pleaded with him to attend an outdoor evangelistic meeting before heading for that city. John went begrudgingly, heard the preaching, got his heart touched by the Lord, heeded the call to accept Jesus, and with hundreds of others went forward, got on his knees, and became a new man."

"Man." I smiled. "Like he had himself a narrow escape."

"Indeed he did. Some others involved with him were found shot to death."

"Anyway," the captain added, "he'll be here in a few minutes. Want to wait, Piri?"

"Why not, Captain? I'd like to meet him," I said. As I did, I dug the word double-crosser bouncing itself into my memory bank. It's a tough and dangerous thing to pull on the streets. Captain Donaldson shuffled through some papers on his desk. I relaxed in my chair and sat back to wait, my eyes seeing PAL awards and pictures on the walls of human beings wearing police uniforms with their arms around kids. And I remembered Momma getting toys a few times for Christmas and I wondered if it had been at this police station. Probably, I thought.

I tilted my head so that my eyes could see who was coming in. I dug a tall and very thin man walk in. He moved lightly.

"John, this is Piri Thomas."

I shook his long thin outstretched hand and dug his face. It was sort of ruddy-colored and like it was alive with a smile, not just his lips, but all of his face.

"Glad to know you, Piri," he said politely.

"Same here, John," I answered on cortesia.

John sat down free and easy. But his eyes were running all over me. Mine were doing the same kind of dance all over him. But it was all done coolly and casually by both of us.

"Piri, John here has come in from out of town," Captain Donaldson informed me. "He's deeply interested in working with children, especially gang kids."

John Clause's eyes and mine were still doing some kind of appraisal job, like a pawnbroker who's figuring out what the merchandise is worth. John Clause broke in.

"Piri, I got a rundown on you."

Rundown? I thought. *This cat sounds like a policeman.*

"Want to fill me in on details about your background?"

I briefly told him things I had done. Then just on general principle, I asked him about his past experiences, although Captain Donaldson had just filled me in. Clause gave me a re-hash of the events, ending by saying that God had put it into his heart to come to New York and work with teen-age gangs. "My background in crime fits me for Christian ministry with these kids," he added, "and, Piri, with your background and new way of thinking, you could be a great help."

I said nothing. John wrote down an address, handed it to me. "Why don't you come down Monday morning. We can talk some more then. I've got a storefront club."

"Yeah, okay," I answered.

"Fine, I'll see you then. Lord's blessing on you, Piri."

"Uh . . . oh yeah . . . uh, the same on you, er . . . Reverend Clause."

"For the sake of the kids, I don't want to be known as a

holy Joe. So if it's all the same to you, just call me John. Okay?"

I nodded, shook his outstretched hand, then waved good-by to everybody. As the door closed behind me, I heard someone say, "See you in church."

I didn't answer cause my eyes were digging Smilin' Jack and Bulldog Drummond walking upstairs with some cat whose hands were handcuffed behind him. I checked out of the police station.

That evening I didn't tell Nita about my meeting with John Clause. I wanted to wait until after I had seen him in more action on Monday.

"Have a good day?" Nita asked as I walked in.

"Si." I was mulling over the offer of working with kids, and the good job I had at Finks. I decided to let the thoughts drop out of my mind until Monday.

"Want to eat?"

"Now you're talking, honey. Whatcha got, eh? . . . Whatcha got? Rice and beans?"

Nita laughed. "Whatsa matter? You think Puerto Rican rice and beans is the only food in the world. We got spaghetti and meat balls."

I laughed and started humming an Italian song called "Sorento." Sat at the table and downed me two plates of Michelangelo's favorite food.

I found my way to the clubhouse near Third Avenue. The door was locked. I knocked and heard somebody moving inside. The door opened. There stood John.

"Come in, Piri."

Once inside I carefully looked around. Things were nicely

fixed up. Soda fountain, tables, chairs, even a small pool table. I had to admit it looked like a club should.

"Like it?" John said.

"Chevere." I kept looking around. "Uh, how come the front windows are painted over?"

"Well." John laughed. "It's because we had some trouble between the Italian kids and the Porto Ricans. The Italian kids felt this club was strictly for them and when I had some Porto Rican kids in here, they broke the front window and tried to come in to fight the Porto Rican kids."

"And what happened?" I asked, still checking the scene out.

"The Porto Rican kids charged at them. Fortunately, a patrol car came by and everybody scattered."

"So that's why you painted the windows over?" I looked askance.

John grinned. "No, I painted them over to hide . . . Wait a second. Come and take a look." I followed him to the front of the club. He pulled some curtain away from the windows and there was a wall of bricks.

"Neat, eh?"

I said nothing.

"Like if anybody tries to break in again, the brick wall will keep them out."

I shook my head up and down in understanding, while digging the workmanship of the brick wall.

"Well, let's go into the office and get to know each other and what the club is all about. Er . . . want a soda? Help yourself." John pointed towards the soda fountain.

"No thanks." I smiled, thinking on how the place looked like a fortress. There were mucho bars on the back windows.

I sat down in front of his desk. John eased himself into his chair and started talking about himself.

"I'm an ex-con like yourself."

"You still on parole?" I asked him, my eyes still digging the bars on the back room windows.

"No, I got a pardon, after I got converted and changed my way of living. Through Christ a man's made anew."

"I'm still on parole. I owe the state seven years. I don't know if I really should call myself an ex-con yet, like owing seven years I can go back to jail-time anytime the parole officer thinks I've blown my cool. Like owing them that kind of time still makes me a con."

"You only have to worry about that if you figure on messing up."

"Don't figure on that. Got a chevere job at Fink Bakery."

John started talking on how he got busted, and he gave me even more information than before on his background. I listened half turned on, half turned off. Like so many of us in El Barrio had been busted at one time or another that having the rep of having done time was no big thing.

When John finished talking, I simply told him I was glad he had made it. Then I asked what was happening with the club and how did I fit in. "What's the deal?" I asked.

"Well, it's like this," John explained. "I've come to work with the ghetto kids here in the Barrio because the Lord has put this into my heart."

"We got a lotta organizations working with kids around here now," I said.

"I know that, but the idea is to change their lives through discipline in the Lord. I want to be able to reach the hardcore kids . . . the gangs."

"Yeah, I know. A whole lot can stand to see a better way of living on this turf."

"Turf?"

"Yeah, turf. Our streets, you know, fulla hot and cold running cockroaches and king-size rats, rotten buildings, like you no doubt have noticed."

"Yes, yes, but a change must take place from within before one can be evident from without."

John was leaning on the desk. His voice sounded muy sincero.

I just thought to myself about how better it would be if both changes could come at the same time.

"Still, John, how do I fit in?" I asked.

"Well, you got a rep with the kids. You're from the streets. You've been through it and you know what Christ is all about. You're of—as you say it—the turf. There are a lot of places I can't go that you can. You'll be able to reach the kids and get them to become part of the club. They don't fully trust me yet. I'm a white man from some other part of the country. Even their knowing I did time doesn't impress them. I'm an outsider, but you're one of them. God, I've climbed thousands of stairs and knocked at hundreds of doors, but most don't open and those that do, shut real fast. I've only been able to get a few kids to respond."

"It would be great," I said slowly, "to get them together with good ideas. Get them to stop bopping against each other. Get them not to drop out of school, to make something out of their lives."

"Through Jesus Christ," John added.

"Of course," I said, "that, too. It's an all-around getting together. Kids with good educations can help get rid of all this dirty-ass crap that's happening."

"Ah, Piri?"

"Yeah, John."

"One rule. We don't use profanity. It's not a good example for the kids."

I just nodded, thinking how adept our kids were at using so-called bad words.

"I mean, you and I can understand profanity, but the kids . . . well, you understand?"

Not really, I thought, *but I could always sacrifice an expressive word such as ass, if it would help ease his sensitive nature.*

"Anyway, if you come and join me in the Lord's work, you'll be in charge of the boys. I'm praying that the Lord will send a woman to head up the girls' unit."

"It sounds like a good idea, but I have a pretty good job at Fink and . . ."

"What do you earn?" John asked.

"With overtime I clear about a hundred and five bolos, sometimes more."

"Look, this is for the Lord. I have to see my Board, cause they make the final decisions. But are you willing to start at a hundred ten a week? There's no overtime pay, but most possibly a lot of overtime work. Your take-home pay depends on your dependents."

"I'll talk it over with my wife, Nita, and let you know, John."

"When? You can really be an asset."

"Tomorrow."

We shook hands. I let myself out, but not before cutting a look at the beige curtains that hid a brick wall.

As I walked home I knew I wanted to work with our kids. I knew that I was gonna say yes to John, and I knew that whatever I decided, Nita would go along with it, as long as it had something to do with the Lord.

A hundred bucks a week. After deductions, maybe eighty-six or eighty-seven bucks. But short money or not, like I hadda do it. Man, like with a Christian organization behind me. Imagine how many Carlitos and Carlitas could be helped and saved all at once.

I climbed the stairs, rehearsing how I was gonna put it into words to Nita about quitting Fink and joining John and Jesus in God's work.

Nita just listened as I laid it on her. What John had said, the importance of the work. I talked mucho and then kept quiet. I walked over and opened a window to let the street noises break up my quiet.

"What do you think, Piri?" Nita walked over to my side.

"I'd like to do it, honey."

"Then do it."

I knocked at the office door and watched Mr. Fink through the glass pane. He looked up and waved me in.

"Hi, Mr. Fink. I got something I'd like to talk over with you and as a matter of fact, with your partner Mr. Rosen."

"Is it important, Tommy?"

I smiled a yes and another smile on top of that, thinking, *Nobody calls me Piri in the bakery. It's Tommy.*

Mr. Fink called on the intercom. As we waited for Mr. Rosen, I remembered all the chevere things Mr. Fink would do to help out his workers. Like lend money for emergencies, operations, cats having to go to Puerto Rico because of family troubles. Like he'd help out. Others messing up on their jobs and him giving them mucho chances.

Mr. Rosen came in and sat down. He asked what the trouble was.

Mr. Fink said, "Tommy's got something he says is important."

"Well, let's hear it." Mr. Rosen pulled out a long cigar and lit it.

I started talking. Letting it all hang out about my past. On being on drugs, on getting busted, doing time for armed robbery, and being on parole.

Both remained silent while I talked on.

"I wanna tell you, like it was a hard knot in my guts. I mean, my working up to second foreman and your trusting me with making out them large orders and handling a lot of cash from the drivers. I mean a real big knot in my guts, not because I was tempted to cop anything that wasn't mine, but like afraid you were gonna find out I was on parole and maybe not fire me on account I'm union, but like worse, like stop trusting me and pull me away from handling cash and credit and all the rest. Maybe someday I would have told you straight out, but I'm telling you now, cause I'm going to have to quit. And I'd rather be the one than anybody else someday coming up to you and saying, 'Hey, remember Tommy, didn't you know you had an ex-con working for you?' I wanted to tell you in case somebody made a mistake with your cash or credit, that I wouldn't get smacked with it. I wanted to tell . . .'"

"Why are you quitting, Tommy?" asked Mr. Rosen.

I quickly explained about my job offer with John and the youth club.

The two men merely looked at each other.

"We had been talking about a night supervisor's opening at night," Fink then told me, "and we had you in mind."

"Thanks, Mr. Fink," I said, "but you do understand how I feel about taking care of business in my Barrio."

"I do. But we hate to lose you. Good luck to you anyway, Tommy. If there's anything Jerry or I can ever do in the future, just let us know."

I shook hands with them and said from the door, "I feel good that you know from where I came."

"Good luck, Tommy."

"Good luck to you." I smiled.

"Shalom aleichem." They smiled.

I cut back to work and gently started taking care of Fink Bread. Had to—that damn bread was mucho hot. *Hey diggit,* I thought, *Shalom aleichem means peace unto you.* I felt good about that but suddenly I screamed out trying to suppress some kind of cuss words on account of some boiling hot bread messing up my hands. Wow!!

16

From lawbreaker to peacemaker

It was a clear, bright sunny morning when I walked into the club to begin my first day with John. Outside the clubhouse there had been some Italian kids who had looked me up and down with a mixture of curiosity and suspicion. I had just smiled and gone into the club.

I nodded at three or four Puerto Rican and black youngsters sitting inside. All were between the ages of fifteen and sixteen years. They seemed friendlier, no doubt because we belonged to the same skin and language club.

I soon spotted John, who greeted me in his usual friendly manner.

"Well, buddy," he said, "besides my introducing you to those already established with the club, you're on your own to make a breakthrough in the community, and like, well . . . I don't see any trouble in your handling that end. Hey, let me introduce you to a few of the guys."

John led me into the game room, where he introduced me to some of the club members.

For a few minutes I laughed to myself. Then, finally, I broke into John's introduction, saying, "Hey, I've seen some of you guys around. Like you're with the Untouchables."

"Yeah, that's right," one fellow called out. "My name's Chinko, and this is Timko and Ace."

I shook hands with all of them.

"Mine's Lil Man," another fellow called out, stepping up to shake my hand. "But I ain't with the Untouchables." He smiled.

"Glad to know you, panin."

"Mine's Shade," another said. "I'm with the Untouchables, black branch."

"Okay, Brother. Glad to know you, too." I laughed.

"Let's see if there are some other fellers outside," John said, and I followed him outside. The same Italian youngsters were outside. As we were walking up to them, I dug them looking our way and what they figured was a whisper between them was really loud talking in my ear.

"Wonder what that con man wants now?" one sixteen-year-old whispered.

If John heard, he didn't let on.

"Hey, Sal, Joseph, Al, I want you to meet Piri Thomas, who grew up around . . ."

"Hey, John," one kid interrupted, "I told you to call me Animal. Not Joseph. S'matter? Can't you remember my name?"

John smiled. "Okay . . . okay, Animal it is. Anyway, Piri's gonna work with the club and you'll be seeing a lot of him."

"Why didncha get an Italian youth worker?" Animal said, looking stareface at me.

"Would you like the job, amigo?" I smiled.

"How much does it pay?" He grinned.

"About ninety-five bucks a week, take-home pay." I laughed. "That enough for you?"

"Naw, shit, that's chicken feed. I pulled down two or three times that much working on the trucks."

"That's pretty cool," I said, almost tempted to have him get me a job working with him.

The one called Sal broke in with, "Well, we don't get along too well with spics and niggers."

I felt myself tighten up, but I kept my voice calm and steady. "Well, that's your problem, not ours. But like the idea of the club . . ."

"Is to see if we can all get along," interrupted Animal.

"Something like that, Animal . . . something like that. See you guys around." I walked back into the clubhouse leaving John to yak with them.

"Say, Piri?"

I looked at Timko, whose youthful eyes were widened with curiosity.

"Yeah?"

"Ain't you the one who done time after shooting it out with the nabs?"

"Yeah, something like that." I smiled. I didn't feel it was the right time to be talking about my past. But I soon changed the subject. "Hey, any you guys play pool?"

"Best stick in town," said Lil Man.

"You're on, Lil Man. Cop a stick."

"Hey, whatta want us to call you?"

"Just by my name. Piri's good enough."

"Break, Piri."

I smiled and broke, spreading balls all over the pool table.

In the long months that followed the clubhouse was always jumping with young bloods. Boys and girls—just relaxing, rapping, and digging one another's vibes. Like mucho things were going on. I was also doing my best to keep the peace between gangs as well as to keep a lot of the group in school and off drugs. *Diggit,* I thought to myself, *from lawbreaker to peacemaker. Who would've believed it seven or eight years ago?*

One night I remember I had just checked my watch and it was about ten and I was about to close up the club. I was talking a bit with a white volunteer worker, Gary. We were just shooting the bull when suddenly I heard an up tight voice coming seemingly out of nowhere at me. It was a pretty Puerto Rican girl named Graciella.

"Petey, Petey," she called, out of breath.

"What's happenin', girl?"

"Oh, man, Petey, you gotta make it. Manuel's gonna kill Timko."

I locked the club, shoved the keys in my pocket, and followed Graciella. I almost forgot the young man next to me. I turned to him.

"Want to come with me?" I asked Gary.

"Sure will, Petey, if it's all right."

The three of us cut down Second Avenue in no time. Funny thoughts ran down my mind. Like why can't there be more people like this cat by my side, who really wants to help? Porque else would he be here?

There it was—right in the middle of the projects, 112th Street between First and Second avenues—Manuel, Timko, and four or five of Manuel's boys. Manuel had his arm around Timko's throat and was pressing a gun against the small of his back. I decided to play it cool.

"Manuel," I said, "man, what's shakin?"

Manuel grinned a bit and then it faded as he dug the white dude, Gary, standing beside me.

"Is that the Man?" He looked dead at me, pointing an accusing finger.

"Nay, baby, he ain't no cop. He's my friend. What's happening?"

"I'm gonna kill this basura," he yelled, turning his head in Timko's direction.

I dug Timko hung up in a real tight sense of helplessness. Who wouldn't feel that way with a gun that could blow a bullet and blast your life away?

"Manuel!" I thought I was shouting it, but actually it came out as a whisper. "Why burn Timko? Can't you beat him in a fair one?"

Timko was about to say something, but I used the best of my street psychology and shut him up. "Shut up, dammit. I ain't talking to you!" I roared.

Manuel had Timko's life in his hand and I had to play some kind of street chess so that Timko could walk away with it.

"Caramba yeah," Manuel said, no doubt hip to my psychology. "I can put this maricon in my pocket."

"Chevere, Manuel."

I smiled and at the same momento dug the relief on Timko's face. Very easy and smooth-like I reached for Manuel's piece, felt it in my hand as he let it go, and put it in my pocket. Manuel whipped his jacket off while breathing all kinds of hells, his fierce eyes revealing his anger towards Timko. I led Timko just a few short steps away. "Deal, baby," I told him. "It's better than a cold pistola stuck up under your armpit. No matter how big your lumps, baby, you at least got a chance of getting up por la mañana."

I looked at Manuel. "A chevere one, fair all the way. I got your word?"

"You got my word, Petey."

And Timko walked away with Manuel.

I let out a sigh of relief.

Gary walked beside me as I left the projects. I dug his voice saying very softly, "Petey, surely God has His hand on you."

I couldn't help thinking that His hand and my own two did beat a blank. *Thanks a lot, Jesus. The worst Timko can get is a closed eyeball and a slight case of knuckled lockjaw and that's better than being a long time muerto. Like next time, maybe the odds will be in his favor.*

I got out of bed very quietly and walked over to the window and looked down from the fourteenth floor and still smelled the kind of funny hospital smell from where I had just come. . . .

I let my mind float out there and put together the bop and how it went down. . . .

I could see the fellas hanging around the stoop. . . . It was on a Thursday night cause Manuel had the fight with Timko on Wednesday.

It was about ten-thirty . . . There was Louis, Little Blue, Johnny, Junior, Torres, about fourteen guys, and . . . .

"Hey, dig, man, ain't that Timko coming here? Man, he looks all messed up."

Louis jumps off the stoop and the rest of the guys followed right behind.

"Jesus, Timko! What the hell happened?"

"Oh them mother jumpers . . ."

Timko's lips are bloody, his eyebrows split. His face is full of sangre. His clothes are ripped and dirty, and he looks like somebody used him for a walking rug.

"Damn, man," screams Little Blue. "What cat did you up?"

Timko leans heavily against the iron railing of the stoop and holds on to his ribs and spits blood.

"Get the guys, man. I got snagged by Joe and Willie up at the San Juan."

"You mean at the upstairs dance club?" asked Louis.

"Like, man, you got some suerte (luck). First yesterday, you deal with Manuel and got all messed up."

Timko's blood-look at Louis makes him back up.

"Damn, man." Timko breathed hard. "I met some of Manuel's boys and they started to sound me low on how I got done up by Manuel, and like, especially by that motherless Joe Buck Tooth."

"Ain't that his war counselor?"

"Yeah."

"I heard he's Manuel's right-hand tight Hermano."

"Yeah, but I checked him out good. I busted his curly head with a full no deposit bottle of cream soda."

"And que paso?" asked Louis.

"Can't you see, you stupid maricon (faggot), I'm bleeding?"

"Well, let's call the shit on." Little Blue is impatient.

. . . . Yeah, I can just see it. I push my mind out a little further into that street and walk with my boys. The tempo speed goes faster and louder and la venganza kick is going down. . . .

"Walk smooth, fellas. Don't pick up suspicion. Don't let the Man see us walking too fast."

"Here we are."

There are the long steps leading up to the San Juan. Dig that smooth Puerto Rican rhythm falling down. Timko is all for crashing the dance hall. He's a mucho angry cat.

"Naw, hold it," says Louis. "I know the guys that snagged

you. Let me smooth-talk them and smooth-walk them out of the joint, and then . . ."

A long pause and Louis rubs his hands and shrugs his shoulders. Little Blue agrees. Johnny agrees. All the fourteen guys agree, and Timko agrees.

"Up there or down here on the streets—makes no difference. I want to cop me some jaws."

I can see your bright shining eyes, Timko. I wonder whose fault it was you got your behind whipped the first time. Makes no difference, the reason ain't the thing. The thing is you got wasted and you want your turn at wasting.

"Yeah, fellas, let's wait down here in the cool down shadows for the meat."

"I'll be right back."

Full of heart, Louis goes into the semi-darkness of low red lights, blue lights, paper decorations, and record music in among the fast-moving mambo feet and the wild fallout of fancy down steps. Smooth guys and stacked muchachas.

Louis spots Ace, one of Joe's boys. "Hey, Ace, come here," he calls.

"What you want?"

"It's Louis, your boy. You know."

"Yeah, Louis, what's shaking? Joe ain't here. He got his head split and is getting it sewed up at Flower Hospital."

"Hey, Ace, can I see you outside, man. It's important. I'm in a jam and I need your help."

"No sweating, amigo. You ain't bothering me."

That's a nice answer, Ace, but you should have said, Some other time, Louis, I'm busy now.

Louis puts his arm around Ace's shoulders, walks him from the dance hall, away from his boys, and whispers confidentially into his ear all his lies and problems.

Now Louis has him out in the hall. All that is separating Ace from getting wasted are a long flight of stairs, maybe twenty or thirty steps. Louis looks over his shoulder, making sure none of Ace's boys have jumped wise and are maybe following. No, nobody is coming out.

"Well, Louis, what's the trouble, what can I do for you?"

"Oh, nuttin," says Louis, "except . . . wambo . . ."

"Oh . . . OH . . ."

Little Blue yells from downstairs, "I think you broke his jaw." Down the long flight of stairs comes Ace, head over heels into waiting hands and feet.

The blood gushes out of Ace's nose.

"Timko, get your kicks on Route Sixty-six," yells Little Blue.

Slam—bam . . . .

"You mother jumper . . . think you're gonna jump me and get away with it?"

Johnny yells out, "Hey, there's two more of his boys coming out."

And two more cats are swallowed up under fourteen pairs of fists and feet. Everybody is piling out of the dance hall San Juan, but just to check out the scene.

"Little Blue, Ace is getting away. Watch im."

Ace, bloody and really mangled, is scrambling, running low from side to side. His face is low and so is Little Blue's foot, and the two meet. Ace's mouth is full of hard shoe leather and Blue's shoe is wet with blood, and somewhere on that dark sidewalk are some of Ace's teeth.

Ace scrambles up and runs, still keeping himself up.

"Man," Timko screams as he digs Ace getting away. "That's my meat, get him."

And then Manuel turns up. Suddenly both sides stand frozen just looking at each other.

"The shit's on with you mothers," screams Manuel. "Call it when you want it. Get your boys. Set the place and set the time. I'm getting you," Manuel screams, pointing at Timko, ". . . and you"—pointing at Blue—". . . and you . . . and you . . . and you . . . all you mother fuckin' punks. Me, I'm gonna put you in my pocket."

Manuel breaks loose toward Timko. Blue pulls out a piece. Somebody yells, "Watch out."

Timko pulls a .32 caliber. Then like everybody freezes solid.

Damn, Manuel, you hadda keep your rep up, eh?

You're a Cobra.

Manuel blows sky high. "Burn, mother jumpers, burn. I'm a Cobra to my heart. Burn!" he cried, then rushed into Timko.

There is some kind of little noises from a .22 and other ones from a .32 caliber.

My mind thought on . . . *and they burned you, Manuel, didn't they? And you fell still screaming, I'm a bad walking Cobra to my heart.*

I went to the kitchen for some Mavi, drank a glass, and went back to fourteen floors above the city and went on thinking how I got the word after having come back with some other kids from seeing the fights at St. Nick's Arena.

I cut out to Metropolitan Hospital, where they had taken Manuel. He was alive, but maybe better muerto. Like one of those bullets had torn up his spine. He was paralyzed from the middle of his body down to the tips of his toes. He wasn't going to walk no mas. . . .

. . . All kinds of hell was gonna break loose, because all

the old Cobras from long ago—I mean cats who were twenty
to thirty-five years old—other angry kids—fifteen, twelve, eight
years old—I mean even those who were unborn in their
mother's womb were calling for the shit to be called on—
like war—

I listened to his boys and heard some fierce talking words,
like mangling and blood and wasting cats up. We're gonna
call the shit on with them Tigers . . . and in my mind I
wondered what I, who was trying to get my people together,
was gonna say, because I, too, wanted to get a piece to fight
alongside my boy's bullet-splintered spine.

Concho, I'm one of his. And another part of my mind,
Yeah, but ain't you one of them, too?

Like both sides are Puerto Ricans. What can you tell a
blood brother in a scene like that?

I whispered into Manuel's ear. "Hermanito, tell our people
the bop ain't on. Let's not tear up cats who didn't have nothing to do with it. We're gonna have all kinds of brother clubs
involved and diggit, Manuel, it's P.R. against P.R. Here are
all your boys waiting for the word 'GO.'"

Swear to God, my mind was jumping all over itself. "Cool
it, baby, take care of it yourself," I said.

Out of his pain, I dug him smile. It was a long, long silence, so long I heard it in my mind as he looked at his boys
and snapped his fingers in mucho pain and said, "Cool it.
I'll take care of it."

I pressed his shoulder and held his hand and then walked
out of that room with all them old cats and young cats and
unborn cats and walked down a long corridor and out into a
real bad breeze street. . . .

I wondered if God really dug about what was happening
in El Barrio?

I kept on walking, trying to keep hurting tears from jumping six feet out of my ojos and found myself split away, alone, from the Cobras.

I stopped near Park Avenue and 111th Street right next to the La Marketa and leaned against a '58 Chevy. Unsaid palabras rushed out of me.

Dammit, if we Puerto Ricans gotta fight, let it be against these rotten putrid conditions, cockroaches, the rats, and rundown buildings, against no good schools, no good jobs, no good living time. Let's get together. If we gotta die, caramba, let it not be at each other's hands. Let's have had it with "Aye, Bendito," and let's get together . . . we gotta bop . . . let's bop against what's choking us to death. Let's take each other's hands from around each other's throats and make for a unity, cause we can't have a mother thing going for us unless we got a unity.

I took a deep breath and looked at the building a few doors down called dignity a million years ago when it belonged to rich people. "The Madison," and I remembered when as a kid we had lived there. It was called a slum house.

Bueno, I thought as I checked my steps toward the subway. *Mañana, we all get up and try mucho harder one more time, and then the next mañana. Porque no?*

17

Water don't know the color of skin

"All right, Petey, you ready to take off?"

I looked at John Clause and answered yeah.

"Where you figuring to take the kids today?"

"I figure on taking them to the same camp I took the Italian kids to a couple of weeks ago."

"Sounds like a good idea."

"I think they're gonna like it, John. It's got a nice diving board."

"Okay, buddy," he said. "Take off."

Funny, I thought, *John always calls me Buddy. Wonder if he means it.*

I loaded all the fellows into the station wagon, and then took off onto the Henry Hudson Parkway, singing in unison almost all the whole time, "I've Got a Sunday Kind of Love."

Driving along, I dug it was a beautiful warm sunny day.

We made it into that swimming camp following the whole line of cars going in there. As I took out a five-dollar bill to hand through the open window, I should have known something was wrong by the funny look that came over this attendant's face as his eyes made a quick rejection survey of some kind of Martian aliens attempting to invade his kind of domain. But that was only a split second.

For, with the most bull crap force of sincerity in his voice, he smiled and said, "Gee, fellows, we're all filled up."

And I heard the *gee whizzes, damns, maybe there's another place* . . . but I knew. Lil Man did, too. Like all of us knew. I pulled the car to one side and watched fifty more cars go in.

I think that the first knowledge I ever had of a country across the Hudson River called New Jersey was when I heard about a fun park called Palisades. But soon found out that they wouldn't let dark people into their most famous salt water pool . . . and all the fun went out of knocking down bottles with baseballs and shooting at candles with a .22 rifle . . . it even blotted out the delight of that fantastic roller coaster and even the fun house became a mockery, not to mention how flat the taste of submarine Italian sandwiches became in my mouth.

All these thoughts ran through my mind as we sat in that Ford station wagon full of Puerto Rican and black kids waiting just outside the swimming camp.

I remember that I had driven up to that same camp two weeks before with a station wagon packed with Italian kids and a couple of Irish kids, and, I think, there was a little white Spanish Jew. The doors opened up with no sweat in the midst of all the swinging sounds of their laughter and the looking forward to jumping into that New Jersey water.

I paid the entrance fee, almost completely unaware of quizzical looks that attendant gave me.

But we had a ball that day. One of the kids had a transistor radio and Bombino did all kinds of high jumps off that board. Everybody just did his own thing, and there were no problems or hassles that day.

My thoughts were brought back to the present, the angry

words of Shade, the black president of the Untouchables. Funny how this kid, who was only about five feet tall and weighed barely 100 pounds, could have such a command over cats who were twice his size. He even had mucho pull with the other Untouchable chapters, which ran through the five boroughs and even into Newark, New Jersey.

"Will you dig it, baby," Shade cried out. "That damn gray told us that there was no room in that swimming camp and dig all them cars going in . . ."

Man, I thought, *the last time I was here was with them white kids. I hadn't been their passport, but they sure as hell had been mine.*

I pushed the car in reverse and headed back to New York, thinking I should have told that attendant, "Funny man, water don't know the difference of skin." I eased the tension amidst all them cries and murmuring of "I hate them white mother fuckers" by the black kids and "que so lo metanpor el culo" (let them put it up their ass) by the Puerto Rican kids, by saying, "Which one can eat forty hamburgers at the White Tower in the Bronx?"

We drove up to that White Tower in the Bronx and I had five dollars expense money and sneaked ten bucks out from my rent money so that I could fill their guts with something more nourishing than that crap we all had to swallow.

Funny, I thought, through a big mouthful of twelve-cent hamburger, *water don't know the difference of skin unless the water happened to belong to white men like that.*

Lil Man had an idea.

"Hey, Piri, baby, let's go to our own beach. I like Orchard Beach better anyway. Ain't that right, fellas?"

"Yeah . . ." they all agreed.

And so I took off for Orchard Beach, with the chevere sound of a beating beat of:

"SCREW JERSEY ONE . . . TWO . . . THREE . . . SCREW JERSEY FOR YOU AND ME."

Later that day I dropped all my young brothers off, parked the car about six blocks away and sat on a favorite stoop that belongs to all of us.

I could feel my legs growing real heavy with weariness and my heart growing real heavy with a true sense of justified hate.

God, where do you come into all of this? My face was cara palo, no expression on it, but if anybody could dig my heart, they could see the blasting and bombing of a pure sense of outraged dignity. I cut myself loose from my thoughts because I wanted to hear the street feeling. A beautiful bolero that somebody was playing out of a fourth-floor window came down to me and diggit, man, straight from my mother heart and soul. That cat that was singing, he sure sang it like it is. It was called "Adelante."

I got up and started walking out toward 110th Street, trying hard to keep my heart from feeling so tight, because I knew with all my swinging soul that I was going to do things right. I was going to take care of straight business.

18

Fourth of July

I cut down toward First Avenue. The evening was mucho hot, like July. I was wincing because all them firecrackers were bursting loose. It seemed like everybody was celebrating the Fourth of July.

I jumped a foot and a half away as a round torpedo came whistling off some rooftop and made an explosion two feet away from my right ear and left it ringing with its message of liberty and independence.

I dug Puerto Ricans and black and white kids whirling sparklers and flinging them from front and side fire escapes. I dug some Roman candles go off a two-story building and make a pretty like splash of bursting color against our ghetto sky. I smiled at the Puerto Rican and Italian parents who were setting them off while gently screaming at their kids not to get in the way on account they could get burnt. I stopped near the corner and watched some kids doing daredevil things like approaching a firecracker that hadn't gone off.

"Hey, kid, better cool it with them duds. Sometimes they take their time going off. Uh . . . like in your hand."

The kid smiled a wounded warrior's smile and held up a bandaged finger and then went about his fooling around with street land mines. He laughed in triumph and broke a dud firecracker in two, lit it, and made a sizzling scissor.

I gave him a two-fingered salute in acknowledgment of his bravery.

I heard a woman's powerful voice behind me, and the brave kid's face jumped mucho scared.

"Hey, Anthony, how many times I gotta tell you not ta fool with them firecrackers when they no go off?"

I turned toward the voice and her soft face made no rapport with her angry words.

"An what the hell is that bandage doing on your finger? You wann maybe lose a hand, eh? My God, I should have quit when I had five. I had to fool around and have had you, uh, Anthony?"

"Aw . . . Mom . . ."

I cut down another block and my eyes dug a lot of American flags waving from fire escapes and windows. Some large and some small. Between them, I dug the flags of the Empire of Puerto Rico.

"Hey, Piri." I turned and saw four young bloods.

"Hi, Lil Man," I said. "What's happening, fellers?"

"Having a ball. Say, you wanna come in with us on getting some fireworks?"

"Like, how much?" I grinned. "Two bucks worth?"

"Yeah, like that's cool."

"Tell you what, who's got a buck?"

Lil Man turned to Blue. "How much you got? And you, Ace, and you too, Chiquito?"

I waited patiently and they came up with ninety five centavos. I held my hand out and received the coins. I eased a five-dollar bill into Lil Man's hands. "Split even, okay?"

"Diggit, Piri, good looking out. Hey, Brother, you sure we ain't putting you out?"

"Nay, nunca." I slapped older skin against young skin.

Lil Man put his arm around me. "Les go and get the fire-works."

"No, Poppo." I put both hands up. "They sound too much like bullets to me. Have a ball and don't . . ."

"Yeah . . . yeah, we know, DON'T GET BURNT."

"Whatta you? A wise guy?" I said, doing my best to sound like a fierce Edward G. Robinson. We all cracked up, and then started to walk away from each other. Then a voice full of hate came rolling down from a stoop.

I didn't hear all the words at first because of the explosions of different degrees going on. I looked at the stoop.

Marco, an Italian kid, was leaning against the doorjamb. He blew out a long thin stream of smoke from a Robert Burns slim-jim cigar. I cocked my head like asking if it were me he was talking to. His expression didn't change.

"You dirty fucking bodega spic."

This time I understood his words loud and above the fire-crackers blowing up all around us.

I said nothing. My face remained cool.

"You heard me! You dirty fucking bodega spic."

I heard the running feet of Little Man and the others coming my way.

"Whatcha mean, dirty fucking bodega spic?" Little Man was blowing his mind. "Whatcha mean sounding Big Bro like that? You dirty . . ."

I reached and grabbed Little Man, who with the other three had mucho ideas of stuffing Marco into his Robert Burns cigar.

"Time, little Brothers. Go on, take care of business. I'll take care of my own digs." I took them aside. "Hey, cool it now. Besides, how would it look for you four cats to be jumping all over that nice kid?"

"Oh wow, Piri." Little Man was practically doing a buga-loo in his anger.

"Go ahead now."

Blue whispered in my ear. "Look, Piri, we know you're grown up and it ain't right to smack a kid unless there ain't no way out, but I don't gotta go by them rules. Just walk away and I'll kick the shit outta him for you, like I'll even let a couple of days go by."

I could understand how these Puerto Rican kids were jumping stink at this outrage against their proud heritage and were all for making strawberry Jello outta bad-mouth. I just shook my head gently in no-time, like I could take care of my share of Puerto Rican heritage with this boy.

"Forget it, will ya?" I gently slapped him on the side of his head. "Tell you what. If I need your help in fighting him, I'll ask for it. Okay? Chevere."

"Okay, Piri."

I watched the four make it up the block, turning from time to time making some kind of bad faces with badder gestures aimed at the Robert Burns kid on the stoop.

I turned to the kid and, gotta give him credit, he might have gotten a shade lighter, but he sure had stood his ground. I took a deep breath and made believe something had caught my attention across the street.

Man, I was like mucho angry. His words burned into my mind. DIRTY FUCKING BODEGA SPIC. I felt my hands rubbing themselves up and down on my thighs. I bit my teeth down hard together and heard them grind like they wanted to turn to white powder. I inhaled deeply and let it out softly. Ever since I was a kid, I couldn't stand to be called a spic or any other crap-sounding name that was meant to put me down. But I was a man now and I couldn't off a kid. I mean, like he was learning now and nobody gets to a kid by just bouncing him around, especially if it's an older like me. I reached my eyes to some sparklers that were arching towards the street and thought, *But sometimes some kids that don't belong to anybody really could use a cool-ass whipping.*

I dug Marco out from the corner of my eye and thoughts of his being one of the kids I was trying to work with eased off some of the sting and some of the anger rolling inside me.

I walked slowly toward him and smiled.

"What's happening, Marco?"

He didn't say anything.

I remembered his real name was Luigi, but he hated the crap out of it and renamed himself MARCO. *Why not?* I thought. *Mucho of us do that when a name don't fit us.*

"Mind if I stand here with you for a while, Marco?" My voice really had no courage in it. I looked up out into the streets and watched a waterfall of different kinds of fireworks. Somebody had set off a half a dozen Roman candles and it was like some kind of rainbow that didn't belong on the streets. I made my eyes see through it, trying to see some kind of image. I guess I was trying to see the face of a Jewish Jesus Christ. I guess I was trying to see out beyond my inner personally insulted self.

I turned away from Marco. We both went into a silent bag, and my thoughts ran back into a yesterday when I had been around his age, and I had been heading towards the Jefferson Avenue Public Swimming Pool deep in the heart of Italiano territory. I dug my amigos waiting.

"Hey, you guys ready?" I slapped skin with Waneko.

"Better believe it."

I counted our numbers and there was only three of us.

"Heard there's been some shit going on in that pool." Waneko's face was kinda grim.

"Yeah," said Lil Louis. "But hell, them Italians don't own that pool, like it's for everybody."

"So let's split," I said. "There's three of us Puerto Ricans." Everybody laughed, digging that I had made that number three sound like three thousand.

We walked to the corner of Lexington Avenue and my eyes pushed out across the border into Italian turf, and our feet crossed over the line. It was like a mucho thing that our towels and sandwiches went under our left arms, leaving our right hands free to defend ourselves—if we were jumped along the way. Even our way of walking changed, like walking with a baddo determination—not like a challenge but like a "ain't looking for trouble but we're ready."

We hit First Avenue and cut up to 114th Street. Some bad looks were thrown our way and the same returned, but nada happened. We smiled at each other. I dug the bright-sticky Saturday sun and couldn't wait to cannonball into the pool.

We paid our way in and got our clothes into a basket, put our tags around our ankles, all the time digging everything around us. We hit the pool and I dug mucho people having a chevere time—and like no up tight tension was going around.

"Hey, looks all right." Waneko smiled. "Les goo-ooo. . . ." And the three of us hit that green water with a GERON-IMO yell.

Man, it was a ball and some chevere hours went by.

"Hey, panin, I'm making it home," Lil Louis yelled at me from across the pool. "You coming?"

"Nah, I dig it here," I yelled back.

"Me too, Louis." Waneko waved at him.

"Okay, see you around."

"Hey, man," I yelled. "Take the bus back, like don't walk." Lil Louis laughed and shouted back, "Like you don't hafta tell me that. Like I know."

I jumped back into the pool and lost sight of Waneko as tiempo went by. I felt a hand touch my shoulder. I looked around.

"Hey, panin, how you doing?" I smiled. It was David, a real nice kid whose father was Puerto Rican and mother Jewish. He didn't look Puerto Rican, but he sure acted it.

David brushed some sandy hair from his eyes. I could tell he was worried about something.

"You better get out, Piri," he said firmly. His eyes were watching in all directions.

"Okay, man, what's happening?" My eyes were doing an all-around number just like him.

"There's a bunch of Italianos I overheard talking about beating up the Puerto Ricans and colored kids."

"When?" My eyes searched for Waneko.

"I don't know, but I already told some of the other kids what's gonna happen. Ya better split."

I started to tell him to do likewise, but changed my mind. He didn't look Puerto Rican.

"Good looking out, David." I slapped skin with him in appreciation, and made my way towards the end of the pool and my feet touched the bottom in the three-foot department.

"Waneko," I yelled. I couldn't see him but was hoping my voice would find him. I dug some yelling and scuffling breaking out in a few different places around the pool and didn't have to think twice to know we were getting a sneak put on us.

I turned to get my behind outta the pool and bango—splat . . . I felt a fist hit me like a rock on the side of my neck.

I splashed around and dug a kid smaller than me aiming another punch.

"Hey, you little maricon," I screamed in anger and disbelief. Like the fist was attached to an Italian kid of about nine or ten years old.

"Hey, kid, I don't wanna hit you." I held the part of my neck that ached. "I'm too big for you, but you try to off me again and I'm gonna kick the living spaghettis outta ya."

And then I heard it, and like knew I was set up.

"Hey, fellers, looka that spic trying to beat up one of our little kids."

"Why, that fucking bodega. Let's make it even."

And my eyes dug about six or seven Italianos jumping feet first into the pool and most of them landing on me. I felt fists coming every which way and getting hit in my mouth, nose, eyes—like all over. I swung out, hitting out at everywhere. I felt a whole bunch of hate-filled fists smashing into me. I was pushed under the water and my eyes vaguely dug the green water turning reddish with salted blood that had to be from my nose and busted lips. I felt somebody's knee make some kind of brave attempt to cave in my skinny ribs. I grabbed at somebody's hair and pulled his head towards my own and smacked my cabeza into his face.

Oh, Jee-suss . . . I thought. *They wanna kill me.* And I squeezed hard in hate and anger. I heard a scream of pain.

"Oh my God, he's crushing my balls."

I felt an arm around my throat and mucho punches that didn't hurt so much. I was swallowing mucho liquid and didn't know if it was blood or water. I kicked. I butted. I bit.

I punched out and scratched with grubby nails and like all of a sudden, I was left alone.

I heard mucho yelling and screaming that sounded like echoes. I pulled myself out of the pool and stood on wobbling legs that felt like somebody had pulled the bones out of them. I could see fighting going on. I felt my fists cocked by my side and sniffing back my chevere blood that was coming out of my nose like one of them lousy broken faucets at home.

"Pobrecito, pobrecito, what did they do to you?"

I recognized the voice as Waneko's. The eye that hadn't been punched as much, dug him running towards me. He put my arm around his shoulder and walked me towards the gate. "What did they do to you?"

I half grinned and said, "Whatsa matter, estupido, are you blind? They beat the shit outta me. Where the fuck were you?"

"Copping a hot dog." His voice sounded kinda sad, like sorry he hadn't been there to share my getting done up.

"Are you hurting, panin?"

I dug his face and his eyes were mucho angry and full of tears that were making destinations down his cheeks.

"You dirty bastards. You dirty bastards," Waneko screamed back at the pool.

"What's the matter?"

I looked at somebody that had a policeman's uniform on. I dug him as one of the two or three policia that were suppose to keep things cool at the pool.

"What happened?" His voice had a casual tone about it.

"What the fuck do you think happened?" I screamed out. "We got sneaked and where the hell were you and plueese don't tell me you didn't see what's happening. LOOK . . ."

And his eyes dug the scufflings still going on.

Policemen were pouring into the pool.

"But like I ain't got no great expectations. Shit, like you're probably Italiano."

"Hey, you little sonnabitch, I'm Irish."

I felt Waneko pulling me towards the gate. The policeman pointed at Waneko.

"Hey, take him to the first aid station. Tell the nurse to . . ."

"We're going home, Waneko." My voice sounded as fat and swollen as my lips, eyes, and nose.

"We'll get that treated first." The cop's voice had some kind of sad-ass tolerance in it.

"I don't want no first aid, no nurse, no bandages. I just wanna get back to my block and let my people know about this shit that just went down."

I felt everything inside me burning.

"You want me to put you on a bus?"

"I don't want nothing from you. Muchas gracias." I bowed sarcastically.

"Take that wise little bastard home."

And the last my eyes saw of him was his shaking his head from side to side.

We copped our clothes and Waneko was leading the way towards the bus stop.

"Hey, panin." I pulled at his elbow. "Let's not take the bus, man, let's walk home right through their territory."

Waneko shook his head and quietly said, "If you're down, I'm down."

"I'm down," I snarled.

"Chevere. We go together." We slapped skin and split for our block with a bad-sounding walk through enemy territory.

I dug people looking at my busted up face. I could feel

some hot blood making a slow river out from one of my hurts and some kind of thundering thoughts bomb-blasting their way out of my mind.

Shit, man. We're gonna teach them not to fuck with us. Concho, like they gonna learn we walk tall or not at all.

I came back to ahora time, with the trailing thought on how I had kept touching my bloody face and checking the sticky sangre on my fingers and how I could taste its saltiness clear down to my guts. I managed a wry smile at the remembrance of the mucho bad-ass bopping that had gone down soon after.

I felt my face and rubbed a little beard and all of a sudden I got this helluva feeling. It came pouring out of me. I didn't look at Marco, and like he wasn't looking at me.

"Hey, Marco, I'm gonna talk. So do us a favor and be cool." My voice was quiet and mucho matter-of-fact. "I'm a Puerto Rican American. I'm a second-generation-born American. Ye-ah . . ." I fought my voice from becoming up tight. "I got Puerto Rican blood in me and it's not so long ago I began to find out what I'm all about. Si, this is my country too, Marco. My people came here from Puerto Rico, but I . . . me, personally, was born here, like in Harlem Hospital."

My voice was now soft and calm but firm.

"Not only this Barrio is mine, but this whole United States of America. There are all kinds of people living in it, but you don't name them Guineas, Spics, Niggers, Micks, Honkies, Yids, Polacks, Greaseballs, Chinks, Japs, Mex, white trash and all the rest of them baddo names. You just name them human beings. Because I bet with all my heart, they mostly was born from a mother who gave them love. And if they grew to hate, it was maybe because, like you and me, they found out that reality is not like you learn in the fairy tale books, but on truthful hard-assed streets. But people got to unlearn bad things and learn about good things, like dignity and respect for each other, and like I got a whole lot to learn too."

Marco said nothing, but I dug he was looking at me, and that was like listening.

"Marco, I don't like hurting words, especially if a person ain't got it coming and like sure I got up tight when you sounded bad on me. Like I'm damn sure you don't dig being called Guinea."

"I've been called that a lotta times and worse," Marco interrupted. I didn't look at him.

"Don't tell me you liked it."

"Nobody likes being spit on."

"So I don't dig it either. Man, I've got nothing personal against you except this sound you put on me, but like, I understand you swinging out in some kind of up tight anger. Diggit, Marco, like I ain't no kid. Like you're seventeen years old, big for your age, but still seventeen. Like when I was seventeen years old, you weren't even born yet."

"So, what's that prove?" Marco's voice wasn't angry, at least not towards me.

I smiled a little and then let it spread all over my face.

"Maybe it don't prove nothing," I said. "Maybe something. Quien sabe?"

"Ya want one?"

I looked at him. I took the offered Robert Burns and he lit it with a gold lighter. I inhaled like it was a peace pipe. I tapped him thanks lightly on the shoulder.

"Look, Marco, if you were an adult and had laid that heavy

stuff on me I would've probably asked you to repeat and then busted you dead in your mouth."

"Yeah . . . and I'da got . . ."

"Yeah . . ." I cut him off. "You'd got your brothers and sisters and uncles and friends and relations and you'd come in cars mounted with cannons and submachine guns and wipe me and all the Puerto Ricans off the face of El Barrio, RIGHT? . . . Aw shit, Marco . . . Right?"

Marco didn't say nada, but his face showed he had been thinking exactly or thereabouts on what I had just said.

"Look, kid, what's been going on has been going on for a long time, before you were even a wink in your old man's eye and that's where that's at. I'm just thinking about tu y yo. Me and you, straight business. We give each other respect, cause a human being's got a right to it and will get it one way or the other. Marco, your family gotta be as poor as the Puerto Ricans living around here. Otherwise they'd have moved away. I mean like, you and your family are running into the same rats and roaches as we are. Let's be fighting these God-damned conditions, not each other. Marco, I give you respect. You gimme the same. Diggit?"

"You got it, Cum."

"You calling me a scum bag?" I asked, kind of heated like.

"Naw." He smiled. "Like me and my boys call each other that all the time. I'm just trying to find some way of calling you paisan."

"Pecalungul (up yours)," I grinned.

"Up yours too." He smiled.

"Take it easy, amigo," I said and walked away from the stoop.

I walked slowly down the street. *Damn,* I thought. *Sure's a whole lot of kids with baddo reps they're building and like Marco's one of them. He's like trying to reach out for some kind of street glory and thinking he's gonna get it by kicking in the faces of Puerto Ricans and black kids.*

I heard somebody call my name from above.

I checked my steps, stopped, and looked up. "Hey, Brother," I yelled up.

"Yeah, Piri." Blue was grinding the juice out of a sparerib bone.

"Hey, Blue. That looks good."

"Yeah-a, come on up, man. My old lady's got two pots full." His face turned into the apartment. "Hey, Martha, set up a big plate. A king's-size appetite is coming up."

Martha stuck her head out of the window.

"Hi, Piri."

"Hi, Martha, it's okay?"

"Are you kidding? Come on any time."

I walked up the stairs. The bad taste of having been sounded as a dirty fucking bodega spic had almost left my mouth.

I'll get the rest of it out with some good grit, my mind said—*even though my corazón's gonna pump with resentment for a while.*

Wow, man!! Sticks and stones will break my bones, but calling me a BODEGA SPIC really hurts the hell out of me.

The door opened and I smelled the spareribs, rice, and black-eye peas.

"Hey, Brother, you're looking good," smiled Martha.

"Yeah," I said, and walked in smiling. Already I was feeling better.

19

Where green grass and trees grow

Nita was taking care of business. She was cooking up a storm. I checked my watch cause Sis, Don, and the kids were coming over for Sunday dinner.

I felt kinda good cause mucho good months had passed and Nita was going to have a baby.

Nita slapped my hand away from caressing her stomach as she went by me. I went into all kinds of funny numbers, pretending she had broken my hand.

Don, Sis, and the kids soon arrived, and the dinner went beautifully. Nita had done it up right. Pasteles (meat pie) and arroz con habichuclas (rice and beans) and pernil (roast pork). After the meal everybody sat in the forest green living room, that is, after Nita took everybody on a grand tour of the place.

I heard Sis ask Nita where she bought the drapes and Nita proudly saying, "Oh, I just made them myself. To buy them is expensive, and they're really junk."

Anyway, mucho talk went down and Don was cluing us in on the virtues of living on Long Island, where green grass and trees grow. He was talking right where I was most weak, white picket fence and all them cosa things, even though somewhere in my mind, bad past memories of Long Island jumped in view via my thoughts.

"I got a good deal for you if you're interested, Piri." Don looked serious.

"Like what?"

"Well, I got a house where we used to live and I can let you have it cheap, and on the lot right next to it there's another house. Of course it needs a lot of work, but I'll give it to you as part of the package."

"Like how much down?" My mind kept seeing green grass and trees and white picket fences.

"We can give it to you for three thousand dollars down." Sis broke in.

I smiled, wondering if they had the thought of selling their property to me all the time . . .

"And the whole selling price?" I looked at Nita, who didn't look too happy.

"Er . . . well." Don hesitated. I could tell by his expression that he wanted to be fair. "All in all, like a giveaway, we can let it go for nine thousand total."

What! I thought within myself, *that's a good deal.*

"Of course there's work to be done. One of the houses needs the whole chimney rebuilt."

Don went on talking, but my mind was already putting my bricklaying expertise to building one.

"I don't know," Nita shyly ventured, and stopped when she realized my eyes were telling her, "We can discuss it later."

The door closed and I could hear Sis and her family making it down the stairs.

Nita and I didn't say much for a while. I helped her clean up and when I came back upstairs after throwing away the garbage, she was sitting at the kitchen table. She motioned my attention to a hot cup of cafe, and I sat across from her, for a long-little while the only sound was our sipping cafe together. She broke the quiet time.

"Piri? You're not thinking seriously of buying the house, are you?"

I looked at the enormous refrigerator and answered, "Well, I'm thinking about it, of course, Nita. I'd like for us to see the house. I mean . . . wow, like two houses for nine thousand bolos sounds like a chevere deal and gee, Nita, a chance to get outta El Barrio and you giving birth next month or so . . . Well, like caramba, it's a good deal for the kid and . . ."

"But we just only have about twenty-four hundred saved and . . ."

"Hey, don't worry. If push come to shove, we can borrow the rest, or make some kind of contract with Don like a second mortgage or algo. Anyway, like they said, we can go and see them el Sabado (Saturday). We don't have to buy, just look. Hey, don't look so worried."

Nita's face had a "I don't know" look on it, but as a good esposa (wife) she said quietly, "If you wish, Piri. Just looking won't hurt."

She washed the coffee cups and watched some television in our forest green living room. Red Skelton was on, but all I kept seeing was white picket fences surrounding green grass and green trees that were growing around a house in Long Island.

That whole next Saturday was spent in going through the two houses.

"I'll admit it's going to take a lot of work to put them in shape, but it's worth it and with a good coat of paint on them, you'll both have something to be proud of," Don reassured us.

"Don and I lived here when we got married," Sis interjected. "Everybody called it a dollhouse."

"You can live in this one and rent the smaller one. That will help make your payments easier to the bank."

I made a face cause the other house had mucho mucho work to be done. Carpentry, plumbing, and a new chimney.

I forced my mind to look at the two "in pretty bad shape" houses and imagine a finished product. I'm afraid my mind overdid itself, for doggone it if they didn't change into something you'd see only around Beverly Hills.

Nita was strangely quiet and remained so till we got home and into bed.

"Nita?" I whispered.

"Si, Piri." Her back was turned towards me.

I reached over gently and rubbed her swollen stomach tenderly and was mucho rewarded by a couple of kicks from a waiting to be born kid.

"Whatta you think? I don't mind working my behind off getting it fixed up. I mean, it's like for you and the baby. Whatta you think, Nita? Mucho clean air, a yard, like no whole lotta garbage. No junkies running around. Whatta you think, eh?"

"I think we should wait until our baby is born and see how we are money-wise."

"Gee, Nita, nobody ever got any place without taking a chance. Man!! Where else can you pick up a couple of houses for only nine thousand bolos?"

"Only nine thousand."

I thought she sounded a little sarcastic, so I turned the conversation off gently and quietly.

"It doesn't hurt to think about it. Does it, honey?"

"No, Piri, it doesn't." Her tiny hand pressed my hand on her heaving tummy and she giggled.

"I hope he's not a cabezón like you."

"I hope she's as beautiful as you." And squeezed back.

The honking of some cars and multi street noises began to make me konk out.

"Nita." I yawned big and wide.

"Si."

"Yo te amo." My hand felt the little life beating inside of her.

"Y yo a ti, Piri."

20

Como, like un hijo is born

Sunday School service was about over. Victor, who had been my best man, was delivering a wrap-up on the heavy responsibilities of being a Christian and the inner strength needed to overcome temptations.

I smiled at him, knowing that he would be at a baseball game at Yankee Stadium and like that was one of the taboos among the church elders.

I caught his eye and made a motion of a batter swinging at a ball. Victor's eyes sparkled like he was cracking up inside. He ended up with, "Although I believe that what is sin to one is not sin to another."

The whole young people's class were mucho anxious in their muy reverent "AMEN."

Victor winked at me. My smiling stopped when I looked at the face of the hand who was tapping my back. It was Tia.

"Piri." She smiled. "Lessen, don't get excited and nervous, but Nita is having her getting ready dolores (pains). It's time to take her to the hospital."

Oh, man, did I freeze inside! I looked over at Nita, who was surrounded by mucho hermanas y hermanitos. Her face was mixed up in sometimes looking relaxed and sometimes twitching up in pain.

I got up and the whole church knew what was going down. I felt hands tapping me as I went to Nita. Like they were telling me everything was gonna be all right.

Outside of me I was cool, like as if this thing came up every day and I was mucho use to it. I got Nita's coat.

"We'll use my car, Hermano Piri."

"Gracias, Hermano Rivera. Are you okay, honey?"

Nita didn't believe in throwing bull around and just answered straight.

"No, ignorante, I'm not. It hurts like hell," she said. But soon she smiled weakly, "Pero don't worry."

I inwardly practiced my expression of looking panic-stricken, but settled for a couple of concerned frowns. I told Nita to hang on for a couple of seconds. That I was gonna call Beth Israel so that Dr. Drew would know we were coming, like Nita was due.

"Imbecil," Nita breathed out between labor pains, "the doctor can wait, but I can't. Let us hurry." She eased her put-down of me with a smile.

Wow, I thought, *her birth pangs must have her up tight, cause in just a few minutes, I've become not only an ignorante but also an imbecil.*

We soon got to the hospital and after going through a whole lot of little hang ups, like checking out the doctor, filling out papers, signing releases in case of death due to complications (which, without saying, made my sangre slip below zero), Nita was encased in a white gown, groaning and moaning, and in between intervals of smiles and light yak was put to bed.

I just stood by her bed and wished I could share some of the dolor. After like about a million hours and Dr. Drew's mucho examinations, he pulled me outside.

"Mr. Thomas," Dr. Drew said as he slipped his rubber glove off.

"Yeah . . . yeah," I tried sounding relaxed.

"Your wife has a small pelvis."

"And . . . and . . ."

"It's nothing serious, except she won't be able to give birth naturally."

"So . . . so." My mind was practically seeing him filling out a death certificate—like due to a small pelvis Nita has gone to be with the Angelitos.

"She'll have to have a Caesarean."

"A what?"

"A section, it's a very simple operation. As a matter of fact, a lot of movie stars have it that way."

Oh, my God, I thought, *Nita's no damn movie star.*

"You'll have to sign and . . ."

"Gimme the paper, gimmee the paper. How long will it be, Dr. Drew?"

"She goes in a while. I want you to wait with her. I think it's a good idea for the man to see what it's all about with the woman during her birth pangs."

I nodded and went in and watched Nita . . . poor Nita . . . who would sometimes let out a screech and roll her eyes and sometimes let an unchristian mala palabra roar out, and then in between relax.

The nurses came in and they rolled Nita out.

I sat near the bed and waited for Nita to come back.

"Mr. Thomas?" a nurse soon called.

"Yeah . . ." I answered.

"Why don't you go and sit in the waiting room. They're a couple of more like you. You can sit up there and brag to each other. It'll be easier on your nerves."

Three other guys and myself sat in the waiting room and there wasn't no bragging, just light talk.

"Hell, I'm late for work already," one guy said.

"So, this doesn't happen every day," another guy added.

"I hope this one's okay, she's had three miscarriages," the third said.

The late-for-work guy asked me, "Your first?"

I nodded a cool yeah.

"You'll get used to it. I got eight."

I smiled weak-like, wondering if the woman got used to it.

Around 9 P.M. I was all alone in the waiting room. The other three cats had gotten their good news and had cut out. The late-for-work guy had mumbled something about the hell with work and going out and getting loaded, and wishing to hell his wife wasn't so God damn Catholic and get herself sterilized or something.

My ears picked up a sound and a nurse wheeling a small white cart stopped and smiled at me. I just stared like an ignorante and an imbecil.

"It's all yours, father, an eight pound three ounce healthy baby . . . BOY."

I staggered toward the little cart and looked down on the hairiest prune wrinkled kid in the world.

"You can see your wife for a few seconds," the nurse informed me. "Cause she's sedated."

"What?" I was only half listening to her. That kid was something else. A big hairy head and smacking his tiny hands at the whole big world.

"She's had injections, so she's kind of in a dream world."

I could understand that. I felt the same. Half an hour or

so, I was standing by Nita's bed. I looked like Dr. Drew with a gown and bandage around my nose and mouth.

"Nita?"

Nita sort of half acknowledged my being there and whispered, "Verdad que ese cabezón (big head) is beautiful."

"You better believe it, Nita, honey. You better believe it."

I kissed her and my thoughts were pushing out words of thanks for being so chevere and my sorriness on what she had to go through.

I made it to the phone booth and called the whole world and told them about MIGHTY RICKY being born, and went to sleep at Tia's house.

I wasn't gonna sleep in our bed until Nita came home.

The next four or five days were visiting days to see Nita and Ricky. Everybody went to visit. I kept bringing flowers.

I dug my son, who was making time with his mother's breast, like there was no mañana and God Almighty, it's a helluva feeling to stand there and watch all the beauty of a miracle doing his thing before your eyes, and I turned and went to pay the hospital bill.

The forest green living room was full of familia and presents. I walked in behind Nita, holding Ricky gentle-like. I remembered walking down the block and people we knew waving congratulations.

"Que es? Dona Chancleta, little lady slipper?" asked one.

No, I shook my head. "It's un machito, man-child." Finally, when everybody left, Nita and I just sat quietly staring at Ricky, who, not digging the quiet, farted gently and began yelling.

I watched Nita take his diaper off and I crinkled my nose at Ricky's production.

"Sure looks like mustard." I laughed.

"Just watch how I do it." Nita's face was impish. I got the feeling I was gonna get tighter with Ricky's mustard than I had thought.

Time passed by and Nita had long finished with her forty days quarantine that she told me about when I had gotten too close to her one romantic night.

"A what? Whatta you mean, forty days quarantine."

"It's something we do in Puerto Rico. We get strong again and rested and part of it, besides eating healthy food like sopa de pichon, y sopa de gallina (pigeon soup or chicken soup), is the husband staying away from you know what I mean . . ."

Nita's face vivid with laughter at my most rejected pained expression.

"It's all right," she calmed me down. "You can rest with me and eat healthy food also."

I don't know how much I rested, but the healthy foods socked mucho pounds onto me.

"Nita?" I heard her making gurgling sounds to a raging Ricky in the bedroom.

"Ahuh?"

I walked over to the bedroom and jumped in the gurgling. If I hadn't loved that kid so much I would have long given him walking papers. The bags under my eyes long having become full-fledged steamer trunks from mucho nights of having put strain on our creaking carpet-covered wooden floors. I swore that beautiful cabezón (big head) must have been born with insomnia. Nita had smiled at that, gently breaking it to me that Don Ricardo copped his nod time during the day. Nights were for going out on the town.

I watched Ricky while trying to bring out a point to Nita.

Caramba, that kid was trying to suck his fingers, bite off his toes and play with his pee-pee all at the same time. I raised my eyebrows upward and down sexy-like and smiled at Nita.

"Kid's gonna be something, eh? He's just a little fart and already he knows where it's at."

Nita laughed and said, "You really think he knows what it's for?"

"Instinctively," I said. "This kid was born ready."

Nita picked up our young sex maniac and we sat in the living room.

"Nita?"

She looked at me.

"I've been thinking about the houses in Long Island and . . ."

"Do you really want to move, Piri?"

"Like to try it. Like, we're both young now and if we start now, maybe someday we can have us something chevere, but we gotta start some . . ."

"Okay, Piri," Nita broke me off. "If you want to, it's okay, you're the man."

I just looked at Nita. *It's okay,* I thought.

Nita was busy feeding Ricky's hungry face. *Kinda go for a white picket fence,* I thought and ran-walked to the phone to call up Don to tell him the deal was on.

21

Back to Babylon . . . one more time

Dig it, world!!!! Did you ever try to buy property? There's a million wheeling and dealings that goes down . . . OH YEAH-A.

On a Saturday afternoon I sat down by my all-alone self and looked at mucho papers, written in lawyers' language—CONTRACT OF SALE. It began:

"THIS AGREEMENT made the 23d day of MAY 1958, between Don Baldwin, residing at 32 Southwest Street, Wyandanch, Long Island, New York, *hereinafter described as the seller* and Piri Thomas and Anita Luz Thomas, his wife, both residing at 201 East 117th Street, New York City, *hereinafter described as the purchaser. . . .*"

I felt joy at holding the contract in my hand.

I heard the key being turned and Nita's coming back from La Marketa and Mighty Ricky's king-size Puerto Rican lungs were like together. Nita dropped off the shopping bags fast-like, her dirty look of, "don't you know how to take care of our kid?" and her mommie sounds of love towards El Gran Ricardo were an all-together thing. I shrugged my shoulders and buried the indignity of being misunderstood by looking at CONTRACT OF SALE. I winked at them and tossed them into the bread box, which never had seen bread. It was like our "keep important things there" strongbox. I put away all kinds of vegetables and meats. I dug the iron-hard hunk of salchichon (hard salami), Puerto Rican cheese, and guava paste.

Nita came into the kitchen carrying Ricky. I gave him a make-believe dirty look for being such a troublemaker.

I pulled the salchichon out of the refrigerator and chopped a piece off. Ricky's eyes followed my chewing mouth.

"Uh-uh, no salami for you, kid. It will make you sick. Nita, we can be ready to move to Wyandanch in about two weeks."

"Are you happy, Piri, I mean about Long Island?"

"Sure am," I said, and thought, *Why not, ain't I suppose to be?*

I dug her soft serious look and croaked at Ricky, "Hey, kid, you happy too, eh? EH? EH??"

I blew it with Ricky. He was snoring his fat culito off and Nita and I just stared at each other listening to Mighty Ricky snore and I guess trying almost scared-like to build a better future.

I checked out how much it was gonna cost to make the move to Wyandanch, Long Island, and it was going to be a lotta bread.

I started off by calling up the big moving companies and ended up with a do-it-yourself Rent-a-Trailer. Don offered to give me a hand. We began the move into Babylon at six in the morning, and it took three complete trips back and forth to take care of business. Nita, Sis, and Carmela stayed in the house on Long Island, while Don, Frankie, and I made the move.

By 11:30 P.M. that night, Nita, Ricky, and I were sitting in our living room in our little house in Wyandanch. All the furniture was in place and everything was quiet, except for

Ricky (who was baby snoring away) and the sound of crickets
outside.

It was such a different sound outside that I started to miss
street noises. Nita and I went and stood outside. I felt the
grass underneath my work shoes. The moonlight did its thing
by giving the warm breeze and green grass and trees a sil-
very glow of shadows and silhouettes. I put my arm around
Nita and hugged gently.

"It's pretty, eh, Nita?"

"Si, Piri. It reminds me a little of Puerto Rico."

I looked at the different lights in the houses of our neighbors and their neat fences. Some made of green hedges and
some of picket fences, and I couldn't help thinking that at
last Nita and I had white picket fences, too.

Time and space went swinging by. I'd spend all my free
time away from work pouring mucho sweat getting the houses
in shape, especially the one Nita and I were hoping to rent
and ease the strain of bank first and second mortgages paid
off on time.

Nita would help mix cement and I rebuilt the chimney.
When it was finally finished, we took all kinds of pictures.
Chito, Nita's nephew, who spent every Saturday and Sunday
with us, wiped sweat off his young forehead.

"It's finished." He grinned.

"Sure is." I grinned happy-like, thinking, *What a loss my
talents are to the Bricklayers Union and to the world.*

I guess I was so wrapped up in feeling happy and proud
of having something that belonged to Nita and me, that I
had forgotten the unfeeling people that don't dig other people
for no reason at all, except that their skins aren't white like
their own.

I got my first taste of awareness to its true face when the neighbors around would pass by and stare. Not just natural ordinary curiosity friendly stares, but stares that were saying, "How dare you move here?" I remember walking back from town and trying hard to hurry before the Dixie Cup Ice Cream melted. I passed a couple who lived down across the road and I smiled at them and winked at their little boy. They smiled back and nodded. They must have walked about fifteen feet away from me, and not knowing how mucho sharp my Barrio street ears were, began to spit their friendly cruel racist Christian talk.

"My God, darling, who could have sold that nigger a house in our community?"

Funny, I thought, *her voice doesn't have a trace of Southernness in it.*

"Don Baldwin did, and that man is not a nigger. He's a Porto Rican. You remember when we vacationed in Porto Rico, they have a lot of dark ones that look like . . ."

The expert's voice on different ethnic people trailed off leaving me up tight.

Woowee . . . so my being Puerto Rican was supposed to put me a notch above being American black. Maybe just the way the Irish were supposed to be a notch above the Italianos. Who makes the damn rules of who's better than who? I looked back at the two so-called Christians walking with their child and just to get their attention, I let out a mighty yell. They looked back and I made a most exaggerated bow and the gesture let them know I'd heard the bullshit that they, white Christian God-loving God-fearing, had put down and that without a doubt, Christ had overheard their words of love and brotherhood.

I walked into our driveway thinking that Christians ought

to stop sending their missionaries to the dark parts of the world to preach Christ and Brotherhood. They should just spread their missionaries among themselves and get their heads together.

Months went by and Nita made friends with some of the neighbors. It was un poco easier for Nita, on account of being fair. I never asked her what she and they talked about, until one night over some pizza, Nita broke her thoughts out.

"Piri?"

"Uhmmmm."

"These people are prejudiced."

"Porque?" I mumbled, feeling stupid for asking, damn well knowing why, but it was the coolest way I could think of to find out what had gone down with Nita.

"It's the way they make friendly smiles and . . ." Nita cleaned some Italian tomato sauce from her chin and looked at Ricky having a ball on his blanket on the floor.

I turned my eyes where hers were and smiled at Ricky gumming a chunk of pizza crust to death.

"And what, Nita?" I pushed.

"I don't know, they said how pretty Puerto Rico is and that they loved it on their vacations and . . ."

"And? . . ."

"They always end up asking, 'Is your husband Porto Rican or is he . . .' How did one put it? Oh, si. 'Is he an American Negro?'"

They meant nigger, I thought.

"All except the family right behind our house. They're Seven-Day Adventist and when you're working, Mrs. Johnson comes over, and I've been over to her house and, well, she doesn't look at things like the others."

"Forget it, Nita." I fought not to let my voice get mucho

angry. "We don't live in their house, we live in ours. We pay our way. Hell, they don't put food in our mouths, we do."

Dammit, I jumped stink inside my head. *One more time. I should have known better than to have come back to Babylon. Christ, won't this ca-ca ever change?*

"What did you tell her? I mean about what I was?"

"What else?" She smiled wide and pretty. "That you're the most chevere American-born negrito Puertorriqueno in the world."

Her hug and kiss told me she was mucho right.

The conversation lost its way on account of the woman wrestlers on the TV. I leaned over and dug my finger into Ricky's mouth, because he was greedily choking on his piece of pizza pie crust.

22

St. Jude the impossible . . . my God!!!

Nita and I stood in the backyard. Wow, it was almost over-run with weeds and grass. I got me a bright idea.

"Honey." My face broke out in a sunshine smile. "Let's grow us a garden, like, you know, we're people of property now. Let's go in for gentlemen farming."

"Cabezón," Nita laughed. "What are we going to grow?"

"Everything. Mangos, aguacates (alligator pears), plantanos (plantains), gandules (peas), coconuts, name it, baby, you got it."

"Bobo, those things only grow in weather like Puerto Rico's." Her elbow smacked gently into my belly.

"Okay, okay." I made a pained expression of having my solar plexus crushed. "We'll grow tomatoes, lettuce, watermelons, peppers, carrots and . . ."

"And that's enough. We haven't got a hundred cuerdas." Nita's sense of reality busted my dream of starting a truck farm.

"Okay, let's start now."

I started chopping brush and Nita hauling them into the woods. The sun was beautifully warm and I stripped to my waist. I cooled a handkerchief around my forehead and laughed as Nita teased me on my pobre imitation of trying to look like an Apache. I ignored her put-down.

"It's good enough for Cochise, it ought to be chevere for you, squaw woman."

The hours went by and the backyard got to look like a clearing. I gulped down lemonade and chewed up a baloney sandwich.

I really could see all them growing things already as the cleared space was about twenty feet by thirty feet. I damn near broke my back forcing a rusty lawnmower past twigs, rocks, and empty cans that got in the way.

Nita raked all the waste into one big pile. I thought about burning the stuff, but decided against it. It all went into the woods.

I stood at one corner of the cleared ground, my foot on a shovel ready to break ground. I nodded my head solemnly at Nita, who was wiping beads of lady sweat off her brow.

"Before I break ground for this year's planting, I wish to dedicate this hallowed ground to the Rain God, Mother Earth, and the gentle rays of the sun that we may have a good harvest and that the horn of plenty will fill our storehouse to a mucho overflow, that who so ever needeth will come and not go away empty-handed during the seven years of famine."

"Okay, Joseph of Egypt," Nita cracked. "Stop wasting wind and start plowing."

I shoved the shovel hard in Wyandanch ground and with arms outstretched beseeched the gods to look with favor on our land. I spit on my hands and brought up a shovelful of half a pound of earth and five pounds of rotten tin cans and broken bottles.

"What the hell?? Like this is garbage!"

The hours went by and between some mild Christian swearing, I finally sat down on top of a mountain of garbage, tin cans, bedsprings, a toy rocking horse, three lampshades, and some unmentionables.

"My God, Nita, we've only got this half done and there's enough garbage under the ground to run neck-in-neck with 117th Street. Enough for now. We'll get at it tomorrow."

I went into the house and got Don on the phone.

"Hi, Piri," Don greeted.

"Wow, Don, did you rent the backyard out as a garbage dump?"

"What's the matter?"

"Nita and I are digging for a garden and have come up with a garbage dumper's dream."

"Oh . . . ah . . . haha, well, when we first got the place we just buried a little garbage there."

"Yeah." I laughed weakly and hung up feeling cheated. Like with all my trying to escape from the crap, here was tons of it buried in my backyard. But never say die and in a week we had two truckloads sent to the dump. I felt like laying the twenty-buck bill on Don.

Later on I felt pretty proud as we dug the neat rows of planted seed and baby tomato plants.

"Now, all we got to do is be patient and we'll soon be eating the fruit of our garbaged labor." I grinned, not even digging the slightest idea that after the bugs, birds, and uncaring dogs, we might end up buying vegetables. But I hadda say one thing, the vegetables that survived the pestilence could have won prizes. That crappy garbage was some hell of a fertilizer.

Don and Sis came over to the house. Sis to yak with Nita and Don to help me with repairs. Don was a damn good all-around man.

The talk got around to my getting a car. Without one I was in bad shape for getting around Wyandanch.

"I got one for you, Piri. You can have my old Studebaker, it's in damn good shape."

"How much?"

"Nothing. We'd like you to have it, make things easier for you."

"Hey, man, thanks." I smiled. But my one unblinking eye wondered if the digging up of the garbage dump had anything to do with an easing of conscience.

A year went into two. My work at the club was going along pretty good. Like I dug changes in a lot of the youngsters' attitudes. A lot of them who had dropped out of school dropped in again. Bopping had fallen off. But it wasn't just because of our club's work alone, because there were many other groups and organizations that were pulling their weight with the kids. Things weren't like we'd like them to be, but at least we were making some kind of dents in the problems of ghetto living, and the best dent was that the people were getting together and involving themselves in better education for our kids, involvement in politics, demonstrations at City Hall, Albany, name it, and the people were into it . . . demonstrations clear into Washington. Rat control, rent strikes, welfare struggles, police brutality, and the most chevere part of it was that the young ones were mucho now aware of what was oppressing all of us. They were becoming better teachers than the olders and that was the best feeling of all. Yet even with all the success of the club, I, myself, maybe because I was living in Wyandanch and away from the heart of the club, didn't feel I was as close to the kids as I wanted to be.

One night I came home dead tired. I just looked at my

dinner and after Ricky went to sleep, I told Nita what was on my mind. "Honey, how would you feel about moving back to El Barrio or anywhere in the City?"

"What!!!" She came on strong. "Is it on account of these shameless ones?"

"Later for them, Nita. Most of these people around here are so damn busy being bigots, they ain't got time for happiness. I put them in my pocket. Before it really use to bug me knowing they didn't want us here, but like no more. We could live wherever we want and screw them that don't dig us.

"Never," I continued. "It's that the back and forth bit is getting to me. I gotta get up mucho early, hassle at work all day, and buck my way back here. I'm sorry, honey, but maybe this place would be chevere if I worked out here. Look, like we can sell it at a better price, get our bread back with something added. We got the house next door rented and the whole place is improved, new parts, cleared land."

Nita laughed.

I gently held her hand.

"Really, honey, it's beating the crap outta me. It's expensive, like the commuting alone runs to twenty bucks or so, plus incidentals and I come in so beat out. I don't feel like doing repairs. Wow, like if the pump don't go, some other thing goes and . . ."

"When do we move, negrito?" Nita's fingers squeezed my hand with mucho understanding.

"As soon as we find a buyer. It will be better. Like it's hard on you too, walking to your job in that sewing machine dress factory and then picking up Ricky."

"But that's just next door and I haven't minded."

"You don't mind moving, eh, honey? I mean, it's okay?"

"I only moved here on account of you, Piri, and I'll move back to New York for the same reason. Besides"—and Nita laughed—"I miss the gossip and Pastor Hernandez and everybody. It's not that the church out here is not fine, but on 118th Street it's like being with la familia."

"Chevere, it's settled. Let me start checking out a buyer. There's a real estate office in town."

I took Nita in my arms.

"You don't mind, eh, Nita?"

"It does get cold here in the winter, Piri, and lonely. You leaving so early and coming back so late. Sometimes even having to stay over. Mind? I was sort of praying you'd want to go back."

Even so, I felt sad for taking away the white picket fence.

Slam Bang, Man!!! I stumbled into the house out of sheer anger. My body temperature was on such a high kick, my up tight eyeballs must have been shooting out fireballs of hating heat.

Nita came out of Ricky's room in time to see me crashing my fist in staccato calle anger into the living room's flowered wallpapered plaster boards. There were about seven or eight fist holes clean through when from far off I heard Nita screaming.

"Por Dios, Piri, Por Dios, que pasa! My God, please stop. What's the matter?"

Ricky began crying because of the racket. I ran into his room and gently snatched him up. I hadda hold on to something like my son to cool la mierda that had just gone down.

I held Ricky close and made all kinds of cooing sounds. I couldn't help noticing that the veins on the back of my hands were bursting with the wanting so bad to have punched that cat all inside his bad-breathed prejudiced mouth.

"Shshshshsh, niño. Poppie's just letting out some kinda baddo steam. I ain't angry at you, lindo."

Ricky believed me and accepted my bo-bo offering and let himself be lowered back into his crib.

I walked over to the living room window and stared at the wilderness out there.

"Que paso, Piri?" Nita's hand made its way gently onto my shoulder.

"Oh man, honey. It's the Babylon bullshit all over again. Just like when I was a kid. Like going down South, like . . . . Oh, wow . . .

"Just like when is this hell gonna stop? When are they gonna stop thinking that White is the National Anthem of the whole world . . . ? When are they gonna . . . ?"

"For God sakes, negrito. Calm yourself and tell me what happened."

I gently cut myself loose from Nita and sat down on the sofa.

"Animales. Honey, that's what they are, nada but animales. Well-educated make-believe white Christian . . . that s.o.b. even had a sign in his window announcing a picnic in honor of St. Jude the Impossible."

Jesus Christ, I thought. *A man shouldn't come into his home and bring in so much storm.*

Nita just stood there watching my face going through all kinds of contortions and talking to walls.

"What's the sickness they got? What is the fever with them that if everything ain't white, it ain't in sight. Damn, man, we Puerto Ricans got a right to live, even if a whole mucho of us ain't lily blancos."

"Por favor, Piri, calmate. What happened?"

I smiled a little, but tight, and drew a word picture of what had gone down.

"Honey, I've been going to the real estate agent for weeks and didn't tell you what has been going down to spare you details, but a lot of crap is involved. Honey, the first time I went down to the real estate office and walked in I saw this guy sitting behind a desk." As I talked to Nita, my mind began to relive what had gone down.

"Er . . . are you the real estate agent?" I had asked.

The ruddy-face man looked up and with mucho politeness nodded yes.

"I'm Piri Thomas and I'd like to discuss some business with you."

"Glad to know you, Mr. Thomas. I'm Mr. Paul Hendricks. Please have a chair."

"Thanks." I let myself relax.

He polite like offered me a cigar as he lit one up for himself. I polite-like refused.

"Well, Mr. Thomas. If you're interested in a home we have some near Gold Farms Road, and some of the best Negro families are located there."

"I don't want to buy, Mr. Hendricks. I want to sell."

"Uhmmmm, seems to me I knew most of the families at Gold Farms Road and I can't come to er . . . place you?"

"I don't live in Gold Farms."

"Oh, no wonder. Your property is probably at Red Creek Road or Maple Lane. I'm afraid I couldn't handle your house, Mr. Thomas."

I watched his cigar smoke making his face look like he was on fire.

"It's not located in either place. It's on Silver View Path, Number Thirty-six."

"But that's, er . . ." Mr. Hendricks wasn't puffing on his cigar.

Damn, but I knew where he was at.

"That's near Clear Water Pond." I smiled.

"Er . . . have you lived there long?"

"About a little over two Christmases." I smiled.

"If you don't mind my asking, who did you buy the house from?"

"Houses, I have two of them. Live in one and got the other rented. Uh . . . I bought them from my brother-in-law Don Baldwin."

Mr. Hendricks' face lit up in instant recognition.

"Oh . . . ha ha, of course, you're the Spanish family I've heard about."

"Puerto Rican," I corrected.

"I see . . . er . . . is there any particular reason for wanting to sell out?"

"A couple. Ahuh, one is that I work in New York and for the kind of work I'm doing I ought to live closer."

"What kind of work do you do, Mr. Thomas?"

"I work with kids."

"Very commendable."

I nodded thanks and went on.

"The other reason is that there is prejudice."

Like Mr. Hendricks didn't even acknowledge my last reason.

"Er . . . do you have a picture of the house and property?"

"Sure . . ."

"Uhmmmmm, they look pretty good. Er . . . how much you asking for them?"

I checked my mind out again and remembered the exact figure Nita and I had worked out.

"Fourteen thousand for the two, Mr. Hendricks. We've put a lot of work into them."

"Would it be all right if I brought prospective buyers to your house?"

"Any time, Mr. Hendricks, except like maybe not in the middle of the night."

Mr. Hendricks had laughed. He had brought out some forms and took down mucho information and after I had signed making him my agent he had put out his cigar and assured me of a best possible deal.

I came back to now time and took a cup of coffee from Nita.

"Nita, remember those few times Mr. Hendricks brought some people to look at our houses?"

"I remember they didn't seem too interested."

"Don't blame them, they wanted something new, up-to-date. What we need is somebody who can't afford to buy something new, like somebody like us. So you know what I did?"

"What, Piri?"

"I went out on my own and got to talking to Reverend Wilson, who's Pastor of the Mt. Zion Afro Church, and he introduced me to somebody who is interested. I brought him and his wife here while you were in church. He liked the price and the idea of being able to rent the other house. So I went back today to the real estate office, feeling like chevere. Wow, did I want to surprise you with a closed deal. Instead . . . oh, dammit . . ."

I saw myself in the real estate office.

"Good afternoon, Mr. Thomas."

"Good afternoon, Mr. Hendricks."

"I'm sorry, but no luck yet. Seems people want something a bit more modern. All the people I've brought over feel they'd rather put the extra monies into a new house."

"I got a buyer, Mr. Hendricks." I felt smug that what he hadn't been able to do I did.

"Well, that's wonderful. Of course I'm . . ."

"The people can't come in till Friday cause that's his day off."

"Wonderful. Can you give me their names and address and phone number? I can call them and arrange a definite appointment."

"I got it right here," and I handed him the information.

"I see . . . I see." His eyes read the piece of paper. "Mr. and Mrs. Arnold Hersh . . . A-huh, 1203 Gold Farms Road . . . Oh . . . uhm . . ."

"What's the matter, Mr. Hendricks?"

"Are they colored?"

"That's right. Why?" I asked, knowing the why all the way.

"Really, Mr. Thomas, I don't know quite how to say this, but you certainly must know that Silver View Path is a, er . . . white community and they wouldn't be happy there . . . and you bought your house from Mr. Baldwin, who's lived here many years and his parents before him and, well, you're being, er . . . Spanish is not like . . ."

My blood was tearing itself up into my eyeball.

"Why don't you just come out with it, fella?" My eyes just stared into his.

"Well, it's not that I mind, but the people, I mean their homes, they've worked hard and they do mind, ah . . . mixing, and well, Dammit, I have lived here all my life. Real estate is my livelihood and if I sold to a colored family property in Silver View, well . . . Can you understand? I mean, put yourself in my place."

"Not on a bet, Mr. Hendricks. I'm selling my property to who the hell I choose and I don't need you. In fact, I'll chop your commission off the price and get the thing along with that much faster."

"Mr. Thomas, you've got to understand my position."

"I don't understand nothing. All I understand is that I'm also a victim to this prejudice shit, too, and my color is my color and speaking Spanish don't make my color any more lighter. So forget trying to get around me with that played-out shit. This ain't my first time in Babylon."

"It would be difficult for Mr. Baldwin." Hendricks' voice came in weak.

"Mr. Baldwin don't believe in that racist crap. He'll stand up under your prejudice weight." I was almost snarling.

"It's not me. It's the position I'm in."

"Well, get up off your hands and knees and walk like you say you are and not because of the position you're in."

"Mister . . ."

I got up and walked toward the door.

"I'm selling my house, or I'm not selling it, but either way, I'm gonna make the decision."

I walked away shaking my head in disgust. My eyes dug the sign in his window.

PICNIC IN HONOR OF ST. JUDE THE IMPOSSIBLE. . . .

MY GOD!!!

"What do you think, Nita?"

I looked at my hands. "I see nothing wrong with fighting

them. It is too bad they are the way they are, but we have the right to sell to whom we please. It makes one feel sick, Nita."

"Si, Piri, but they are the most sick."

St. Jude the Impossible . . . .
MY GOD!!!!!

23

You better believe it, son

Couldn't keep my mind from churning. All through dinner I forced myself to go through everything that seemed normal —even to the making believe that I was hungry.

That sign in Hendricks' window, ST. JUDE THE IMPOSSIBLE, kept raging through my mente. *Damn,* I thought, *how long ago did that happen?* And the calendar in my brain answered, *"Hey, stupid, about six weeks ago."*

"Was the food okay, corazón?"

I looked up at Nita, who was hung up between feeding herself and keeping Ricky from greasing food over himself like the champ he was.

He's grown, I thought. *My kid's beautiful, gonna teach him what the world's all about.*

"Food's chevere, baby. Como siempre."

"I'll get you more." And Nita tried to balance Ricky's determination to wash his hands in the bowl of habichuelas (beans).

"I'll get it, honey."

I walked into the kitchen, not really hungry, but a man's not supposed to turn down food cooked in love, no matter how up tight he may be. On my way back I slapped Ricky's hands. He used his hands to make hash outta them beans.

"Nita, teach him better, eh?"

Nita's hurt look made me add something like, "I mean, teach him to use a fork if he wants to make hash outta the beans."

Ricky must have caught wise. He left the beans and copped himself a ball. By taking care of business with my plate, I gave him a Poppie's loving dirty look and smeared a little bean juice on his nose. My son-of-a-gun muchachito dug the action and slammed a tiny fistful dead into my face.

Nita laughed.

Ricky laughed.

I just smiled. "Rotten kid."

Ricky did Puerto Rican baby gurgles with a rotten kid pleasure. I laughed with pride. My closed fist under Ricky's nose didn't move him at all, like he was in his glory declaring war on his old man with P.R. Red Kidney Beans.

We all dug each other and for that short while time, all the dark out there was shut out.

"Come, bandido, time for a bath," and Nita hauled mighty fighting Ricky toward what to him was splashing time.

Ricky was in the tub doing his thing.

"Going to take a walk. Need anything?"

"No, honey."

"I'll see you. Hey, champ, learn how to swim, uh?"

"Poppie . . . Poppie . . ." Ricky's arms reached out to me. I bent over him and he gave me a wet hug.

"See you later, panin."

Ricky smiled and his thumb went into his mouth like Custer's Last Stand.

Outside was kind of crispy. I walked to the back and had a passing thought of all the garbage I had dug out of there.

The sun was making its mind on when to set. I decided

to walk in the woods. It was kind of pretty, like autumn to me always is . . .

I looked around to see if any catbirds were around, but all I could see were the tougher sparrows. I crunched my way through the woods and broke into a clearing, and a side road. I walked along kicking little rocks and hunks of dead wood. I heard a car behind me and got off to the side of the road.

"Hey, Brother Piri."

I looked at the driver. It was Reverend Wilson.

"How are you, sir?" I smiled at him but my heart wasn't in it.

"You sure look down in the dumps," he said.

"Hell's bursting, Reverend. A whole lot of ca-ca going down."

"Want a lift?"

"Ain't going nowhere, Reverend. Just walking."

"How about coming over to my house, meet the missus and we eat us something?"

I started to say I wasn't hungry, but didn't want to turn down his chevere courtesy.

"Why not? Thanks Reverend Wilson."

"Call me Jules. My whole name's Jules Tall-Tree Wilson. They say I got some Indian in me, mostly lost. The black in me is more outstanding."

His strong-looking dark copper-skinned face was smiling. I dug him to be about thirty-six or thirty-eight years old. He was built with mucho muscles—with hands that could hide a football damn near. I climbed into his truck and sat back for the ride to his place.

"Where you live, Reverend . . . er, Jules?"

"About two blocks up on that hill."

"Here in Silver View Hill?"

He must have dug my face, cause he just smiled tight, but gently-like, and said, "Yeah, Brother Piri, just you and us are the only ones on this side of Wyandanch. Here we are." His truck made wheels into a driveway of a house that was tremendous, but wasn't finished yet.

It looked as if only one man had been working on it.

"Built it myself. Some help from brothers from the congregation, but at the beginning, only me. It's taking quite a long time, but I had to give a lot of time to the Lord in starting Mt. Zion Afro Church, but ole God's been good."

"Catch much hell? I mean, living here, Jules?"

"They don't dare hang me, but they've tried everything but. Hey, there's my love."

We got out of the car and walked toward a pretty woman who was standing in the open doorway.

"Clara, this is the young feller I was telling you about. Clara, Piri . . . Piri . . . Clara."

"Glad to know you, Mrs. Wilson."

"Clara will do, Brother Piri. Won't you please come in?"

We sat in the unfinished kitchen and I listened to Reverend Jules talk about his moving to Silver View Hill. How he bought the two acres from a good white man, and how for the last four years he had been struggling to build a beautiful house on a shoestring, with secondhand lumber, secondhand everything, except his labor and love, which were firsthand. And how a civic committee called "Better Civic Improvement Committee" had been fighting to get him out of there, trying to find mucho violations.

I heard his voice full of anger but with no defeat in it talk about how it was gonna look when it was finished and everything that had happened in the last six weeks blew my mind. My voice sounded gentle-like.

"I know about that group of S.O.B.s called the 'Better Civic Improvement Committee.'"

"Figured you'd found out, Brother Piri."

Sister Clara put some hot coffee and ham and cheese sandwiches on the table. Reverend Jules got up and lit some dim bulbs.

"Gotta keep cost down, no matter what. Don't mind the low-watt bulbs." His laughter was mucho tall.

I didn't laugh too good.

"Got bad times, eh?"

It blew out of me. "God dammit to hell, you're damn right." I looked quickly at Sister Clara.

"Sorry, Sister, I mean for cursing. It's . . ."

"No need to be. A man's got a right to say damn and hell, specially when so damn many of us are living in a damn hell."

Sister Clara's voice was quiet and mucho for real.

"What went down, son?" Reverend Jules bit three quarters of his sandwich off at one clip. "I blow off steam once in a while."

Sister Clara laughed. "Once in a while, but dear Lord Jesus, them once in a whiles makes a volcano look like a teapot."

"Man's got a right to get mad at other folks' stupid way of thinking." Reverend Jules picked up the rest of his sandwich and it left the world.

"And a man's got a right to live on land he bought with honest sweat. I reckon I could live elsewhere with a whole lot of more peace, but I'd probably have troubles there too. Nope, one's gotta make a stand on his land and fight if need be for his right to live there. Nothing comes easy, son, especially living . . . and like I'm saying, if I got to put away my

Bible and pick me up a gun, there ain't no way the Lord's gonna mind."

"Mucho tearing points, Brother Jules. What do they fuck-" I felt my adam's apple buckle at the forming cuss word. Brother Jules's face changed no expression.

"Fucking want?" He finished it for me.

I smiled. I didn't even mind the dim light bulbs.

"Brother Piri? They want our blood, our talent. They want our sweat. They want our labor and they want—period. Life ain't a living with them. It's a business, born and bred on a mountain of anything that ain't white. It's just an unnatural greediness . . ."

"And," Sister Clara gently interrupted, "when they ain't got us to worry about, they out of force of habit, start taking care of each other, but like that's only just to keep in practice."

"I know that from way back." I attempted to bite into my ham and cheese sandwich. "But what do them racists want in the end. I mean, what are they striving for? What's their goal? I mean, what kind of world are they aiming for? Damn, God, don't they even realize that anything born in hate dies in hate? Damn, Brother Jules, like all the history I've read, and all the history I've lived, all I've seen is that the good people of the earth with beauty to give have just been crippled, slaughtered, or rewritten into history as a culture of nothing. God, they wrote the history of the Alamo, like it was the Mexicans' fault. The massacre at Sand Creek like the Cavalry had fought its way out of an ambush. They signed peace treaties like they had all the ink in the world, and their word was gospel truth until it didn't suit their purposes, and then game-time for the trusting ones."

"We got some sassafras tea, Brother Piri. Would you like

some?" Sister Clara's face was most cara palo and gentle-like.

"Sugar, Brother Piri?"

"Uh? . . . Yes, thank you."

"What went down, Brother Piri?"

"Jules." My voice was in a quiet-like way holding in some kind of a bomb to keep from bursting out.

"In these last six weeks a whole lot of things have gone down. You remember that man and his family, Mr. Hersh, who wanted to buy the two houses? Well, it seems that the Better Civic Improvement, or whatever that committee is . . ."

"I know what you're talking about, Brother Piri," Brother Jules said, sort of looking at the wall.

"Well, they got to him," I went on. "Cause I called him up the other night and he said to me, 'Mr. Thomas, I don't want any trouble and I just got a little money and I'm trying to put it into a house. We've been staying at Gold Farms with my sister-in-law since we just came in from Alabama and I've gotten phone calls not to buy the property. I don't want any trouble, Mr. Thomas, so if it's all right with you, I'll look around a little longer."

Sister Clara made some kind of funny laugh and gently, matter-of-fact quietly-like just said, "Lord, if they keep scaring our people into not taking a chance, we're going to keep pushing peanuts with our nose."

"Oh, Christ, let me get it out," I said. "I went over to see my brother-in-law Don and told him what was happening."

"You talking about Don Baldwin?" Brother Jules cut in.

"Yeah, he's a for real cat. Anyway, he got real angry and my sister said something about that committee being nothing more than being headed by a Nazi."

"What are you planning to do, Brother Piri?"

"I'm planning to fight this all the way."

"That's where it's at." He smiled. "Black Jesus did it, ain't no reason for a brown Jesus not to do it, especially when they said only a white Jesus could do it."

I tasted my sassafras tea. *Hey caramba, this homemade brew is all right. Sassafras tea,* I thought in my mind, while even the hotness of burning way down in my throat did nothing to cool the anger that Mr. Hendricks and their committee for Better Civic Improvement had shot up in me.

I made my way down the road and Brother Jules's words kept breaking themselves on my back.

"Brother Piri, you sure you don't want me to drive you back?"

"No, I'll walk. Thank you, Sister Clara, for your hospitality."

"Hey, Brother Piri."

I looked back and said, "Yeah, Brother Jules?"

"Someday I hope to visit Puerto Rico."

And I said, "Me too, cause I have never been there."

"Don't let your anger get you down, boy, cause if you do, it'll consume you and they'll have you in their pockets."

I roared out laughing and Wyandanch's woods reverberated with my sound.

"Hey, Brother Jules, you don't know my background, but I've seen hell just like you. I'm just trying to save some of my strength to finally see the beauty where right now there's nothing at all."

"Hey, Brother Jules."

His voice seemed further away when he answered, that was because my feet were walking away. "Yeah, Brother Piri?"

"Build you house chevere here on Clear View Hill."

And his voice came floating down to me like some kind of preacher on an altar on a hill.

"You better believe it, son . . ."

You better believe it, son . . .

You better believe it.

24

White picket fences not spelling love

The moon was out as I cut through the woods on my way home. *Funny,* I thought, *how the earth looks the same when you're walking through the woods.*

I pushed the door open con cuidado, trying not to wake the two corazónes inside.

"Piri?" It was Nita. "Everything all right, negrito?"

"What isn't, honey, we'll fight to make it right. Uhhh, how come you sitting in the dark?"

"Lights wake up Ricky."

"Nita?"

"Si?"

"I made arrangements to move back to New York."

"Para El Barrio?"

"Brooklyn project, same thing."

Nita got up and stood by the window. I walked over to her side. There were no words. We just looked out the window at shadowy trees and bushes, and we listened to the strange-sounding noises that were alien in whatever barrio we were going back to.

"Negrito?"

I was watching the rays of the moon fill the living room.

"Piri?"

I made my ears strain for the sound of Puerto Rican music.

"Piri?"

I strained my nose for the familiar smell of Puerto Rican food.

"Negrito, why are you so quiet?"

I pushed the hurt in and made me cara palo tall inside. I thought of the mountain of garbage Nita and I had seen materialize before our garden came to be.

"Piri, please, papito, say something."

I dug the sky upstairs, my eyes looking for the Dog Star.

"Piri?"

"Si, Nita?"

"Have faith."

My arm went around Nita's waist. My hand touched her stomach and felt its chevere swelling.

"Nita?"

"Si, Piri?"

"What's it gonna be, honey? Machito o chancleta, boy or girl?"

"Cabezón, big head." Nita laughed, washing away baddo feelings. "What God gives to us. What would you like?"

"A girl," I whispered, wondering about white picket fences not spelling love.

25

Tantas guerras (so many wars)

How much time had gone by? Two, three, six months. Like time had lost its mucho meaning, it don't add or subtract, it's a dimension of its own.

And here we were in a project house. No white picket fences, no chirping birds, no racist neighbors.

I walked around, like pacing up and down. I checked Ricky out. He was most chevere asleep. I dug my mind talking to him silent-like.

Your father and mother give you their beauty, walk tall or not at all . . . Adelante.

I checked my watch. It was seven-thirty. Nita would be back from her sister Carmela's around ten o'clock.

The in-between hours were busted up with some phone calls. Lil Man or Tracy. Bop gonna start. Italianos getting back. Blacks jumping stink. Crazy Horse getting busted. Lena's old man tried to stomp her into the ground. Grandstand Louie just got over an overdose.

I made me a cup of Cafe Bustelo and gave thought that the young ones should stop their negative kick, put their beauty of brain power a la positiva, and then the system of racists and exploiters would see the handwriting on the wall.

I downed the cafe and felt its hotness reach itself down

into my ice-cold stomach and play games with my belly
button.

I sipped coffee . . .

I listened to the street noises . . .

I dug my knuckles on both hands like with mucho
scars . . .

I listened to the most chevere sounds of my son's Puerto
Rican breathing . . .

I fought down a feeling of nausea like vomitando . . .

I thought of all little children of all the chevere pretty
colors, like the making up of a Barrio rainbow . . .

I listened to a record from an apartment below, *algo chevere* by Bobby Capo . . .

I held my face cara palo, like they can't beat us. We walk
tall or nunca at all.

Caramba . . . caramba . . .

"Popi, Popi."

I turned and gave mucho recognition to a tiny hand tug-
ging at my pants and like trying to climb into my lap.

"Hey, papi. Hey, tall little one. What are you doing outta
bed?"

"Popi?"

"Si, hijo." I let my hand be a climbing tree and son Ricky
climbed into the saddle of my right leg. "How come you ain't
taking care of business by copping some chevere sleep?"

"I'm not sleepy. I want cornflakes."

I laughed.

"Hey, can't you pick something else like . . . ?"

"Cornflakes I want."

"Don't have any. Hey, look in the refrigerator and
pick . . ."

"Popi?"

"Sí."

"Y Mommie?"

"She went out."

I dug my son's eyes making a quick looking thing around the kitchen.

"She'll be back soon, papo. Here, take care of business." I handed him his bottle of milk and cookie with butter. Held him tight with gentle warmth and pointed his culito toward the bedroom way.

I listened to his moving feet make their way towards his bed. I listened to his settling down. I listened to the swallowing of a cookie with butter and my thoughts smiled and went back to thinking of all that had gone down in Wyandanch, a good Indian name.

I dug the calendar on the wall and admired the picture of a white blond little girl hugging a collie puppy. My eyes walked their way to the date—March 14, 1961—and lazy-like, I remembered the hassles of having moved on New Year's Eve 1961—and furniture laying all around and the noises of people partying and Nita and I standing in the midst of all the confusion of unpacking and looking at each other and wishing each other a "Happy New Year" and going back to unpacking listening with half an ear to Guy Lombardo's "Ole Lang Syne."

It was the middle of January or February that I went back to Wyandanch to see if I could sell the house. I wanted to go alone, but Nita gently insisted on coming along. We left Ricky with Carmela yelling his lungs out at rejection.

We drove toward Wyandanch past La Guardia airfield. Grand Central Parkway made the turn into the Northern

State Parkway. The further we went into Long Island, the colder it got.

Snow was on the ground and ice was all around. There wasn't much talking between Nita and myself.

I was thinking about the almost new car we were driving that we could almost afford. It was a pretty soft yellow Ford. I turned the radio on, trying to find a warm blast of chevere music and heard the last part of some kind of beautiful speech by Martin Luther King. I swerved just a little bit to keep from getting hit by a mucho anxious taxicab, changed the stations to WVNO. Might as well hear some Spanish music, and ran into the news broadcast on how lousy the world situation was.

"Do you think we can sell the place, Piri?"

"Hell, yes, Nita, don't worry about it."

Hell, yes, Piri. Don't worry about it, I thought within myself. We turned into the road at Clear Water Pond. We got out in front of the house. Nita was carefully trying to crunch her way through knee-deep snow. I was wondering if it was worthwhile to have dug all that garbage out of the backyard.

Got my keys out and we both looked at each other kind of funny-like because the door was wide open.

God, as I walked in a funny smile crossed my face. It was dog shit all over the place and I saw from the inside what I hadn't seen from the outside. Some windows were broken out. My eyes touched the water faucet in the kitchen and the water had been turned on so that the pipes would burst.

"Oh, Piri, who has done this?"

"Wow, there is no name. Like whoever did this, Nita, this is not the work of human beings. This is the put-down of master haters."

Nita and I walked around from room to room and I didn't hate the dogs for their dog shit. I hated the humans who were really the dogs.

"Let's go home. Nita, don't worry about it. I'll take care of it." And I did my best not to notice little swelling tears of hurt welling in Nita's eyes.

I walked to the bathroom and washed my face with cold water. I dug my face in the mirror, the muscles making all kinds of up and down facial motions fighting for some human sense of control.

"Son bestias (beasts)." Her voice was angry. Her anger real.

"Let's go home, Nita," I gently said.

I held her close, trying to find some kind of warmth in that ice box that was once our home.

"They are not going to heaven." Nita's voice was mucho adamant.

"No sweat, woman. They have already chosen hell."

"Bestias."

"Shus . . . shus . . . shuss . . . Nita, let's go home."

The phone rang. I reached over and picked up my coffee. I lifted the phone.

"Quien es?"

"Nita."

"Hi."

"I'll be home in a little while. Is everything okay?"

"Porque no? Oh yeah, we almost lost Ricky."

"WHAT!!!!!!"

"Nada mucho, Nita. He didn't sit on his potty. He sat on the big one and almost got swallowed."

I heard Nita laugh. It was intermingled with mucho concern.

"You better start teaching him how to balance his culito on the big potty." I laid fatherly advice on her. I heard Nita make madre sounds.

"He wants to fly even before he can run. I'll be home soon."

Nita hung up while I was saying, "They can't beat us Puerto Ricans."

Moodiness settled over me . . .

Anger settled over me . . .

Alone-ness settled over me . . .

And I let my mind's memory bank make a moving picture of what had gone down in Wyandanch.

"I want to sell the house, Sis, and they say I can't sell it to anybody that ain't white."

Miriam looked at me.

"They are Natzi."

"You mean NAZIS."

"The leader of the Better Civic Improvement Committee is."

"Did you and Don know them?"

"We did and don't want to any more."

"I'm glad you and Don ain't prejudiced . . ."

"We don't want . . ."

And the rest of my remembering went by the wayside. Suddenly I thought of the child Nita was carrying. *Quien sabe? Hope it's a little slipper, a Lady Slipper, a beautiful flower that will grow well among the weeds.*

I thought back to how I had asked John Clause what we could do about it. I felt sure a Christian like him would rally to the cause of right and justice. But when I had asked him, his most hallowed voice had just answered, "Why don't you take it to the NAACP?" Great God Almighty! Oh, well, I had shrugged my shoulders. *Take it to the Lord or the Commonwealth of Puerto Rico.*

"Nita?"

"Si?"

"We lost the houses, like I hope you don't . . .

"Caramba, Nita, I hope you don't think I let us down. I fought them, honey, right up to the town hall, but like they kept slapping one violation after another on the house. Jesus Christ, they got so much money behind them. How do you win?"

"Bueno, when people like us get together."

"Honey, I know all that. It's us I'm talking about. All the sweat and work we put into our property, plus mucho hard-earned money." My voice started rising with a whole lot of anger. "We've lost the houses, dammit!!"

"Negrito." Nita looked half at Ricky's room, half at me. "Callate (be quiet). You'll wake up Ricky."

"We still owe some money besides that."

"Let's go to bed. You have to go to work tomorrow, and mañana's otro dia."

I started to say something else but just let my mind become blank-like. *Yeah, mañana's another adelante day.— What you say, Brother Jules, about putting aside your Bible and if need be, picking up a gun!*

"Yeah, honey—let's go to bed."

26

The great church downtown

Like mucho Sundays before, I rode around picking up the kids to go to Sunday School. The majority of the kids were waiting at the club. It was only hard to reach kids that the club made a special point of picking up.

I honked my horn at Dee Bruce, who was working with the girls' youth club. Her car was making a turn into 108th Street. There were seven girls in the car with her.

"Hi, Dee, what's shakin?" I hollered.

"Having a ball trying to wake up some of these lazy bones."

"I can tell." I smiled, looking at three of them asleep. The other four were fast on their way.

"So can I." She dug the guys in my car and they were pulling the same number.

"Well, whatta you expect? They spend Saturday night partying and breaking night all the way into Sunday morning. It's a miracle we even got the bodies to move at all."

Dee Bruce laughed. "Yes, it seems these young ladies have never heard of getting their beauty sleep."

"What young ladies?" wisecracked Lil Man. "Them ain't no ladies and there ain't no amount of sleep gonna give them beauty."

"We are too ladies," came back an angry shout. It was buck-tooth Rita.

"An we don't need sleep to stay beautiful," screeched skinny Alice. "We're just naturally so."

"My God," Blue mimicked skinny Alice's voice. "I've seen better beauty behind bars at the Bronx Zoo."

"You better keep your mouth shut, Cheetah, or I'll send you back to Tarzan." Skinny Alice was getting mucho up tight.

"haw . . . haw . . . haw . . . Augg, Augg . . . arawow . . . ugg . . . ugg . . ." Lil Man went into a Cheetah improvisation, adding in a high falsetto voice, "Here comes your man, skinny honey, pucker up for a jungle kiss."

"Give it to your mother," a disguised voice screamed from Dee Bruce's car.

"Oh, you wanna play rough, eh?" Lil Man said. "Well, tell your mother that I . . ."

"Whoa, down, Lil Man, you ain't gonna play the mother game on a Sunday Morning," I said.

"That's a perfect example, man. A perfect example," screamed mortally wounded Lil Man. "You call that being ladies. Amazons is a better word." Lil Man extended his head out the car window. "I know who made that crack about giving it to my mother." He didn't really know, but he was hoping the voice would slip so he could identify it and lay some mighty blows on its owner, but the owner was mucho smart and answered back.

"Sorry about sounding your mother. Give it to your sister."

"Ya see . . . ya see, they ain't no ladies, they's GORILLAS."

"So's your father," came another disguised voice.

The other kids in the car were falling out with laughter at seeing Lil Man getting wasted by the girls, who were scoring mucho points on him, and this only made Lil Man jump more stink.

"Ladies, my behind. You ain't ladies, you ain't nuttin but cachaperas (lesbians)."

"If you say so, faggittito," came another disguised voice.

"By the way, wasn't that your daddy I saw wearing drag the other day?"

Lil Man's neck got all full of exploding veins and he was trying to open the door with clear cool intentions of wanting to off the Ladies in Dee Bruce's car, but was being held back by the rest of the kids, who were still laughing their heads off.

I made a motion to Dee Bruce that she'd better take off. Lil Man's ego was shot to hell and only two or three little ladies being wasted was gonna cool his outraged dignity.

As we pulled away from each other a voice not disguised at all yelled back, "Yoo-hoo . . . Oh, Lil Man . . . I'm still your girl, ain't I? See you in church hon-nnnnnnnnnnnnnnn-bunch . . ."

By the time we got to church Lil Man had cooled off and was laughing with the rest of us. His only act of revenge was to jump in front of his girl and do a most chevere impression of a gorilla paying court to his beloved.

Anna laughed so hard she jumped into a bad case of hiccups and the mixture of the two made the rest of us crack up and then like a cool breeze, all the put-downs between them became a thing of the past . . . like forgotten. Lil Man put his arm around Anna and his lips got real tight with her ear with some soft whispered words that had the mucho tender sound of love.

The last of the volunteer cars drove up and our kids piled out of them.

"Is that the church?" I heard a young voice ask.

"Ain't you ever been here before?" somebody questioned.

"Naw . . . first time. Man, like this is a church and a half."

"Yeah, but we ain't going there, like we use to but they gave us our own place in that loft across the street."

"How come?" first-timer asked.

"I dunno. I think they figured we'd like a place of our own."

I looked up at the big towering rich church that stood on this clean street downtown and my mind did a flip backwards into time . . .

I was in the club . . .

"Hey, Piri."

I looked up from my desk towards John's voice. His face was smiling mucho.

"What's happening, John?" I smiled back.

"I made a contact and got us a church that we can take the kids to for Sunday School classes and let me tell you, it's really wonderful of the church to open its doors to the underprivileged kids."

"Yeah, ain't it?" I waited for John to keep talking.

"You know the Great Church downtown?"

"I sure do. It's like a thousand of our small storefront churches packed into one . . . like that's rich country."

"Well." John looked pleased. "They've consented to have our kids come every week for Sunday School classes."

"That sounds cool, John." I tried to make my voice sound as pleased as his but it just came out matter-of-fact.

"When do we start, John?"

"Tomorrow will be the first Sunday."

To tell the truth, I had all kinds of mixed feelings as

John, me, and about fifteen kids walked into that big rich church. Not even a squeak came out of some of our kids' sneakers as we made our way on the soft expensive wall to wall rugs. My God, the inside of that church looked like a golden temple . . . and the brethren and sisters that belonged to it dressed accordingly. Our kids were mucho awed by it and were talking in soft hushed whispers, smiling back at all the hundreds of welcoming, smiling faces. We were led past rooms that had classes going on . . . and there was a couple with young people sitting there. I figured we'd be going into one of them, but like, nay. Our guide kept leading us and finally stopped in front of an empty room filled with empty chairs and John motioned for us to sit down and everybody scuffed quiet-like and sat down. Like a little bit uncomfortable. Man, like that millionaire church had impressed us so much, we were bent out of shape, feeling out of place. A man, whom I figured was a deacon or somebody on the VIP board of the church, stood before us and our ears heard mucho brotherly sounds coming from his smiling mouth.

"We of the Great Church welcome you in the name of Jesus Christ."

We all listened intently.

". . . and wish that you all feel completely at ease. This is your church and together we can worship our God in Christian fellowship."

We all listened intently.

". . . and feel free to bring all your friends so that we can all share together in the love of Christ."

My ears were hearing right. I listened to the sounds of his voice.

". . . We want the beautiful children from your neighborhoods to feel welcome. As Christ once said, 'Suffer the children to come unto me, for such is the kingdom of heaven.'"

The words went rolling on and I could feel the kids' apprehension of being up tight in this billion-dollar church begin to ease away, mine included.

We went into our Sunday School lessons, sang some songs like "What a Friend We Have in Jesus" and "Nearer my God to Thee," and after a prayer and a reverent Amen, left the Great Church downtown in rich town feeling like great at how they had put out the welcoming mat for us and had smiled us out of sight. Man, we almost felt like wanted altogether children in the Great House of God.

The Sunday rolled into other Sundays and the kids got over their hush-hush entrance into the church and would talk freely and laughed . . . that is until the mucho "shhsss" started to come from the regular Christian membership. Then feelings started to change—on little things, like the kids singing "What a Friend We Have in Jesus" in five-part harmony on a fast up-beat a la street scene. The disapproving frown on a non-understanding face told us that it should have been sung slow, like on a funeral kick.

Some of them people I dug with mucho heart and soul didn't want us there . . . and it was only their so-called commitment to Christ that kept them from throwing us out super-duper fast . . . but they said it without words. They said it subtly with their eyes and protected facial expressions and our corazóns began to get up tight and our souls mucho cold.

27

I believe Christ is for the truth

Things began to change between me and a certain brand of Christianity. That pink cloud of togetherness was beginning to dissolve. I had noticed things I hadn't dug before or perhaps hadn't wanted to dig in the white Christian/ghetto relationship. It was like we weren't equals. It was as if they were the chosen ones—despite the teachings in their Bibles—like they were sent to save us by getting us a hearing with Christ. But like it had to be on their own terms.

I let my eyes do a 360 degree turn around the inside of the church. It looked like the inside of a saved Madison Square Garden. The pews, the carved woodwork, the pulpit were like the kind found only at Tiffany's. I dug the people were really inhibited. Like they were afraid to bend and put a wrinkle in their elegant clothes. I overheard someone saying that one of the newly appointed deacons was a Wall Street broker. I soon spotted a nervous, middle-aged man up on the pulpit. I dug his fingers playing with gold cuff links that let out sparkling flashes of lights to attest to the fact that diamonds were inlaid on his cuff links. I dug people staring at us. Some smiled. Some whispered. Most ignored us. I dug their voices in prayer. I dug their voices lifted in song to God, and like I realized that what a difference there was between our storefront churches in El Barrio and this one.

Like ours are poor in bread, but really rich in spirit, and this was just rich in pesos. Maybe I'm wrong, I thought, but they're here in God's house acting like it was some kind of business appointment.

They looked at each other in a kind of "Who's Who" attitude, and regarded us with a *Suffer the Little Children to Come unto Me,* that is, if they ain't dirty little ghetto kids. Caramba, I knew inside me that all Christians weren't tied up in this kind of hypocritical bag, but those that were sure were muffing it for the nitty-gritty ones.

Man, I said to myself, *they even say Amen like they're counting money.*

After one particular service, I approached John. I tried to remain calm as I explained that we all felt out of place in this church.

"It's nothing they say, John," I explained. "It's in their looks. The kids aren't stupid, John. Lil Man and a lot of the kids got to me with their feelings. Like if we're suppose to be part of their Sunday School, how come we gotta be in a room all by ourselves?" I fought to keep my voice non-angry —but blew it. "Dammit to hell, ain't we good enough to sit with their young white sons and daughters. We ain't stupid. Their smiles and attitudes are so damn condescending. We're tired of feeling hung up in a hypocritical bag by those who hide themselves under the heading of Christian Fellowship. They can lie to themselves and try to lie to us, but dammit to hell, if God's so powerful as they make Him out to be, how can they be so stupid as to think they are pulling this bullshit over His eyes?"

John was quiet for a while, minutes. Then he said softly,

"You mustn't let the devil come into your mind with false words."

"Oh God, damn it, John. Don't come on so weak."

"Well, you are young in the Lord, Piri, and there are many things you still don't understand. You must . . ."

"Yeah, John, I know. It's like we always must give in, must do right, must follow, must bow and scrape . . . smiling our behinds off and hanging on by our chins while the rest of the world lives on in some kind of glorified splendor. Bull Shit."

"You're not showing respect for the Lord, Piri, and you're certainly not showing it towards me."

"If talking nitty-gritty means no respect for the Lord and you . . . well . . . tough shit cookie."

"That's enough, Piri." John's expression was kind of stern and grim, but he smiled and added, "We'll just have to take all these feelings to the Lord in prayer."

"Or some place else, John, maybe some place higher."

"Maybe some place higher?" His voice didn't believe what he was hearing. "Like who?"

I smiled. "Maybe like to the Lord's grandfather. I'll see you later, John." I walked away but stopped at his voice.

"You ought to pray more often, Piri."

"Prayers gotta be strengthened with some kind of action, John. Without disrespect, amigo, if you've read history, too, you'd know many people have been taught to pray and when they finished praying and looked around, their land and respect was gone—taken away by the ones who had taught them to pray."

"Piri, don't let the devils use you."

"Don't worry, John, none of them will use me—or any of us if we can help it."

After the talk with John, I was up tight for a while but soon calmed down. I put myself to thinking about our own lil church across the street from the Great Church. If those people were for real, I knew, we might just see some kind of heaven together between the two churches. My God, some humans name this world Earth and some animals make it HELL.

28

Mayday—Mayday

It was a really beautiful May day. I mean, what was beautiful about the day was that the sun was shining, and the air felt warm and fresh, and merry old spring was blooming greenly all over the place. But the streets weren't like the weather or the time of year. Instead, they were up tight and tense. Mucho gang clubs were all for making hell break loose. I felt it brewing for a couple of weeks while walking down the streets and talking to the kids from all the different gangs involved. I remember talking to Shade, the president of the Untouchables, the black gang, and Lil Man, the president of the Puerto Rican Untouchables. It was on the corner of 108th Street and Lexington Avenue.

Being brought up in the ghetto streets, where everything is like so for real, you kind of sense that something's going to happen, even if it's not put down in black and white. You sniff the air and know that everything ain't right. You feel some uneasiness like in the pit of your stomach.

"Shade," I called to him as I saw him walking down my way.

"Yeah, Brother."

"I think we got some problems on our hands. Things are going to start wailing in a few days?"

Shade smiled. Like always he looked young, tough, and

nitty-gritty. He was black and beautifully proud, but not really arrogant.

"What's been happening?" I asked him, even though I had talked to other people. "I like to get the story straight, cause I like to see that right is a true might."

Before Shade could answer, Lil Man jumped in fast.

"Concho, Piri, like the Hawks went into the Red Wings' territory and then started to walk around. So they jumped on some of us Puerto Ricans, talking to the Red Wings and thought we were joining with them to jump them and then the Untouchables, Shade's people, were talking to our Puerto Rican Untouchables and they thought we were going to join forces to gang up on them. Then the Monitors, trying to decide which side to join, and then the Turbans, our Puerto Rican brother club, automatically jumped in on our side. Now we got brother clubs coming up from the Bronx and from the Lower East Side and nobody knows where it's at, except that there's going to be a awful bip bop."

I motioned for them to sit with me on the stoop. I just shook my head up and down to clear the confusion of the rapidly relayed information.

"Yeah, Lil Man is running it to you straight," Shade added. "Like all the zip gun factories and all the homemade grenade factories are in full blast. Man, if we gotta, we'll make us a fuckin' atom bomb."

My hearing copped a deaf. I was just thinking about the ingenuity that destructiveness forces people to have. *Homemade hand grenadas*, I thought. *Damn world, you know what it takes to make one of them?* An empty shoe polish can stuffed with gunpowder, or whatever else you want to put into it, different kinds of metals. Then you put black tape all around it with a little hole on the side where you can put in a little firecracker fuse, maybe about six inches long and light it up, throw it into your so-called enemy, and slam-bam, there's a whole lot of blood and agony, and now Shade's talking about producing El Barrio's first atom bomb.

I quickly thought things over and decided what to do. "Now look," I told Lil Man. "We got to get all the fellows together, cats from the Turbans and every place else. I'll reach Juju from the Red Wings and Crazy Horse from the Hawks. You get the cats from the Monitors and different brother groups and any cats who you think should be involved. Go down and see Little Maverick and tell him to spread the word out to all the other people."

"You want me to see the Dragons?" Lil Man asked.

"No, I'll take care of them. I'll go see Jerro and take care of the Viceroys also."

"Hey," interrupted Shade. "Don't you know that the Dragons and Viceroys have been fighting it out for a long time?"

"Sure I know. Just spread the word that I don't want every-body coming. I just want the presidents, the war counselors, and the prime ministers. Or the ambassadors from each to come, because we can't fill up the club with hundreds of cats."

"When you going to set it up for?"

I looked up at the May night.

"The day after tomorrow," I said. "Okay, baby, take care of business." I slapped skin with these two young warrior brothers. I got up from the stoop and cut out.

I called John Clause and told him what was happening and that I felt it would be a good idea to get them together before hell broke loose.

He said, "When can you get them together?"

"Day after tomorrow. I'll call you and let you know if it's been set up."

Time was passing. It sure took a lot of walking from block

to block talking your googy off, eating up hearts and minds, because a lot of them didn't even want to talk. They just wanted to go on burning, like "rep" was all there was and reasoning was a thing of the past.

The day of the meeting the club was filling up slowly but surely. I stood at the door carefully eyeing everyone who walked in.

"Nobody's packing?" I had to ask that even though I knew that each of them had something on him. It takes a brave man to come into enemy camp unarmed, but in street talk, only a fool comes in unarmed.

Juju, President of the Red Wings, walked in with his proud sense of arrogance, holding on to one of the most killer-diller looking mutts I'd ever seen. It was a pure thoroughbred Doberman pinscher and one man-killer dog. In spite of myself, I had to smile.

I went to the office and phoned John Clause.

"They are here, John, and things are down pretty pat. It's a little hectic. Can you make it? If you can't, okay. I'll take care of business."

"I'll be right down," he answered.

I walked back to hear all the discussing and murmurings and cursings. How about that! It was like the Tower of Babel. Puerto Rican cats were talking Spanish. The Italian cats were talking Italian. The black cats were talking swing talk. Like everybody was trying to make his own kind of secret Morse code so that if jump came to jump—and stomp came to stomp—and burn came to burn—each one would have the upper hand.

I turned around and walked back into the back room. I went into the toilet, took care of my bladder, examined my teeth in the mirror, and asked God to give me some kind of wisdom to say the right words so that these young beautiful kids wouldn't have to send themselves into a worse kinda hell than the one they were already living in. The Tower of Babel was still going on as I walked up into the main room of the club.

"How many can speak Italian over here?" I said.

Naturally all the Italians raised their hands.

"How many can speak Spanish?"

And naturally all the Puerto Ricans raised their hands.

"And how many can speak jive talk, soul talk?"

And naturally all the black cats raised their hands.

"All right. How many here can speak English? I mean talk like straight English?"

Everybody, of course, looked at me kind of funny, because everybody here could understand English. I smiled to ease the tension.

"So for the sake of communication, let's speak the bad English we all know, so we know where we're all at."

It was quiet for a little while and I felt each of these young minds turning and churning, wheeling and dealing, wondering if they were going to give up the secret weapon of their own language's secret code and let their coats be open to the enemy. I walked over to the soda fountain and started to pour myself soda water. Hell broke loose. I turned my head fast and I saw a brave young Hawk attempt to pet Juju's black Doberman pinscher with a friendly hand, like all kids like dogs. Man, mucho hands made a fast grab for zip guns, or real ones, that would have made Billy the Kid look like he was retarded in slow-motion time. I yelled out, "Hold tight."

Juju, with his majestic air, said, "Down, down," and then as an afterthought, said in Italian some kind of words that sounded like "Pecalungel."

The pressure there was so great in that little club that I walked over to the front door, held it open, and yelled back at the kids: "I invited you here as men to talk over what's happening and find out where we're right or where we're wrong. But if I'm talking to a bunch of shit-assed kids . . ."

I heard mumblings from somewhere. "Piri's cursing."

Right in the middle of what I was saying, I stopped and told them, "You're damned right, because I'm burnt. I invited cats over here that I believed to have a whole lotta heart. But to have heart is not enough. You've got to have a mind. So to those of you who just have heart and no goddam mind, get your asses out of here."

"We'll stay," Lil Man cried out nice and clear. And one of the Monitors echoed, "Same." Never much of a talker, Juju added, "Us, too, paisan," and a black said, "Yeah, baby." And so on and so on. Only one cat walked out, but he said he'd be back. Everybody looked at him wondering if he were going to get some bomb or something. He smiled kind of shyly and embarrassed and made his excuses for having to leave. "I got my girl knocked up and it's visiting hours now, so I'll just shoot over there and I'll shoot right back."

"That's what you get for shooting so straight, ya shudda used blanks," Lil Man cracked him.

I closed the door behind him. Some were laughing and telling some strong jokes, while others were still stone-faced, looking at other faces remembering broken jaws, bad insults, and other cats who were of their own who had kicked off dead in the great bops of kid warfare.

I spent some time walking and talking from group to group, guy to guy, so that all would know that I was, with all my heart, without nationality, color, or creed. Like I was a human being because wasn't that the way that Christ ran it down to us? Like we're all created in each other's image and all men are brothers.

A loud bang, bang, bang at the door. Everybody stiffened and became alert with a self-defensive movement which made their bodies jerk straight and stiff. I cut over to the door to open it and it looked like every cop in New York was out there. Squad cars with little red Christmas bulbs going around and around. People up on the sidewalk, some ministers, some Youth Board workers, some anxious parents.

One police officer attempted to come in. I closed the door and said to the cats inside, "Stay cool. They aren't coming in here and besides"—I smiled—"none of you are carrying any pieces, are you? But don't worry. They aren't coming in here."

They couldn't come in here, I thought to myself. *The club would look like an armory if the kids were ever frisked.* A thought flashed in my mind of this one cat who walked in with a certain limp because he had a sawed-off shotgun tucked inside his trousers. I opened the door and walked out into a whole lot of flack. I told the policemen from the Twenty-third Precinct that we were taking care of business to avert a gang war from breaking out.

One cop said, "Look, Piri, I mean, you know this is our job." I tried making my face as cara palo as I could and said, "I'm willing to put me down on the line. Let me take care of business."

For about ten minutes all this yak went on with mothers, police officers, neighbors, fathers, and, finally, they called it off, and then everybody left. But with all the raw discussion on the street, I couldn't help hearing with sharp street ears that inside the club, everything was like "kid quiet." I

imagined what were some of the things the kids were thinking, like, "Damn, if my old man finds out, he's gonna kick
the shit out of me." Or maybe, "Aye Bendito, whew! You
know, I hope Mom doesn't find out about this shit." Finally,
the policemen said that if I needed them I should call. I
thanked them, knowing that the plainclothesmen in plain
old cars were going to be going around and around this block
like in a funeral procession. I hugged all the mothers and told
them not to worry. Still standing at both corners were the
older Italian killer-dillers, who had no wish to get too close
to the cops as well as having no wish to get too far away
from the young Bambinos.

I opened the club door with my key and walked back inside and made small talk. Then the door opened and in
walked John Clause. I was sitting on one of the chairs, and
I nodded hello.

"Hi, buddy," he puffed out.

He made a motion for me to come to the back office. I
followed him in. He quickly asked for a rundown on the
situation. I ran it down to him as fast as I could in the space
of a minute or so, and then we walked back out. I introduced John to the group.

Meanwhile, I was making a mental picture of Juju's black
Doberman pinscher, who was the coolest piece of living proto-
plasm in the room. He was yawning. I looked at John and
said, "Okay, John, it's all yours."

John said, "You're doing fine, you take care of the meeting,
Piri."

I shrugged my shoulders and jumped into peacemaking.

The presidents spoke their piece, their advisors whispering in their ears. Some started talking in their own language,
which I corrected not because of lack of respect for their

ethnic background, but rather for the sake of understanding and communication. Some of the talk was rough and rough it had to be . . . talk about past injuries, not trusting, "japping" (pulling a sneak, a back job, stabbing in the back).

I found myself talking about what the essence of humanity is, of dignity in street talk, of respect, of how where there wasn't a bridge from one block to another, that it was up to us to build that bridge together. Finally, it was all over and I don't remember how long it took. But there wasn't going to be any gang bop.

John and I were left alone in the club. "It went off pretty good, buddy, eh?" he said. And I smiled, "Why not? With the Lord Jesus Christ on our side, how can we lose?" And my eyes looked dead into his for a long long time.

Somewhere in the back of my mind, I was thinking of that big church and the rest of churches all over where certain Christians had bought up all the shares on so-called Salvation. I watched John drive off to his home in the suburbs. I walked around my Barrio. I saw there the Puerto Rican kids, the black kids, the Italian kids, the Irish kids, the you-name-them kids. Name their ethnic backgrounds.

I checked into the playground on Park Avenue and 208th Street and sat on a bench and watched mothers of all colors giving their kids some kind of air and some kind of exercise to drive out of their lungs the stench of garbage, futility, and despair. I kept thinking, *God, Jesus Christ, if you're for real, come on down and we'll walk nitty-gritty out of their lungs, the stench of garbage, futility, and despair.*

I was beginning to fully distrust John Clause. I couldn't figure out exactly why. But I didn't think I could ever be easy with him again.

29

El block party

Time went swinging by. John Clause was providing openings for some of the more articulate kids, like getting them
jobs in a bank.

The chevere thing we agreed on was education. Like without it our kids were like lambs in an arrogant racist structure of wolves.

I tried ignoring the little things that annoyed me about
John. But what I couldn't ignore was his self-imposed image
of great spiritual elder, of the great white father.

I walked down to Madison Avenue heading toward 104th
Street. I checked my watch and como, it was like 8:30 P.M.
I looked up at the warm, almost friendly Friday night and
smiled inside of a long-ago memory when I was a school kid
and dug the scene on a Friday night, cause on Saturday
there was no school.

I shook my head and broke out in my own thing smile,
cause I had learned better. School and learning was not just
in a building. It was also in the everyday stick of living.

"Hey, Piri, whatcha smiling about?"

I dug Lil Man, Chiquito, and their girl friends, Anna
and Rosie.

I laughed. "Aw, I was just thinking on something funny."

"Hey, cool it, Piri. I had a tio who blew his mind like that. Use to go around talking to himself."

"Damn, man." I threw a light left hook, then followed it with a light right. Lil Man ducked, bobbed, weaved, and came back with his own brand of boxing skill. He threw his fists but with a young brother's restraint.

"Hey, Piri," he said, "you gonna make it to the block party tonight?"

"I'm on my way there now. I'll probably see you guys there."

I watched them walk away and Lil Man broke the romantic dignity of walking around La Plaza with their novias to jump into a boxing match with his buddy Peter.

I walked toward a whole lot of music going on. The block was shut off to traffic. Even from two blocks away, I could hear and see the different sounds of people getting together.

I dug, as I got closer, the smell of all kinds of goodo comida, like the mommies of the block had gotten together and there was mucho arroz con gandules and lechon asado (roast pig), mucho cuchifritos, mucho warmth, mucho togetherness, and mucho most chevere Puerto Ricans.

I walked into the block in time to see some young bloods taking care of business with steel drums and the sounds jumped West Indian as played by Puerto Ricans. *Adelante, together now*, I thought.

The smell of the food was good. Some was free, some was being sold. I dug into my pocket and bought me un bacalaito (salted dry codfish mixed into a flour paste and fried). I bit into it and like always, our bacalaitos tasted outta sight.

Another group took over and the great roar of applause as they were introduced gave proof that they came out of our Barrio and were like real pros, known all over with mucho sides to their credit and ours. They went into a let it all hang out Afro-Latin buga-lo and the street and sidewalks became alive with dancing.

Somebody tapped me on the shoulder. It was Chiquito. He presented his girl Rosie to me. Rosie and I danced together. Then we walked back to Chiquito, who was doing all kinds of bowing acts. I acknowledged his overtures of praise and nodded my head towards Lil Man, asking his permission to dance with his girl, Anna. The music was something cool and romantic.

Lil Man looked up tight. He came up close and whispered, "Bro?"

"Yeah, que pasa?"

"This one's a favorite with me and Anna. Uh . . . like this song brought us together and I hope you don't mind if . . ."

"Wow, Lil Man, nay, nunca. Go take care of your beautiful together thing."

"You can have the next."

And Lil Man and his Anna were gone.

One of the block mommies pushed an overloaded paper plate of arroz con gandules and pernil in my hands.

"Eat, Piri. It's cooked with love."

"Chevere, Dona Luisa. Gracias."

I picked out an unused stoop and copped a squat. I balanced my alma comida on my left knee while the fingers of my right hand kinda tender-like touched the side of my face where Dona Luisa had kissed me and my mind went back into my mommie's own time and in the middle of our Puerto Rican block party. Painful memories of the past entwined with gentle ones dug their ways into the present, and soon I was lost in these memories.

My God, dammit to hell, Mommi. What happened to us, Mommi? I can almost remember your feeding me leche from your breasts. I can remember your love. I can remember muy malo and muy good and your warm smile and overwhelming words of, "Aye, negrito, when you were born, the mold was broken." I can remember my looking at you in question-like awe and wondering why something had to be broken because I had been born. How could I as a child cause anything to be broken? But somehow your affection lulled me to understand that I was something special to you. *Diggit, Moms, you sure are together. How old was I? . . .* And my mind shut out all the sounds of the block party . . .

Going on some kind of sixteen, my mind answered back. *And what went down? Something like the hard-ass truth of reality.* My mind shoved its answer into my guts and other wondrous words from my majestic madre made remembrance pour into my mind.

"Ay, hijo, por favor, remember always what you build with one hand, do not destroy with the other."

"Mommi, why do we gotta live like this?" How old was I? Thirteen?

"Study, Son, and you will help us not to live like this."

"Gee, Moms, why can't Poppi get us out of this? Golly, Mommi, porque?"

"You listen, son." I could almost hear the anger in her voice. *"He does the best and you don't know how bad these mundo ees here in Nueva York."*

My mind remembered keeping quiet out of respecto while wondering if she thought I was blind to the hot and cold running cockroaches and king-size rats.

"Your father is a good man." I smiled in present time and thought to myself, *Wow, kids sometime get the mucho idea*

their poppies and mommies are gods and goddesses and like
the truth where it's really at is that they are pure and simple,
nada mas, poppies and mommies doing their best for their
kids.

Suddenly the sound of a voice jarred me. I came up out
of yesterday in time to see one of the youth workers walking
up to me.

"Hey, Pappo, you're killing what was killing you?"

"Yeah, Moncho, like this is some good food." I offered my
plate to Moncho.

"Later, Piri. I'm stuffed to the last gut."

I nodded and kept on chewing and swallowing. I dug
Moncho. Came up from our neighborhood, went to college,
and was working with our kids as a youth worker. I couldn't
say the same for all the youth workers, or some of their
bosses. Like many of them came into our Barrio with lots of
theory and no experience and in two weeks somehow became not only experts on the art of street Barrio living, but
also had suffered more than the people themselves. *God bless*
them, I thought. *I wish there was some way I could help*
them.

"Hear what's happened?" Moncho had waited until I had
finished gritting and wiping my mouth. He even waited till
I downed half his beer.

"What's happening, Moncho?"

"I just got the news, Piri, straight from my office. Straight
from the P.D. and . . ."

"What's happened, Moncho?" I finished off his beer.

"You know an Italian kid called Marco, right? And you
know that he's been some kind of holy terror on Puerto
Rican kids, beating them just on general principles?"

"Oye, Moncho, I know all about Marco. I know all about

his being down on Puerto Ricans. I know he figures he's fighting for his territory. I know he got all kinds of cute names for anybody that ain't Italian. Like that's what he's been taught. If you're gonna tell me he ain't loved by a lotta Puerto Rican kids, forget it. Let me put you wise. There's a whole lot of his own young paisans that don't dig him either. That kid's rough and makes his own rules. I've had a chance to er . . . uh . . . feel a little of his put-downs and . . ." All of a sudden something dawned on me. "Hey, Moncho, whatta you mean, *he's been* some kind of holy terror?" I asked.

"He's dead."

"When?"

"Nobody knows yet. They haven't performed an autopsy on him yet, but a rough guess, about three days."

"How did he get wasted?"

"Stabbed."

Shanked, I thought.

"They counted about a hundred and twenty stab wounds on him. Whoever done it had to be a psycho."

"Where did it happen, Moncho?"

"It could have happened anywhere along the East River, Piri. That's where he was found. I don't know, it could have been near 116th Street, near 120th . . . But they found him somewhere near 103d or 101st Street, and that's what the big shit is all about."

"Si, Moncho. You don't have to tell me. That's where mucho Puerto Ricans and blacks live and I can make mental pictures of what's happening. Marco is found in the East River on Puerto Rican and black turf. Conclusions of Italian kids is that Marco got done up by Puerto Ricans or blacks or both. Oh shit, and none of them will probably even think about the river current. He could've been wasted in his own block."

"Piri, you know as well as I that most kids think of current in terms of school current events, not this kind of current. Where Marco was found, that's where they feel they gotta pick up."

I almost smiled at Moncho's slip of grammar. Like he went all the way to college and his "GOTTA" was still street talk.

"You're right about that, Moncho. If it was a Puerto Rican or a black kid, the same would probably be thought."

"That's not all." Moncho reached for his beer and finding I'd left him none, he just made a face of "like be my guest."

I ignored him and asked, "What else, Moncho?"

"They got some crap out about ten for one, blacks or Puerto Ricans for Marco."

"Without proof?" I softly asked.

"What do you think?"

"Without proof," I answered in agreement. "Naturally, some shit-ass code, man. The enemy is always wrong and your side is always right. Man, what a fuckin way to do things, to jump shit-ass stink without no proof."

I looked up and dug the block party going on full blast. Everybody was having a ball and even the few angry arguments had a brotherly love sound about them.

"Let me move around some, Piri." Moncho got up. "I'll see you later."

"I'll be here for a while. Check me out. Uh . . . thanks for the beer."

"De nada, hustler." He grinned.

My head bowed in appreciation. I watched him walk away and I thought about a whole lot of blood being spilled.

Lil Man came up with his girl friend, Anna.

"Your dance, Big Bro."

I took Anna by the hand and led her into the street gutter dance floor and took care of business to some fast fire music with much conga sounds. After it was over, I took her back to Lil Man and with much exaggerated courtesy, bowed and said, "Zank you verre much for the privilege and honor of being allowed to wail with your muy chevere chamaquita."

"De nada." Lil Man bowed back, took his old lady's hand and split back to the dance floor of 104th Street.

I dug Moncho coming towards me with two cans of beer in his hand and he was like smiling. He handed me one.

"What's up, Moncho?"

"It looks like everything is going to be cool. I checked in again and la policia busted somebody for Marco's killing."

"Puerto Ricans or blacks?"

"Neither. Marco was involved with some money and other things. He got wasted in a personal involvement . . . and like the word's gotten out so it looks like everything's going to be cool."

Lil Man and six or seven kids were coming up fast towards Moncho and me.

"Ya hear Marco is dead and that the word's out the shit's gonna be on. Like we're suppose to have offed the cat and like that ain't so. Man, shit, we gonna get ourselves together. Marco's boys are talking some shit about ten for one. Later for that."

"Ain't nada happening, Lil Man. Moncho just found out that the police busted the one who offed Marco. A personal happening between them."

"Is that straight business?" Chiquito's eyes were dead small.

"Straight business," Moncho said. "I swear. I just got the word."

"That's cool," said Lil Man, "but just in case, we're putting the word out to all our people to be on their toes. Better be ready than be a dead Freddy. Fair enough?"

"Fair enough." I smiled seriously.

"Hey," I said softly, "why don't you all go get some of that good dancing on."

"Yeah, good idea. But we still gonna stay ready. Like we didn't do it and we ain't paying for it. Hell, man, we've paid for enough. Shit, we ain't responsible for . . ."

"Amen, Lil Man. Amen," I whispered.

They all walked off and there was a mucho murmuring of strategy talk going off with them.

"I'm glad that's cooled," Moncho said afterward. "But if these kids get jumped on after their being innocent, like I'm gonna be on their side."

"Amen, Moncho, Amen, like me too."

We both sat there quiet, digging somebody singing a Bobby Capo hit, and I did my best to enjoy the scene.

"Hey, Moncho," I asked, half mildly. "Who teaches anybody this kind of hate, man?"

"No se, Brother. I really don't know. Unless it's them that ain't got no love."

I nodded my head and smiled at my college hermano's AIN'T and my ears picked up on some of the words of Bobby Capo's song. It was saying something about love.

Moncho pulled himself up off the stoop . . . slapped good skin with me. As he walked away, I returned his "hasta luego" with a wave of my hand, made my behind mucho comfortable on that hard stoop and once again let my mind blend backwards into tiempo . . . I was starting to think of Moms again.

"Would you like something else, hijo?" someone asked.

I looked up. It was Dona Luisa.

"No, gracias." I made a punto smile back.

"You look so see-ri-ous, negrito. What's the trouble?"

I made my smile bigger. "No trouble, just thinking, Dona Luisa, just thinking."

"No think too mucho, hijo. Sometime it's no good for your head."

She patted me on the back and then departed to take care of anybody who was hon-gree. I just smiled back. I picked at my food and went back to thinking about Mommie and total recall made mucho thunder in my mind.

How did you die, Mommie? Why did you have to die this way? Rotten . . . like real rotten. You should have had the beauty of dying in an essence of dignity. Shit! It killed you, Mommie, these warped-up fucked-up garbage lepered streets made up of ghetto pain. Wow, Moms, I can hear your pala-bras, "Be a good human being, son."

Wow, hung up in all this ca-ca and meanness and my Moms still had the guts to take time out and be a most chevere Moms. I made a much honored salute to all the chevere moms of the world within the closeness of my corazón.

Gee, Mommie, they sent a telegram to tell us you had died. Didn't they know I knew already? This fucking ghetto hell had killed you long before. You don't know how I strug-gled to read your request of Psalm 102, Psalm 105, and the goodo Psalm 23d in our Puerto Rican language.

Gee, Mommie . . . like your first words when I went to see you in the hospital were, "I pray to God. He sent you to me before I die."

Gee, Mom, when I went back to the hospital to pick up your belongings . . . I walked out of that hospital, Moms, with your worn-out clothes wrapped in a bag . . . and your biblia, Moms, worn, read, and reread and I held the bundle, Mom, I held them mucho close and couldn't help thinking— Mommie, Is this all that's left of you? I remember how close I held your clothes and Bible among staring-eyed people who were wondering why my tears were making such big waves down my cheeks. With a bundle under one arm and a worn beat-up Bible in my hand, gee, Mommie, it was such a bad blippy lonely subway ride back to El Barrio. I dug the stops go by. "Gee, Mommie, don't die."

"I don't die, hijito." Diggit my Mom's face had a most pretty smile. "I go to sleep with God. I go to sleep." . . . The train blasted a roar into a stop called mi Barrio and I got off thinking, JEE-SUSS, what's a kid got to hang on to?

30

Where you at, John?

A Christian group in New Jersey had invited some of the kids to visit it. The getting together was to be held in their hall and all the Christian people there had cooked food so that the kids could have a good time.

I looked at John Clause and asked, "How many kids can go?"

"Well, as many as the two Volkswagen buses can hold, you know, twelve kids . . . thirteen . . . fifteen."

"Great, I'll make up the list."

"I want you to invite Puerto Rican kids from the Untouchables and the Italian kids from the Red Wings."

My mind began to jump three thousand beats at one time because I knew he was asking me to mix kerosene with gasoline to make an explosion.

"John," I said, trying my best to explain the situation to him. "Not only is there animosity between the kids, but the Italians are Catholic and the Puerto Ricans are Catholic and Protestant, and they don't mind going to a Protestant church. But the Italian kids will . . ."

"But it's not church services. It's a party . . . games, food," John insisted.

"It ain't going to work, John. We're going to have problems."

I looked at his face. He looked right back and said, "I don't know what you're worried about. Everything's going to be all right."

"Okay, if you say so, John," but he knew I didn't believe it.

John smiled. "The Lord's work has to be done. It's not a matter of Catholic or Protestants. It's a matter of kids learning to get along together."

"Okay, chevere." I opened my eyes after having closed them for a long time, holding the bridge of my nose with my left hand between my thumb and forefinger. His words intruded into my mind.

"Will you do it, buddy?" he asked.

I nodded "aha," but I told him he was wrong.

"Let me be the judge of that," he responded.

It was cold as I walked out on that street. We met all the kids as they piled into the buses. Pat, a volunteer worker, took all the Puerto Rican kids, the Untouchables, and I took all the Italian kids, the Red Wings.

We drove to New Jersey and when we got there caramba, it was something beautiful to see. Beautiful people, especially the young Christian people, were there with their arms open. They had all kinds of goodies and, by God, I kept looking to see a reaction or something but their arms were really open. They started to get into a circle to play games with a whole lot of good feeling. The Red Wings went over to one side and the Untouchables went over to the other side and I could feel the tension. Somebody was saying, "We are gathered here in a sense of brotherly love and we thank the Lord that we are able to share. Welcome to all you young people. Make yourselves feel at home."

Then they said a prayer and it wasn't a Catholic prayer

in Latin or an Ave Maria as said in the Catholic Church. One young Italian reacted and said, "I'm no Protestant. I'm a Catholic."

Lil Man replied, "I'm a Catholic also, but my old lady said to respect another religion."

Then someone shouted, "Shut you mouth, bodega."

From there, it went on to outcries of, "Guinea," and, "Spic," and "Hi-fidelity m.f.s." It almost came to blows but never got there. I opened my mouth and yelled, "COOL IT!!!"

There wasn't time to explain to these good people, who stood by in a state of horrified shock. I just told them, Thank you and good night.

"Everybody outside," I was shouting. "Let's get outside, I want to run something down to you all."

The Red Wings and the Untouchables walked out and it was snowing something fierce. They were looking at each other's throats.

"I don't care whose bus you get into," I said, "but if you don't get into some bus I'm gonna start tearing up some ass."

I wondered if I could ever bring myself to really hurt one of them. Pat was by my side. I looked at his face.

"We'll meet back at the club," I said.

The Red Wings went into my bus and the Puerto Rican Untouchables went into Pat's bus. Lil Man jumped out of the bus and ran over to me. His teeth were chattering because it was so cold.

"Piri, you going to be all right with them?"

"Porque?"

"You know, like . . ."

"Ah, get back into that bus like I told you."

I got behind the wheel and took off, keeping my eyes on the road. It was really snowing. Rolling along, we couldn't see and behind me all kinds of threats of what they were going to do to the *bodegas* and how no Puerto Rican was worth nada and that they were going to try to take over their territory and their turf . . . and on and on . . .

I kept my eyes on the road, thinking that in the other bus similar threats were being made. It soon got pretty bad, because they were working themselves into a full rage. So I decided I was going to scare them out of their anger. When we got to a place that I felt was cool enough, I made the Volkswagen bus skid, ride, and slide, like we were going to be out of control. I heard some kinda gasp. "Hey, Piri, is anything wrong?"

I said, "Yeah, it's kinda dangerous driving," and made a skid again and stopped.

"Get out, clean the windshield. You, get into the back and brush off the snow. You, check the tires. You, rock the VW a little bit to see its sense of balance."

One voice came out from a cat. He was Irish and I thought all along he was Italian. He leaned over and whispered into my ear, "Is there anything I can do, because I know damn well that what you did here was just to cool it."

My car scare worked. And the rest of the ride back to El Barrio was quiet and like mucho friendly and warm.

As we pulled up in front of the club I felt a hand touch me. It was the Irish kid and he squeezed real hard on my shoulder and without taking my eyes off that snow-covered street, I slapped his hand. Everybody soon filed out and then went their different ways. I listened to the different conversations. "Like, man, we had a narrow escape" . . . "Man, like Petey can really handle the wheel" . . . "Wow, man, that cat is something else." I thought to myself, you cats are a handful too.

A voice roared out from a block away. "Hey, Petey, thanks a lot. When we going for another ride?" I took a deep breath and let it out just as fast. "I'll let you know, paisan." I heard laughter. "Okay, paisan." I heard a few other conversations from ones that had been talking about threats and murmuring about violence. Then I was all alone.

The snow reminded me that I was pretty cold, so I opened up the door to the club and went in. By this time, it was very late. I looked around to check the schedule for the next day.

Then there was a big rapping at the door. It was Pat and the Puerto Rican Untouchables, Lil Man, Batman, and Chiquito. They were *mucho* excited and Pat said in a whisper, "They thought they were going to kill you, Petey, and if they didn't find you here, they had promised an oath they were going to play 'knock-knock.'"

"Knock-knock" means that if you can't find the one responsible when you knock on his door, whoever opens it gets blown away.

I started to laugh. "Hey, que pasa con ustedes? They behaved themselves pretty good."

"You're not telling the truth, Piri," said Lil Man.

What could I say? "Why don't we meet mañana?"

"Piri, they didn't hurt you?"

"Will you guys get one thing straight? This whole thing is about to bring a unity, an understanding."

"But caramba, Piri," said Chiquito, "like you know we love you and we think a whole lot of you."

"Como who?"

He laughed.

"That's for me to know and for you to find out." I slapped

him on the side of his cabeza. "Hey, cut on home. Caramba, don't you think that I get tired?"

They walked out and Lil Man said, "If they ever try to hurt you, we'll call a shit on, sight unseen."

When I was alone, I hit the walls with rights and lefts as hard as I could, like letting it all out. I took my hands and nursed them, trying to keep from blowing my cool.

I flopped heavy-like into my desk chair and kinda lazily shuffled the stack of papers around in front of me.

I picked up a folder marked REPORTS and soon my eyes were reading words of past happenings.

Reports, I thought to myself. *Here I am trying to take care of mucho chevere street business and then I gotta come back and fill out reports.*

Man, the kids' thoughts and feelings can't be summed up in two paragraphs. But John had given the word: file a daily report.

I wonder who he's really checking up on. Me or the kids?

I smiled to myself as I started to read some of the notes. Like the big stink John made because a group of the kids decided to lay some of their art work on the club's front door. (I'd seen worse in museums.) Some choice street words and names proudly written in indelible ink proclaiming to all who passed the chevere immortality of the signer.

REPORT—Piri Thomas   May 8th
Also, I believe some of the young Wings kind of messed up the front door. They took away the brass numbers and painted their names all over the door. We will check into it to see who's doing it and put a stop to this.

We really nipped it in the bud, I half-jokingly thought,
because two days later part of my May 9 report read:

The front door is really now getting messed up. Names
have really been put over it with this indelible pencil.
I believe it is because we have turned to this new policy
now where no club has a definite set date for meeting.
Giving the Italian boys Friday, Saturday, and also Mondays,
since this has been cut out now, I think they resent it a
bit. We will try to get to the bottom of this and get the
word around that this stuff will have to be taken care of,
that the door must be cleaned and so forth . . .

 END OF REPORT.

I remember scrubbing some words off the door that read:
"Dear Lord, we were only trying to communicate when
we say mother-fucker . . . Amen."

My thoughts jumped to the more serious problems, like
the kids getting busted and the hours I'd spent in juvenile
and criminal courts representing them.

"Are you the attorney," the judge would ask, and I'd answer that I wasn't. "I'm Piri Thomas," I'd say. "I work with
the Club."

And the judge would reply, "Oh, you're that Piri Thomas,"
and then the most beautiful words in the English language
would come down from that mighty chair.

"In that case, the Court hereby places the defendant under
the supervision of Mr. Thomas, under his own recognizance."

How about that? The Court letting me, still on parole,
make sure these kids would get more than half a chance.
Wish there were more judges like this most chevere one.

Si, most chevere, because in between going to court and

meeting with probation officers, employment officers, school principals, guidance counselors, my daily reports were slowly falling behind.

Have been working with the boys now and they seem to be in accord with the idea of getting together all their pieces and guns and turning them over to the club. Today I have two or three zip guns, but the heavy stuff is what they're going to get me. They claim to have a sub Thompson machine gun and a Military 303. I've told them I'd rather see action than just to talk about turning them in. They seem to be sincere. We'll wait and see.

We waited, and little by little more pieces started coming into my possession. I was respected and trusted by these kids and giving up their weapons, leaving themselves unarmed, was something they did because they knew I was for real. It took a lot of heart, but they had it.

Man, the club was functioning. The kids were beginning to realize that bopping was played out, like a blank, and they started getting themselves together. Like some were even beginning to dig the religion bit.

It wasn't easy getting these kids to listen to talk about God and Christ, but somehow we managed.

Like the time at summer camp when the kids were about to go to bed and Lil Man piped out of semi-darkness and said:

"Hey, Piri, how about, you know, saying prayers for all of us before going to bed."

Lil Man, I thought, *a stone killer-diller asking me to say a prayer for all of us.*

There was a very quiet atmosphere in that little log cabin

as sixteen boys kept quiet as I brought us all before the Lord, and at the end of the prayer, there was a very reverent Amen in unison.

Lil Man's asking me to pray brought out some long-ago memories. Like when I was a kid. Mommie use to sit us around and she'd read the Bible and afterwards we'd make a circle of prayer with everybody on his knees. Each of us, James, Frankie, Miriam, and myself, would then pray in turn. I usually asked to be last. I remember one time waiting for my turn to pray.

I watched out of one open eye some roaches making their way up the side of the wall while at the same time I tried to analyze Mommie's words of, "If you are good, you'll go to heaven with God and if you're bad, you'll go to hell."

My mind was digging the idea of going to heaven, but not buying the one of going to hell, cause damn-slam, weren't we there now?

Getting back to now time, I realized success with bringing religion to the club was our real accomplishment.

Yeah, it takes corazón to stop a bop, and sure it takes mucho courage to walk through alien turf not knowing if that cat on the roof has a piece pointed at your heart. But it takes a man, a real macho of sixteen or seventeen to say he's beginning to dig the Lord. With all the hell these kids have been through and are going through, they come to know that there's a light in all this ghetto darkness and it's that bright ray of Christ coming through loud and clear and telling each one of them young bloods individually that he's on their side and no mother could ever stop him once he's placed his life in His hands.

I lit a forbidden cigarette and as I tossed the match into the ashtray, my eyes caught some more reports.

REPORT—Piri Thomas   May 5th
9:00 went to Children's Court on 23 Street. The case
of little Louie Cruz. He has been on probation now because of taking articles from the club. He has been behaving himself, been going to school, staying out of trouble.
It's still under our supervision as long as he behaves.

                          END OF REPORT

REPORT—Piri Thomas   June 22nd
On Romero killing, the word is around that after ten days
if the guilty one or ones are not found somebody is going
to pay. Community is alarmed and tension is pretty high.

Appeared in court for case of Jerry Salgado. Traded bike
for gun, gun went off, wounded friend in leg. Tried
crude surgery with razor. Not a bad kid thru and thru. Bail
reduced from $2,000 to $1,000.

REPORT—Piri Thomas   June 28th
Court case: Charlie Sanchez. Adolescents Court. Spoke to
girl's mother, Edwina. Girl's name is Gloria. She states
she was baby sitting. She had known Charlie about two
weeks, not too well. He twisted her arm, forced her to
climb to attic roof where he asked her to have sex relations with him. She refused. He punched her on the
breast and manhandled her and forced her. She broke
away and ran and got Police Officer Reyes from 25th
Precinct Detective Squad. Charlie admitted the charges
against him. $2,500 bail, lodged in Brooklyn House of
Detention. Girl is 15. Her mother is quite angry at abuse
against her daughter.

REPORT—Piri Thomas   July 8th

Charlie Sanchez, on a charge of attempted rape, reduced
to a misdemeanor rape and part of Youthful Division. He
has been referred to Probation Officer Ryan to whom I
have spoken and is having a pre trial investigation. I told
Mr. Ryan that we have been working with the family and
that we have known them for a period of two years and he
asked me how I came to know them, and I told him that
we knew a first son by the name of Pablo, who was doing
wonderful until he was shot this month through mistaken
identity. We asked Mr. Ryan if he had any further questions to contact me at the club.

I reached into a drawer looking for some paper on which
to write out my report and pulled out a magazine. I started
to put it aside and my eyes dug the heading on it: "YOUNG
HOODLUMS FOR GOD." *Hey,* I thought, *this got to do with that
big bop that almost broke out that May day, with all kinds
of hell trying to break loose here in the club.* I started to
sort of glance through it—my eyebrows shot up in some kind
of amazement. I went back to the heading. "YOUNG HOODLUMS
FOR GOD."

One evening last May, hundreds of teen gangsters
blocked off Second Avenue in East Harlem, N.Y.C. Cursing and wild talk filled the air as members of the Red
Wings gang demanded the Untouchables' blood.

Representatives from the Red Wings, Untouchables,
Monitors, and Turbans swarmed the East Harlem Club
house. These were the top brass: presidents, vice-presidents,
war counselors, and a few prime ministers. Many carried
concealed zip guns, knives, or brass knuckles.

A major gang war was about to erupt, but the leaders had agreed to give ex-gangster John Clause, director of the club, one chance to arbitrate. Clause had been intercepted by a phone on his way to conduct a meeting. Now he was weaving in and out of expressway traffic trying to cover the 20 miles back to Manhattan before the first knife was pulled.

Inside the club, assistant Piri Thomas, a Puerto Rican parolee, converted in a Spanish Harlem mission, was dramatically challenging the stormy mob "to can the jive and hold on until John gets here." Just as one of the gang presidents was about to jump one member of the rival gang, Clause's car screeched to a stop outside.

While cops swarmed all around, Clause reasoned with the gang leaders.

"The hand of the LORD was upon us and we were able to work out a truce," says Clause. "Many lives were spared the bloodiness of a major gang war. We were able to win confidence that will in turn win a hearing for the gospel."

I couldn't believe my eyes as I sat there, shaking my head and staring at the printed words in disbelief. There was a knock at the front door. It was Lil Man. My face must of said up a storm, cause Lil Man was quick to check my mood out.

"Que pasa, Piri?"

"Little Brother, do you remember that trouble we almost had that May day?"

"Sure do, panin. It was like World War Three was gonna break loose."

I handed him the magazine. "Is this the way it all went down?" I asked.

"Holy shit," Lil Man exclaimed after reading the article. "Where's this cat at? According to this, he's like some kind of super hero."

I walked back and sat at the edge of the desk.

"Wow!!" Lil Man's voice showed surprise. "He came into the club and didn't say hardly a word. Like you took care of business with all the fellers and like according to this, Piri, only his getting to the club on time stopped that bad-ass bop from breaking loose. Tell you the truth, Piri, most of the cats don't dig him—or trust him. I've even heard some of the older Italian cats saying he ain't nothing but a con man, and like me being Puerto Rican, I ain't got too much in common with Guineas, but like they're right. John ain't for real." Lil Man shook his head from side to side in obvious disgust.

We both were quiet for a while. Then Lil Man broke out with, "Damn, wonder where John's really at?"

Yeah, I thought, *where you really at, John?*

31

Knock-knock

"Hey, Piri, want to come into the office for a sec?" I looked up from the pool table where Lil Man and I had been playing a mucho ferocious but fun game. I nodded to John sitting in his office.

Once I was in the office, he invited me to sit down. He gave his very best Christian smile.

"What's shakin?" I asked.

Funny, how the wall between me and him was growing higher and higher. Like I dug working with the kids and was mucho willing to bend backwards and like not let personalities get in the way.

"Listen, buddy." He looked at me thoughtfully, while I winced un poco inside at his ability to make the word *buddy* sound like brotherhood. "There's a film crew that wants to do a movie on the work the club is doing and I feel it will further the Lord's work."

"They ain't Communists, are they?" I gently broke in.

"Uh . . ." He looked askance at me.

"Well, like don't you remember the man that came by some time ago and wanted to do a film on the work being done on the streets. Remember, when he came out of your office he talked to me and said that you put thumbs down on a crew following me around and filming what was happening nitty-gritty."

"Yes, I remember." John was looking at me.

"Well, remember, he said your objections were that it would interfere with the work."

"And . . ."

"And like he told me he was from the United Protestant Council and after he left I put the question to you on how come no and you said the council had a lot of Commies on it." I smiled. "And like, John, I've always heard Communists were atheists and like whoever heard of a Christian Communist, although I've heard goodo Christo has been called one."

John's tone of voice told me he wasn't digging my humor. "Let me be the judge of who has anything to do with this club," he said tight-like.

His uptightness annoyed me, and I suddenly decided to let him have it.

"By the way." I leaned over and pulled open the bottom drawer of the desk and pulled out a copy of the Christian magazine. I dug the heading one more time: "YOUNG HOODLUMS FOR GOD." "Have you read this one?" I asked as I handed it to John.

He acted nonchalant-like.

"I have and what's wrong with it?"

"DID it really happen like it says here? I mean, your part in it?"

His face reddened before he answered. "For crying out loud, Piri," he said. "Don't you know that people misconstrue things once in a while. I said it one way, and they wrote it up another way."

I quickly let him know it wasn't the first time this kind

of thing had happened. "I've noticed it in other articles. I've gotten a lot of weapons outta the hands of kids, right?"

"That's right," John answered quickly.

"And in other articles I've read how *you* got them from the kids, like a long blade I turned in to you, and the next thing I know I read about you giving it to some bigwig politician for a souvenir and how you've collected so many weapons, you've got a young armory."

"My God, Piri! This is all for publicity! I say one thing and it's interpreted, and something else is written. You can't believe everything that's written."

"Not even what's in the Bible, John?" I was amazed that even with the tension of the conversation, we both were trying to make it friendly enough to be just short of war breaking out between us.

John threw up his hands to break the tension and laughed, "Come on, Piri! We're not going to let Satan tempt us in wrong thoughts. Hey, remember, we're a team. Give me the benefit of the doubt. I know what's shaking. Whatta you say, buddy?"

"John," I said, my smile mucho tight, "I don't feature it when you make it pretty clear in mucho ways that you don't consider me your equal."

"I don't understand . . ." John broke in.

"Time now, John. TIME . . . I'm talking about when we're alone we're partners working together, but when VIPs come down to the club, I'm introduced as one of the club's street workers. When time comes for some kind of interviews to be given out, all of a sudden I got some other work to take care of. Remember the time some out-of-town people came to the club and you said, 'Hey, Piri, want to get the front part of the club straightened out, it's a mess.' It was a put-down, John, and that's why I told you in front of them that it could keep till after the get-together. 'Heck, we can both clean up in no time later on.' You almost choked when I said that, John."

John said softly, "Lord's honor, it wasn't meant to sound like that." He dropped his eyes for a second to some papers on the desk, but I had already seen his anger in them. And I knew he was putting on some kind of pious act. It was like some kind of chess game between us.

"What's so tough about talking things over with me," I argued on. "I know my streets a million times better than you. You can make a decision without talking it over with me, and you could be putting my life up for grabs as well as a whole lot of other cats. There's a whole lot of times I don't dig your stick at all."

"Hey, come on, Piri. Just remember, we're a team. Give me the benefit of the doubt that I know what's shaking. You know I can't do without you. Let's forget this misunderstanding."

I tighten up inside at his use of "what's shakin," like somehow it sounded alien coming out of his boca. I just nodded and straddled a chair and rested my chin in the palm of my hand and thought, *Yeah, let it lay for now.* "What's shakin with this film crew?" I asked, making my voice sound interested and thinking that we both didn't dig each other any more—if at all ever.

John looked at me like he was trying to figure out what was going on in my head, but my cara palo expression didn't leave him much to go on, so he took a deep breath before speaking. "It's a film that can further our work—the Lord's work. Some of the crew will be coming here today. In fact," he added, looking at his watch, "in about a half an hour."

"Who do they wanna film, John?"

"Everything. The work here in the club. The kids. The winning a hearing for the Lord."

"Where do I come in?"

"You'll take them around. They won't interfere with your work. They'll just film and won't get in your way."

I nodded, wondering how they wouldn't get in my way.

"Are you willing?" John asked.

"Porque not?" I shrugged my shoulders. "If it helps the club help the kids, why not?"

I walked out into the bright street scene and killed time watching a couple of dogs trying to decide whether to make love or chew each other up.

"Hey, perros," I yelled to them. "Peace, uh?" They just looked at me for a second like I was some kind of estupido and went back to taking care of business, like one way or the other.

When I returned to the club, I walked into John's office and dug a couple of men sitting there.

"Come on in, Piri." John smiled. "I want you to meet Carl Stevens and Bill Waters."

I shook hands with them and returned their "glad to know you."

"John tells me you people wanna make a flick out of what's happening," I said.

Carefully eyeing them both as I spoke, I noticed that Bill Waters was very white-skinned with sandy-colored hair. He was no more than six one and about 190 pounds, without much fat. On the other hand, Carl was about five seven, ruddy-complexioned and slimmer, to the tune of about 140 pounds, with a crew cut of black hair that showed a little baldness coming through on top.

"That's right," Bill Waters said, suddenly interrupting my thoughts. "And we'd not only like to film what's happening in the club, but also out on the streets."

"And we'd sure appreciate your co-operation," Carl interjected.

"It's all right with me," I said, "but I think it's a good idea if the fellers got to know you some. Like you're strangers and pointing a camera at them is gonna make them self-conscious and up tight to say the least. And like being frank, there's been people coming in to film and like having left fast minus their cameras and etceteras."

"That's understandable," Carl said. "What we'd like to do is get to know the kids, their families, and for them to get to know us and what we're about."

"What are you about? I mean, what do you want to film? What do you want to show on the screen when it's finished?"

"Just what's happening. The truth as it's happening, Mr. Thomas."

"You can call me Piri." I nodded. "I'll be calling you by your first names."

"Okay, Piri, but to continue, we'd like to film things as they naturally happen."

"Kinda hard." I smiled. "All you got to do is point a camera and if our people don't begin to ham it up, they might get up tight."

As I talked I couldn't help remembering the scene of what had gone down between John and me. I couldn't help thinking that I might be used by these two film cats in more exploitation of our calles. I wondered how I would've felt if they had been Puerto Ricans. Jesus, I blinked my eyes hard to clear my thoughts and listened.

Give them the chance, my mind said. *Let's see where they're at.*

"I ain't gonna be a party to having anything acted out by our people. If you film, it's what's happening."

"That's what we want." Bill seemed sincere. "That and only that. Our film is a documentary and it has to be for real. We're willing to shoot thousands of feet of film and won't use anything that's not a natural happening. Even if it's only a hundred feet of film out of a thousand feet, we'll scrap the rest."

"And we ought to add this too," Carl cut in. "When the film is done, you're both welcome to see it and anything that's a put-down or not in its true light won't be used."

"What do you say, Piri?" John smiled.

"I'm game, John. Like I said, anything that will help the club to help the kids, I'm for it. How soon you starting to shoot?" I got up from my chair.

"We'll be able to start in a few days." Carl stood up and offered me his hand in a shake.

After they were gone, I left the office and walked away. Half smiling, I said to myself, "So now we're going to be in the movies!" I looked for Lil Man and Blue to help me spread the word that we were going to be gen-u-wine MOVING PICTURE STARS, but only if it was filmed for real, like where it was really at.

The film crew lived up to their promises. They got to know the kids and their families. There was a young black woman who was part of the crew, named Margo, who was so together she got renamed Sister by the kids.

I felt chevere that the film crew was for real, and when I heard that they were getting all kinds of invites to eat at the kids' homes, I knew the film was gonna be a together thing.

The young bloods got to be so tight with the crew, they didn't even notice the hand-held cameras any more. In fact, they broke the ice whenever the crew went into blocks where they weren't known and there were no big hassles except once. I heard about it from Carl on how Blue had got him out of a bad scene with some cats that had ideas about checking Carl into a hospital and his camera equipment into a pawnshop. I had smiled thinking on how baddo Blue could be and like he really had to dig anybody in order to go to bat for them, and especially for a gringo. There wasn't a drop of Uncle Tomming in Blue's blood.

But even though the film work was going well, other things troubled. I guess it showed, too.

"Got something on your mind, Piri?" Dee Bruce asked one afternoon as I walked into the club. I could tell she wasn't prying, that she was only concerned. I smiled to assure her that it was okay to ask.

"Er . . . I've noticed you're kind of quiet."

I calmly sat at my desk. "Yeah, you're right, Dee. Like there's a sorry-ass scene that's building up."

"Like what, Piri?" Dee's face had a serious look on it, that was always there whether she smiled or not.

"Like bopping may bust out."

"Porto Ricans and Italians?"

"Naw, Puerto Rican kids against each other. AW HELL!!!" I jumped up from my desk chair. "Dammit! There ain't enough ca-ca happening to them, they gotta get into wasting sessions with each other."

"I don't quite follow on what's causing . . ." Dee broke in. I shook my head and lowered my voice. "There's some trouble that's jumped up between two of the fellers that belong to the club. Each belongs to a different clique. Lil Man belongs to the Untouchables. Chinko belongs to the Turbans. They fell out with each other and the word came down that the shit's on between the two gangs and como, like I'm doing my bestest to get Chinko and Lil Man to cool the stink between them. I've asked them to come to the club so we could talk it over."

I dug my watch and it was about ten minutes past the time I had set up. I looked over at Lil Man, who was at the pool table, sinking his usual impossible shots. His face didn't reflect concern about the up tight bad-ass vibrations shakin between him and Chinko. Like as if the only things he was thinking about was his impossible shots. I smiled and thought, *Like he's playing it cara palo but he's thinking about all the baddo side of bopping. I'd bet my last cuchifrito that's where he's at.*

The door opened and Chinko walked in. He was smiling and wore his red beret almost down to his right eye. Lil Man looked up from his pool table for no more than a split second and then went back to piling points. Chinko just stood and stared at him and his smile had mucho nth degrees of ugliness about it.

I motioned to Chinko to go into the room. Dee clasped her hands together in a "good luck" gesture. I grinned a big yeah-eeah.

Lil Man was chalking his cue tip and with mucho coolness didn't acknowledge Chinko's existence. Chinko kept staring at him and his smile didn't change for the better.

The phone on my desk started ringing and like always, it sounded important. I looked at Chinko and Lil Man and said, "I'll be right back, Hermanitos. Be suave y con calma, okay?"

Their heads nodded okay in my direction. Chinko didn't take his eyes off Lil Man, who hadn't taken his eyes off his shot. I walked back into the office and pulled the door behind me, leaving it about an inch open. I picked up the phone and my voice jumped with impatience. It was from the furniture store and the cat at the other end was putting down some ca-ca about me being overdue on my payments. I tried to assure him I'd take care of it. But he just went into his bag of you'd better, cause we don't want to summons you, and if we have to reclaim it, you'll lose whatever you paid out already.

"Diggit, mister, why the hell you gotta jump so stink about your lousy TV. I said I'd take care of catching up. Damn, man, just by me getting it on credit alone you're getting twice what the bleep-tube's worth."

"You'll send in the payments?"

"Yeah, that's what I said." I slammed the phone down thinking on how great it is to be able to buy for casho.

I walked back into the room. Chinko and Lil Man were doing exactly what I had left them doing.

"You fellers ready to talk things out?" I asked.

Both nodded their okay.

I leaned against the pool table felt. I decided to sit on it. Chinko sat down in a straight-back chair and tipped it against the wall, while Lil Man sat on the windowsill and began doodling by applying coat upon coat of blue chalk on his cue tip. *Lil Man really digs pool. Maybe he can become like a Willie Hoppe if he wants to.* I quickly tossed that thought out of my mind, wondering why the heck I was thinking about that instead of getting to the serious business called being a peacemaker or something.

"Let's start from scratch, Brothers." I watched them shift uncomfortably, like as if they were very far from digging each other as brothers. "And let's find out what's the catastrophe that went down with both of you that's so damn bad, so bad that it's got you two calling bopping season on between your cliques."

Lil Man let out a long breath. Looking dead at Chinko, he said in a bad street tone, "It's that faggot's trying to impress me on how bad he is by always giving me his Dracula Evil Eye look. Shit, he can't even scare one of them thousand of cucarachas he's got in his house, let alone me."

"Later for that shit, Lil Man. I don't live in a rat and roach reproduction center like you do. I live in the projects, diggit, and talking about faggots . . . Mother jumper, you better check out your undercover faggotty father and your mother, whose . . ."

Lil Man's two hands all of a sudden was holding his pool stick like Roberto Clemente with baddo intentions of batting 500 all over Chinko's head. Chinko flew from his chair and grabbed two pool balls with serious ideas of braining Lil Man with them.

"Time," I screamed. I heard my voice coming in like a whispered roar. Lil Man and Chinko didn't move. We all just stood there frozen, eyeing each other for a baddo long-little up tight while.

I walked towards them casually. I slowly reached out and closed my fingers around Lil Man's pool stick. He tightened up on it. My face didn't show any expression. But he knew I was silently saying, "Gimme the stick." Lil Man held on for a couple of seconds. Then he smiled. Relaxed, he shrugged his shoulders and turned the cue stick loose.

I turned to Chinko and held out my other hand. He put the two pool balls into my hand with an exaggerated care that bordered on sheer sarcasm. I placed them just as carefully on the pool table alongside the cue stick, sat back on the table, and dug the floor for a poco while. I talked to the floor while sensing all the way that they were bad-eyeing each other.

Look, panitas (buddies), with all the put-downs that this messed-up racist system is pouring all over us, tell me what's the sense of us screwing each other up some more?"

"It ain't got nothing to do with no racist shit here," Chinko cried out. "It's just got to do with me and that big mouth over there."

"Your mother's got a big mouth," Lil Man shouted.

I gave a mucho patient look at Lil Man. *Damn*, I thought, *I wish he would keep his big boca shut.* But he didn't.

"And you can tell your people the shit's on, diggit." Like now Chinko's face turned into one big evil eye and his voice sounded pained with anger like somebody was rubbing his behind with number three sandpaper. "Just name the place where it's gonna be at, you pink-ass m.f."

I kept quiet to dig where this communication was heading for. Lil Man went into his role of looking up at the ceiling as if to wipe out Chinko's physical existence.

"No set place, faggot, no set place, where me and my people find you and the rest of your faggots. There's where we'll waste you. So you all better walk in bunches and like sleep in the same bed, diggit?"

"Okay, okay, chevere." Chinko's head slowly nodded up and down. "We go all the way and you can go back and tell the rest of your tit-sucking punks that we gonna play knock-knock with each and every one of you till your club is wiped out into past history."

Lil Man looked down from the ceiling and his whole expression was sick tight from an almost insane hatred. "You'll play knock-knock, you'll play knock-knock, you'll play knock-knock." Lil Man sounded like my old man's old broken-down wind-up record player. It was always getting stuck. "You'll play knock-knock," he shouted again.

I got off the pool table, put up my hands shoulders high. Then kneeled and tied my shoelaces. "Look," I said as I got to my feet, "let me run something to both of you nice and easy. Esta bien? I took their bad-vibrating silence to mean it was okay. I looked at Chinko and couldn't stop my voice from coming out loud. "Chinko, what the hell's happening to you? You're talking all this crap about playing knock-knock. Is this where you're at? Man, bopping is bad enough, but playing knock-knock is about as dirty pool as anybody can get. Don't you remember what happened with them two cliques up on 119th Street. What the hell is their names?"

"Tall Crowns and the Blue Demons," Lil Man yelled out.

"Yeah, that's them, remember Chorizo and some of his Tall Crowns went up to one of the Blue Demons' house . . . er . . . I think he went by the name of Yellow Hand and how when his kid brother, who was only about twelve, opened the door, Chorizo shot him. The damn bullet hit his shoulder, but it damn well could've blown away his heart. And like what happened next, uh? Well, one of you guys tell me, or don't you know?"

I felt myself getting up tight inside and made the feeling check out. My voice kept talking on a staccato kick. "Some-body-got-back-at-Chorizo's-by-going-up-to-where-he-lives-in-the-projects-and-ringing-the-doorbell-and-when-an-eye-showed-through-the-peephole-opening, that lunatic somebody rammed a DAMNED ICE PICK INTO IT and, like only some kind of miracle made who was behind that door jerk back enough so that it didn't go maybe into the brain, but not nearly enough to keep from losing an eye. Do any of you bad machos know who was behind that door?"

Chinko and Lil Man nodded a yeah.

"It was Chorizo's tia, his aunt. Not only she got one eye now, but her mind ain't all there from the shock of that maldita experience."

I looked at Chinko for a long while and then let out my anger at him. "And you got the culo to include knock-knock as part of you people calling the shit on, like, if you can't get at each other, you'll just knock on each other's door and whoever opens it—man, woman, child, or beast—is gonna get wasted. Caramba, Chinko, you got a mother, a father, three sisters, and two brothers and you got the lack of heart to stand there and scream that you're gonna play the game of knock-knock. For God's sake, man. The world's outlawed using gas and bacterial warfare cause like the wind could carry that stuff anywhere and some innocent neutral country could get wasted. Man, that stuff was so bad, even the warlover didn't dig it and that's what knock-knock is like. Whew, Chinko."

I slapped my forehead in disgust. "When you opened up your BIG BOCA and let that weak ca-ca come out, didn't you think about your family?" I mentally rested my case, took me a deep breath and let it out slowly, watching Chinko's badlooking face change into an expression of deep thought as his mente was absorbing my words. I could sense him imagining his mother or one of his family getting shot, or an ice pick through their eyes, and diggit, I swear to a mango, I dug him shudder ever so slight while he adjusted his mucho beloved red beret, hooked his thumbs into his pockets, and then stared at the floor. I heard one pool ball gently tapping another. I looked at Lil Man, who, also lost in thought, was knocking the pool balls against each other.

"Fighting's bad enough, amigos, if it's just between armies, but it's mostly the innocent that get chopped up." My voice matched the quietness of the room, and the gentle clacking of pool ball against pool ball. "It's the same with you two. These up tight bad feelings between you don't just hang you both up, it hangs up your boys and . . . your familias."

I stopped for a minute. "Uh, you cats still feel the same towards each other?"

I didn't need no affidavit. Chinko's evil eye jumped jet speed into focus on Lil Man, who back-stared him with a deathly smile that would've made Jack Palance proud of him. I clapped my hands softly a couple of times and said, "Okay, chevere, you both got corazón, right? So how about dealing a fair one just between you two, like nobody else is involved, just you and you? How's that sound?"

Both nodded that it sounded okay.

"And win or lose, all this talk of bopping and knock-knock is game-time."

"You got my word, Piri, but how about him?"

"Mine too." Lil Man stopped rolling the pool balls against each other.

"How many of your boys you're gonna bring so I can bring the same? And I pick the place and time?"

"There ain't going to be nobody's boys along when you two deal and I'm picking the place. Chevere," I said sad-like. "We take the car and go over to Randall's Island. Let's go."

We cut through the office and I saw the other room was jumping with fellers and those that didn't belong to Chinko's clique belonged to Lil Man's and the talking stopped and some kind of waiting grabbed the air. I dug all them caras waiting for some kind of signal from Chinko or Lil Man, gestures signifying asking questions whether the bop was on or not. Both Lil Man and Chinko looked at their boys and smiled appreciative for their loyalty.

"It's just between him and me," Chinko said, adjusting his red beret.

"That's right, it's gonna be a fair one and nobody's coming except Piri and us two."

"Hey, man, that's a drag. Shit, we wanna see you cats taking care of business," someone yelled out.

"Conyo, man, we got a right to be there. Ain't we your boys?"

The thirty or forty requesting voices were putting on mucho protest as we walked on.

"What the hell kind of shit is that?" a diehard voice sneered out.

"See it on the replay. Like this is a closed-circuit fight." I waved to a couple of volunteer workers. Closing the door behind me, I walked between Lil Man and Chinko to the car. I took a couple of deep breaths and dug the clear sky. The stars were doing their number and the moon was taking care of business too.

"I'll sit in the back." Lil Man smiled and then went into a Jack Palance number at Chinko.

"Anywhere you want, chump," Chinko said softly and mean.

I was behind the wheel, but I bet myself a thousand to one, good old chevere panita Chinko has his evil eye a-working one more time. Chinko sat next to me. I threw him a look and, diggit, I was one thousand mental pesos richer.

We drove towards the Triborough Bridge. Lil Man was humming a disguised tune that sounded mucho like "Hearts and Flowers." And every time I checked my rear-view mirror, Chinko's good old evil eye was reflecting itself back at Lil Man.

The bulbs on the Triborough Bridge blurred by and I slowed down and dropped a quarter into a hand without a face. I turned the wheel towards the right and followed the sign to RANDALL'S ISLAND. All of a sudden, I dug that there was no more sounding going on between Chinko and Lil Man.

I cut my eye to Chinko, who was staring straight ahead with his arms crossed. I checked Lil Man. He was looking out the window. I knew this mess didn't have to be. But I'd been to Randall's Island to be this kind of referce before, and as bad as it was to see a couple of chamacos beat up on each other, it was better than an all-out wasting session between two gangs.

I pulled the car into the big field. My eyes were watching out for patrol cars. I'd never run into one, but figured I could run it if any cops showed up.

I jumped out first. The moonlight lit up the whole field. The shadows of trees and bushes and the silence gave one the feeling of being way out in the country instead of just garbage distance from El Barrio. We walked about ten feet from the car. I didn't go into a long line of Queensberry rules of fair play. I just grunted, "Square dealing. Remember, win or lose, no bad bopping after. Check?"

They both nodded their cabezas. I pulled back about five feet. "Start dealing," I said. A fight that could have involved a number of thirty or forty was being put on with a party of only two.

Chinko flipped his red beret at me. I plucked it out of the air like some kind of flying saucer. I watched Chinko and Lil Man moving around each other, ducking and whipping out, throwing left jabs and right crosses. Some landing. Others just making soft breezes against a face. There were few sounds except that of cars going over the bridge. An occasional horn honked. The crickets sang their song, too. But the main sounds were of fists smashing.

I dug the faces of both chamacos. There was no bullshit there. It was for real. Lil Man's mouth caught a right and let the world know it as blood flew out from a smashed lip. Lil Man spit gently and dug a left in Chinko's stomach. Chinko momentarily dropped his guard and while doing so he caught about three right and left combinations that melted his knees. He fell into a praying position. Lil Man rushed toward him to finish colding him, but he must have remembered the rules, cause he checked himself and just stood straight. I walked over to Chinko.

"Enough, panita?" I asked gently.

"Nay, nunca. I'm okay. That punko got lucky." He got to his feet and put his evil eye back on. *Lil Man knows his stuff,* I thought as I looked at Chinko's bleeding nose make like a water faucet.

Chinko leaped towards Lil Man, who merely danced away with mucho pretty footwork. Lil Man was getting real confident. I could tell by the way he dropped his hands and did different cute ring numbers that somebody does only if he is damn good. Or damn crazy.

Suddenly, Chinko's right fist blew up against Lil Man's face, and Lil Man fell, sliding on his backside a couple of feet on some dew-wet ground. But soon he bounced up as if his ass had been made out of rubber. Immediately he stopped his game of acting cute. He moved back and kept circling around until his right eye could focus again. He gingerly touched the eye with his closed fist. There was no doubt that in the morning it was gonna look like a balloon. Chinko charged Lil Man. His head lowered on his victim like some bull that had blown his mind. But Lil Man caught Chinko on the side of his jaw with a roundhouse right. Then Chinko dropped on all fours until his elbows gave way. He laid there trying to get up with his mucho corazón. Lil Man was holding his open right hand under his left armpit and the pain on his face said it had paid a price for the victory. Chinko again tried to get up but Lil Man's fists got beau-coup ready again. Then I stepped in. I tapped Lil Man on the shoulder. He nodded. He was the winner. I helped Chinko to his feet and handed him a handkerchief. Lil Man was quietly dabbing the blood on his lip and closing and opening his hurting right hand.

Nothing said for some time. Finally, Chinko looked at Lil Man and nodded, as if to say, "You beat me square business." Then he smiled. But Lil Man didn't smile back.

"Maybe some other time we try again, eh, Lil Man?" Chinko said.

Lil Man grinned. "Quien sabe, Chinko? Quien sabe?"

I flipped Chinko's beret to him. I put my arms around him and Lil Man. Then we walked to the car. Lil Man got into the back seat. I dug him say, "Hey, Chinko, sit in the back with me, panita. Let's make like we got some kind of chauffeur, okay?"

We drove back to El Barrio and in between listening to my own personal thoughts, I sometimes would listen to some of their words like, "Diggit, Chinko, when we get back to the block, we'll both say it's a draw."

"Conyo, man, you won fair and chevere."

"I know, papo. Pero it was close, you just lost your head and I got lucky. Like if you hadn't blown your cool, quien sabe? And diggit, we're both presidents and like our boys gotta have respect for us and . . ."

"Yeah, I dig." Chinko said softly like he knew he had lost, but he also knew he had to save face. Now Lil Man was offering him a chance to save face like a peace pipe for friendship. Usually, the victor in any fight would brag his cuchifritos off by low-rating the beaten one into a greasy spot on the sidewalk.

"Okay, Bro. You're square business," Chinko added softly.

"You, too, panin. Hey, you know something? I'm glad like we didn't fall into no bopping."

"Yeah . . . knock-knock would've been a bad mother fucking scene." Chinko sniffed. His nose was still bleeding.

Our car came off the Triborough Bridge. As it did some kinda last thoughts jumped into my mind. *Blessed are the peacemakers,* I said to myself, *cause they got a rough way to row.*

32

Chiquito crucified

About a week later I bumped into Chiquito. His eyes were full of tears.

"Hey, panin, que tu pasa?"

"They're trying to get me busted," he cried. His voice shook with an insecurity that should never have been part of a fourteen-year-old Puerto Rican called Chiquito.

"Hey, panin, it ain't that bad, is it? Come on, run it to me nice and easy, baby." I did my best to smile some kind of assurance. Hell, there ain't nothing worse than tears on the face of a kid.

"Just because I cursed," he sniffed. "Just because I cursed that guy, what's his name, Jerry Steele . . ."

"Yeah," I said, "he's one of the volunteer Christian workers."

"Si, the one that's got yellow hair with the crew cut. He said I wasn't supposed to curse because that's taking the Lord's name in vain. He said that if I can't behave like a Christian, I wasn't going to be part of the club any more." He finally broke down, choking to hold back the tears and sobs. He was trying his best to act like the fourteen-year-old man he thought he should be. What in hell could I do? I extended my arms and hugged him real close.

"You're a man, ain't you?"

"Like I told you, Piri. I cursed and Jerry Steele, he chopped me with other things. Like if I don't do it the way it's supposed to be, then Christ ain't going to be my personal Savior. Like, you know, I tried to explain and he wouldn't understand and then he threw me out. John wants to see me now."

"Anything else?"

"Yeah, I wrote a couple of bad letters and told him I was going to get a gun and come back and kill everybody here. Swear to God I didn't mean it though. I was just so fucking mad. Damn, I didn't kill anybody. I just cursed."

In the Bible it says that Christians are supposed to go to spread the word, but God Almighty, I think they at least should try understanding the people they're spreading the word to. Don't these ivory-tower Christians know anything except their own stick of living? I kept my thoughts to myself. All my face held for Chiquito was a smile. "Okay, let me check it out with John," I said.

I walked into the club with him. "Sit down over there, Chiquito." I made a motion to a chair. I went into John's office. There sat Jerry Steele and a group of others. I didn't notice who they all were. Before I even opened up my mouth, John motioned me into the back room. Immediately, he informed me that Chiquito had threatened the life of a volunteer worker. He let me know about the threatening letters Chiquito had written, too.

"Hey, John, whoa now. I mean, you got all those people out there in the office, and you're going to bring Chiquito up before them. I mean, like the kid just cursed."

"Listen, Piri. You're young in the Lord. I've told you many times, you still lack discipline." John continued talking. I let him go on. After all the hell I had been through, I wanted hard to believe in the "unity" and "brotherly love" that mucho

Christians were putting forth. A verse from a chorus I had written popped from nowhere into my *mente:*

Savior—Savior, Hold my Hand
Lead me on to Freedom's land
Help me try to understand
That a man's a brother to another man.

Finally, when I thought I had heard enough, I cried out that I thought he was wrong. Chiquito should be left alone. I was trying hard to keep my cool.

John looked at me. With a smile he said, "Your hesitation is understandable, being so young in the Lord. But self-discipline must be entwined with the salvation that only our Lord Jesus Christ can bring us. It will be best for Chiquito."

My mind ran with remembrance of words spoken at a street meeting by a Puerto Rican Evangelist: "A nugget of gold, no matter how big or small has to go through fire to be refined and worked on by a master craftsman in order to become a fine work of art . . ." I was still adamant in my belief that Chiquito was right in his feeling. At the same time, I was torn between John's words of discipline and the love that Jesus Christ had expounded.

"Remember, Piri, just because a father castigates his children, it does not mean he does not love them."

"You think this discipline will help Chiquito, John?"

"I do, sincerely," he said.

I nodded and walked back into the office, thinking *One more time.*

The meeting with Chiquito was like a court trial. Before I walked in John had told me I had to be strong. I allowed this man to eat up my mind. Chiquito sat in front of the desk of the volunteer Christian workers, and I began to mouth words that were alien to my heart.

"Chiquito," I roared at him. "You come into the club and you say you're going to kill one of the social workers, and you write filthy letters."

Chiquito lowered his head. I reached out and took his face between my hands, "Look at me," I said. "I'm talking to you. I'm not a dog."

My insides were torn to hell before the beautiful reality that this kid was. Looking into Chiquito's reddened eyes, I asked myself if Christianity was a legend or a reality.

John commanded Chiquito to come to him.

I heard Chiquito try very hard to say, "I'm sorry." And he said it again, "I'm sorry."

"You're sorry," roared out John. "You're sorry. The Lord is good. You're on your way to jail. Don't you believe in God?"

And Chiquito cried out, "Sometimes I got no place to sleep, so I go to sleep on the roof and I cry and I pray to God and he don't hear me . . . He ain't worth a damn."

Dios Mio. I was trying very hard to keep from puking up. Is this what Chiquito is all about? Isn't Christianity entwined with love and mercy and understanding?

But like maybe I was too young to know the essence of being a true Christian. Like I thought the true price of being a Christian was to be thrown to some kind of lions or to be burnt alive at the stake. But caramba, doesn't a true Christian forgive the mistakes of a fourteen-year-old Chiquito? I became angry within myself because I felt Christ meant cruel discipline and I started to reach over in anger towards John, but checked myself.

"Chiquito, step out now," John commanded. "We're going to decide what to do."

I watched Chiquito walk out. My heart went with him. He had no place to go. Nobody knew Chiquito's feelings or mine at that moment. Nobody except maybe God and Christ, if they were for real.

"John," I finally cried out. "He's all hung up with frustrations. His grandmother brought him up. He's lived in cellars, parked cars, and rooftops. He needed somebody so badly that he married at thirteen years, a year ago."

John's words snapped back at me.

"That's no excuse for him to threaten the life of a youth worker."

His eyes hit mine. He seemed to be asking, how dare I doubt the words of Christ and what had been written in the Old and New Testaments? Everyone else in the office was so quiet that I could hear the silent tears of Chiquito in the back room.

John Clause ordered that Chiquito be brought back. A young white volunteer Christian worker was about to say something in the kid's defense. But he stopped himself when he saw John's face turning red with anger and distaste. I quietly opened the door and told Chiquito to come in. He came in sort of crushed and sat there. I felt like nowhere.

John said, "Where do you think you're going from here?"

"I guess to jail," Chiquito replied.

"That's right. That's where you're going."

Soon afterward I found myself sitting in John's car. Chiquito between us. John's voice seemed far off to me. My mind was someplace else.

"This is the first time we ever collared a man, ain't that right, Piri?"

I couldn't answer.

I silently looked at John. He looked at me. I knew I believed in the beautiful philosophy of a Jesus Christ. I knew this man claimed to believe in the same Christ.

As John Clause drove off, I was hoping the entire time that God would kill one of us for being a hypocrite. I hoped it wasn't me, because I was only learning the meaning of Christ. We ended up in front of the precinct station. I sat there quietly expecting John to take Chiquito inside. But he said, "You take him in, Piri. I'll see you later." Then he drove off.

I did as he instructed. I talked to the sergeant and told him what had happened.

Once inside, the sergeant left the room for a minute. Chiquito and I looked at each other . . . Fourteen-year-old Chiquito and thirty-two-year-old Piri. We both knew immediately that neither was to blame for the hypocrisy of others.

I left the precinct very quietly, and let my feet take me on some long kind of walking while my mind went on some kind of flying that had mucho to do with John's attitudes. *Diggit, John,* I thought, *you can't handle people's lives like they were wooden puppets. God, no wonder I use to feel uncomfortable everytime I've gone up to your house. Your wife and kids would walk tippy-toes around the house like as if they were afraid to breathe. Diggit, John, like anything you said was law, you roared at them the same way you did at Chiquito. I ain't got no doubts you provide for them mucho good up in that pretty house, but you sure hand them some kind of hardbrand love. Shit, you may rule your house with some way-out iron fist, but here in our Barrio, we're tired of being pressured by all kinds of half-ass white rulers. Diggit, John, I hate your guts and am damn sure you hate mine. But why is it that you haven't fired me, John? Don't tell me. Let me guess. Yeah, it's because you can use me.*

I walked on for mucho blocks. Somebody yelled out some

greeting. I just nodded. I couldn't speak because all that was running through my head was something Chiquito had said. "I got no place to sleep," he had told me. "So I go to sleep on the roof, and I cry . . . and I pray to God and he don't hear me . . . He ain't worth a prayer . . . He ain't worth a damn."

Chiquito was born in the ghetto just like me, and he was trying to learn just like me.

Sometime much later, I ran into Chiquito on 111th Street next to the corner of La Marketa. I was talking with some kids and I heard someone call my name out. It was him. He came across the street, running and yelling to everybody who was there, the people selling aguacates, the people walking by, whoever was there. "Hey, everybody, he's like my father."

We hugged and held on tight.

"Hey, Piri, Children's Court cut me loose. Glad to see me?"

I couldn't help remembering the inquisition he had gone through. Chiquito had been crucified. But now he was resurrected. "You bet I'm glad to see you." I laughed, hugging him tight one more time.

33

You say you're a Christian

Man, I thought as I laid in bed one night, *like mucho times human beings gotta go deep inside themselves and dig among the dark for some kind of light.* This was one of those times for me. Like digging what had gone down with Chiquito made me feel rotten every time I thought about the incident.

The words of Christ were beautiful. But like in the hands of the wrong ones, they could be a devastating spiritual blow to those who wanted to believe.

I was hung up in the middle. I wanted the kids to be helped. The club had the money and means to make that help a reality. But was it worth it to take abuse and the feeling of being used? My mind ran it to me in punto analytical thoughts, but my street corazón wasn't buying it. Conyo, if I sold out what I believed in and copped a plea from la verdad, I wasn't only walking a lie-rope with the kids, but I was bullshitting all of us out of our right to dignity and walking tall. My thoughts must have put my body into action cause I heard Nita's sleepy voice.

"Since we went to bed, you've been tossing and turning. Que te pasa?"

"I got things blowing up in my mind."

"It's the club, verdad?" Nita raised herself up and rested

her face on her elbow. Her face had a deep thoughtful frown. I couldn't help digging the moonlight shining on her. It gave her face some kind of silver glow. "It's John, isn't it?"

"That's about the size of it, Nita. John's got all his Scriptures down pat but he doesn't have the understanding of what we're all about."

"Why don't you quit, negrito? I'm not blind, honey. I see you coming home at all hours knocked out and it's not from working with los muchachas, it's from trying to cope with John's lack of understanding. Listen, honnee, if you ask me, that man is out for himself."

"I'm only trying to give him the benefit of the doubt," I mumbled.

"You're not Cristo, Piri, and you're not a fool. You know where he's at. I know that you don't want to quit because you want to be with the kids. Tell him to go to hell and find someplace else to work from with them."

I turned over and closed my eyes. "Let me think it over, Nita. It's like real deep with me."

"I know, negrito, pero, por favor, don't let it burn you up inside."

I felt her soft kiss on my shoulder and went my way into some kind of sleep, thinking up a breeze. *"Hey, Chiquito, never again, papito."*

It became harder and harder to disguise the bad feeling between John and me. We each knew where the other was at, but like my face always stayed cara palo and didn't let it show.

I walked into the office one afternoon dripping wet from some welcomed rainstorm that was washing the Barrio outside and was introduced to a young cat sitting next to John.

"Piri, this is Lenny Roberts. Remember, I told you some months back about getting somebody else to help us out in the Lord's work?"

I nodded yeah. Quickly I ran my eyes over him. He was dressed in slacks with a herringbone sports jacket and brown and white shoes. His hair was cut GI style—that's real short— and his blue eyes were looking me over curiously. I nodded politely, and his deeply suntanned face made a smile back to me.

"Well, as I told you, he's a minister and his ministry is working with youngsters, and the Lord has put it into his heart to come up from the South to join with us in furthering the Lord's work."

"Ah'm glad to meet you." Lenny's blue eyes shone with friendliness. He got up and shook hands with me. He almost reached up to my five nine, cause I just saw over the top of his brown-haired head. He was built stocky.

"Same here." I returned his courtesy. "Ever been up North before?"

"For short visits. Mah work has been over different parts of the South."

"Ever work with street kids before?"

Lenny's eyes looked at me curiously. I read his face and it said that John had filled him in on me, among the least that must of been said was that I was a very undisciplined Christian.

Lenny glanced at John and back at me and softly said, "Wal . . . kids are kids, aren't they?"

"Depends whose kids you're talking about. If you're talking about working with white kids in the South or . . ."

"Oh." Lenny laughed. "Ah see youh point. No. I've worked with colored children also."

"How about Puerto Ricans?" I asked.

"No, but Ah've worked with Mexican kids."

I just nodded my head. "Well, one sure thing is that we need workers who will go all out to understand what the kids are all about."

"That's where you come in, Piri." I looked at John. "Introduce Lenny to all the kids, their families. Show him the ropes, his help will be invaluable and it will take some of the weight off your shoulders."

"Okay." I smiled and walked out of the office, but not before I caught John and Lenny giving each other some kind of patient glances. *Diggit,* I thought, *I know I ain't thin-skinned and I'm not jumping into no kind of hasty conclusion, pero, but I'm getting bad vibrations from this scene. I'll just be cool and check him out.*

As the time went by I kept checking out his attitudes. His way of talking to white kids was mucho diffcrent from that of talking to the Puerto Rican or black kids. He was relaxed with the white kids, but ever so slightly reserved with the others. If he caught me looking at him, he'd attempt to be even stevens with all the kids. And these happenings weren't just outta my own mind. The kids, who were super-tuned to sincerity, were dropping gentle hints to me about Lenny's attitude.

"You think that cat's for real?" Lil Man asked me.

"Why you asking?"

"Cause most of the guys feel uneasy with him. I don't want you to take this a bad way, Piri, cause you're with the club, but it's like the same feeling we get with John. Like he's up there and we're suppose to be down here."

"Time will tell, papo, let it ride. Cat may just be nervous being new here and trying to find his bearings."

"Yeah, that could be it." Lil Man looked questioningly at me while his face told me he thought otherwise.

It wasn't long before me and Lenny had a run-in. He complained to John that I wasn't taking him with me as much as I was suppose to. John later hit on me about it.

"Look, John, if Lenny got anything to say about what's happening, let him come to me. We'll get it straightened out. I'll talk to him."

"Okay, buddy, it's just that he's anxious to get into the feel of things. I'm depending on you to break him in."

I nodded. Afterward I approached Lenny in the gym.

"I'd like to talk to you, man."

"Gladly," he said.

"First of all, if you ever got something on your mind that concerns me, check it out with me. Like it's kind of weak to run to John so he can deliver me your feelings." I did my best to speak without anger. "Secondly, I can introduce you to everybody I know in El Barrio. But that's only an introduction. You got to earn your own way into being accepted."

"I don't understand what you mean. *I've got to earn my way into being accepted.* I've come here to help these people. Nobody forced me to commit myself to the work that's to be done here."

"That's the trouble, Lenny, with muchos like you who come to El Barrio with their great, liberal willingness to help. They come here gung-ho as groovy soldiers of Christ, armed with mucho acceptance of us and popped-eyed with the burning zeal to spread God's word among us. Then like they totally forget that everybody—don't matter who you are—has to *earn* acceptance.

"For God sakes, Lenny," I continued. "The Bible and Christianity aren't nothing new here in El Barrio. We got more storefront churches than Carter has liver pills. They may be poor but they're beau-coup sincere. The trouble is with the outside people from nice well-to-do churches who sincerely send people to work among us armed with all the knowledge of the Bible and a complete lack of understanding about what makes us tick. Christ sakes, Lenny, if you come to spread God's words, then just come and let us teach you about our humanity, and don't look on us like something that lived in the Stone Age."

"I don't see how you can talk to me like that." I could tell he was getting up tight.

"I'm just running it to you straight, man to man. Cause like we're equal, ain't we?"

"Of course, but your tone of voice leaves much to be desired."

"Oh hell, feller." My voice was getting stronger. "You better learn that we talk pretty frank and pretty strong in these streets and if you're expecting everybody's gonna 'sir' you to death, forget it. If you're respected, it's because you've earned it. If you're for real, it'll come through, but if you're just trying to store up points in heaven, forget it. We know what life's all about, like from bigotry to balling." I dug Lenny's facial muscles tighten up. He was boiling inside, but I didn't let up.

"You're a Christian, right, Lenny?"

He just stared at me.

"Well, I'm gonna ask you a question. Being a believer, you know that God will dig it if you're lying. Uh . . . are you prejudiced against non-white people?"

Lenny's face flickered just a little bit. I stood and waited for his answer and he let it out a little slow, but clear.

"Ah do have my prejudices . . . but being a Christian, I seek to overcome them."

"Without you saying it, the kids notice it and, Lenny, our kids don't need nobody with bigoted hearts and minds to pile more weight on them. You've dug that I don't particularly like you, and you're mucho right. You say you're a Christian and I say you're nothing but a hypocrite." And there's a lot like you, man.

Lenny's face got more up tight.

"You dare say that to me? To cast aspersions on my sincerity as a Christian?"

"Yeah, feller. I dare that and more if need be."

"You're the one who's not a Christian."

"You could be right, man. You could be right."

I walked away. As I did, I wondered how long it would take the message to get to John.

I never heard about it from John, but Lenny, from that time on, happened only to be where I wasn't.

34

Hung on a ghetto cross

Flack started coming in from John on how the documentary film was being shot. I knew something was wrong when I saw Carl coming in day in and day out with a frown on his face.

"Que pasa, Carl?" I said one morning, trying to find out what was bugging him. "You run out of film in the middle of something good?"

"Oh, hi, Piri. No, nothing like that," he answered.

"Let it out, Carl. Some of the fellers giving you a bad tiempo?"

"No. Hell no. But what is it with John? He seems to feel that we're not going about the film right."

"And . . ." I helped out.

"Well, he wants more of the club filmed."

"Ain't that happening?" I checked out Carl's face.

"He wants more of inside the clubhouse and we feel that where the thing's happening is out on the streets."

"That's for sure," I agreed.

Carl grinned. "We told him as much and that we'd be glad to film whatever he felt was relevant inside the club, but we felt that outside with you and the fellers was where it had to be done."

"And . . ." I checked a broken fingernail.

"He said he was the club and not you."

All of a sudden it started to roll and boil inside of me. A feeling of anger and disgust. I felt all my blood corpuscles speed up to ninety miles an hour.

"What do you think, Piri?" Carl didn't notice my catching fire inside.

"I think, Carl, that you're the people making the film. I think you gotta work it out with John and . . ." My voice trailed off and said something in a "fuck it all" whisper.

"I didn't catch what you said, Piri?"

"I just said, 'Later for John, like I quit.'"

"Sorry, didn't hear you again," Carl said.

I checked my voice and it was still whispering almost without sound.

"Nothing, Carl, you'd better take the filming up with John. See you around."

I found myself cutting out of the club and sitting on the stoop in front of my house. Lost in some sorry-ass hurting mean thoughts. Mierda, enough, I've had it, had it, had it.

"Hi, Piri."

I looked up at a girl-woman's voice and dug Rachel, Nita's cousin who had come in from Puerto Rico just a short few months ago.

"Hi, Rachel, como esta nina?" (How are you girl?)

"Bien, Piri, and Nita?"

"Okay, she's upstairs."

"I speek her in telephone," she said, very proud of her English.

"Thatta girl, Rachel, hang in there and you'll be socking the Engleesh all over the Barrio."

Rachel blushed kind of pleased and kind of embarrassed.

I smiled an encouragement at her brave attempt at el American language.

"Hasta luego, Piri."

"Hasta luego, Rachel. Uh . . . tell Nita I'll be up in a while, por favor." I grinned at her blushing.

She smiled and went by me like some sort of perfumed breeze found only in Puerto Rico.

I don't know how long I sat there watching my Barrio's people blur by and thinking hot thoughts of *"I've had it . . . I've had it . . . I've had it . . . . Dammit to hell, I've had it . . ."* Wow, like I went into myself and when my eyes focused on the street scenes again the sun had gone away and some kind of purplish evening light was taking over, giving the stars a chance to pretty up the Barrio with their shining eyes. I smelled a Puerto Rican perfume and looked up at Rachel.

"Bueno, Piri. Nita wan know eef you going sleep on steps?"

I matched her laughter. "No, Rachel, I'm going up soon. Uh . . . you want me to walk you home?"

"No, gracias. I haft to learn how to walking alone."

"Chevere, Rachel. Buenas noches. Give my regard to Carmela, OK?"

"Bien, Piri, adios."

"Adios, Rachel." I watched her nineteen years of life make its way up the block. I thought something gentle like they sure grow beautiful flowers in Puerto Rico.

I dusted my backside free of stoop dust and made some angry steps.

When I heard the elevator was broken, I calmly climbed up my mucho stairs and with every step I psyched my mind not to let Nita know by any tone or expression how up tight I was feeling. Y caramba, by the time I copped the fourteenth floor I had my face looking like I'd won the whole sixty pieces of a Puerto Rican lottery. But oh, man, como—like all that psyching up my mind went down by the wayside cause no sooner did my key let me step into our apartment than Nita cut through my Halloween mask.

"You quit, eh? Bueno, Piri, it's about time."

"You can tell, eh?" I asked solemnly.

"Si," she said. "I heard you were sitting downstairs with fire coming out of your eyes. Want to eat?"

"Later, corazón." I flopped on the couch and quickly removed my shoes. I refused to acknowledge Nita's dirty look. I whiled away some time by staring at some mosca (fly) doing his thing upside down on the ceiling, either because he had sticky feet or hadn't read Newton's words about some kind of gravity or . . . ahh . . . didn't have the sense to know it couldn't walk upside down. I dug another fly make its way upside down and start some kind of communication with the other fly.

"Piri?"

"Uh?" I looked over at Nita.

"Did you tell John you quit?"

"No, not yet."

"What are you waiting for?"

"Cool it, Nita, it is just today I found out I quit for real. Caramba, Nita. So much can be done for the young ones, what a shame that some of those who have the power to do good are so full of their own personal ego bullshit. Oye, Nita," I said pointing to the ceiling. "Do you think those flies up there are more humane than us?"

Nita's voice got mucho concern. "What do flies have to do with what we're talking—are you loco?"

I smiled at Nita to assure her that I was lucid and sane. I now watched the moscas with a philosophical interest.

"Nita? Flies don't lie about what they are. They have always made me shudder in disgust along with los ratones y cucarachas. But like they have never lied about what they are. They are moscas, rat-ones, y cucarachas. At least they ain't hypocrites."

"Negrito, negrito. You feel betrayed."

"Not just me, bon-bon. All of us, Nita." I didn't feel like talking. I just wished we could just be making love, without hassles, without hypocrisy, without . . . *corazón*. I took my eyes off the flies.

"Ayee, Piri, you have not lost your faith, have you?" I noticed now that the flies had cut out.

I turned to Nita and gently told her, "No, I ain't lost my faith, chica. I've just grown up un poco wiser, like that Solomon cat in my own calle way."

I got up off the couch and felt kind of ashamed, cause my most beautiful son Ricky was smiling at me from the bedroom. My being so wrapped up in baddo things had made me forget my beautiful youngblood. I watched him stumbling to make his way towards me. I covered forty miles in four or five steps and grabbed him before he fell. I hugged my chevere child of this earth con mucho gentleness and joyfully I accepted his wet kisses and searching love.

"For you, pa-pee," he communicated.

"Thanks, papito," I said as he handed me some chewed-up banged-up beautiful toy he loved. He stood my hugging for a little while and then pushed himself away. I dug the sign and put him down with a light love smack on his culito and dug him make his way back to his bedroom with some kind of haste that looked like he was worried his other toys were feeling ignored.

I stood there for a while watching him make his getaway and with half a thoughtful smile.

Nita looked at me and put her hands out in a gesture and said, "Well, what are you going to do about it?" I was so wrapped up in thoughts that I didn't pay attention to her question. My eyes dug her cut into the kitchen and like it wasn't till I heard her washing dishes and setting them down real hard that her question dawned on me.

I jumped on the phone and almost drove my forefinger into Bell Telephone's ear and dialed with such a damn urgency that seven numbers won some kind of Nobel prize for sheer mother-loving speed.

"John," I said when the phone at the other end had been picked up, "this is Piri."

"Hi, buddy."

Buddy, shit!! I thought. "Por favor, John, don't call me buddy. Diggit!! I quit. Like you ain't for real."

"Let's talk this over, Piri. Remember us talking about you becoming an Assistant Director?"

I jumped back on his voice, that was coming on weak with its great white father condescending tone. "Look, there ain't no more to be said. Like I'm a human being, John. I ain't no broom in a corner . . . and like, John, I've been bending in all kinds of shapes on account of the kids needing all the help they can get."

"Look, if you're angry about something, we can talk it out. Haven't we always been able to reason things out?"

"John," I cried, putting all kinds of brakes on my voice cause it was jumping into all kinds of different angry octaves. "I didn't mind you copping credit every time I turned in some guns. I even accepted a lot of the other crap you were putting down as long it helped the kids. But it's game time now . . . Pure and simple, I QUIT."

"You never had it so good, Piri." John's voice lost its cool.

"Well, I'm gonna have it better, man. I QUIT."

"If you quit, I'll see to it you never work around this area again."

Oh Wow, I couldn't believe my ears. "Diggit, John." I felt hot tears jump into my eyes. "I was born around here. I live around here and this is still gonna be my Barrio long after you're gone."

My angry eyes focused on Nita. Finally, I just crashed the phone into its cradle.

I sat there shaking with a hot and cold shivering anger. Some five minutes passed. Then the phone rang again. I picked it up and dug John's voice.

"You can't talk to me like that."

"I just did, didn't I?"

"Look, Piri, let's talk this over. I called Captain Donaldson and told him how you felt. He suggested we three get together."

"It's not going to change nothing, John." I was regaining my cool.

"You're certainly not afraid to sit with us and discuss this, are you?"

I smiled at his dime store psychology. "You know better than that."

"Fine, how about meeting up at his office or at mine?"

"How about us meeting on my turf, like . . . I'd feel more comfortable in friendly surroundings."

"Okay, buddy, name the place."

I winced at his hypocritical "buddy." "We'll meet at Rev-

erend Hernandez' church. You know the one. Tomorrow at
noon."

"See you then, buddy."

I hung up slowly. Then I dialed Reverend Hernandez and
gave him the rundown.

The church looked strange as I walked in. It seemed
lonely because there was no congregation there. Reverend
Hernandez sat in the front pew.

"Hi, Chaplain."

"Hola, Piri. Como esta?"

"Still struggling." We made small talk and that broke off
when I heard approaching footsteps. I watched John and
Captain Donaldson come up to us. They went through the
courtesies, cheerfully greeting Reverend Hernandez and me.
I sat down on the upraised platform in front of the pulpit
and waited silently.

"John's told me about the differences between you." I nodded at Captain Donaldson.

"There's good work being done with the kids and there has
to be an atmosphere of discipline."

I nodded and just listened. I barely heard John's side of
it. I almost knew it by heart. Reverend Hernandez was quietly
listening. I looked at Captain Donaldson and simply said,
"I Quit, pure and simple. I quit."

Captain Donaldson said something that bounced inside my
head like a cracked liberty bell. "Piri, listen, you got a great
opportunity to do an important work for the Lord. After
all, John has a great deal of interest in you and you've got
to be appreciative. After all, he picked you up out of the
gutter and . . ."

My mouth dropped open with astonishment.

"What did you say, Captain? That John picked me out of the gutter? Maybe that would be true some long years ago when I was all hung up on a drug ride. But when I met John, I was walking tall, clean, a good job and all my dignity. That's some kind of mentality, Captain." I shook my head from side to side. "Out of the gutter, out of the gutter. Wow, hey if anybody's gonna take credit for picking me out of any kind of gutter, let's give it to the good-o Lord and some co-operation on my side."

"Well, what I meant was that . . ." Captain Donaldson's eyes were hung up on mine digging him in pure amazement.

"With your permission," Reverend Hernandez broke in. "Piri is right. Although I do not like this term of gutter, he was out of the gutter long before he was set free. I know Piri better than you two gentlemen, and when you met him, he had dignity and knew how to care and how to love. With your permission, your terminology is very wrong, Captain."

John stared at me and Captain Donaldson shook his head.

"Then, Piri, you have done what you feel is right," Reverend Hernandez said softly.

"Well, I guess there's nothing more to be said, except that we'd like you to appear before our Board to let them know your reason for resigning." John's voice sounded like it was repressing anger.

"Fine with me, John. I think they ought to know too."

"I'll let you know."

I nodded and listened while the courtesies of parting were exchanged between the two reverends and Captain Donaldson. I stared up at the wall, digging the painting of a white dove which represented the Holy Ghost.

"Well, Lord's blessing on you, Piri."

I nodded to Captain Donaldson and watched him walk out with John. I couldn't help thinking that the captain had a good rep in the community, but caramba, *outta the gutter*. I must of said it out loud, cause Reverend Hernandez sat down next to me and punched me gentle-like on the shoulder.

"Hey, Piri, remember that piece of twig that became a flute?"

"Yeah." I grinned. "But outta the gutter!"

"Si, but you and I and most especially God knows better. No es asi?" I looked toward the entrance and saw John talking something out with the captain.

I got off the subway and made my way to a tall building. I ran into Dee Bruce.

"Hi, Dee, what you doing here?" I asked.

"John asked me to come to this meeting also." Dee was not acting like Dee.

"Oh." I looked at her dead calm. "You know I quit?"

"Yes, I know." We kept walking. "And you know that everything that's gone down is like the truth, don't you?"

Dee Bruce didn't answer and it was as if some kind of struggle was going on inside of her. We got on the elevator and there was no conversation at all. The door opened and I caught a glimpse of the street below. We were up so high the people down there looked like bed-bugs.

We walked into an outer office. John was there with Lenny.

"Whenever you're ready, John. I'd like to have my say to the Board."

"Well, I'm going in first, so if you please don't mind waiting."

I sat down watching him disappear into another room. I

caught Lenny looking at me. It was a look of "You're going to get put in your place."

"How you been doing, Lenny?"

Lenny wasn't too good at disguising his malo feelings towards me. He glared and remained silent.

"Uh . . . nice day, eh, Lenny?"

Lenny's jaw muscle twitched.

"You think the Giants will win the pennant?" I went on as if oblivious to his mucho hostility. "Ummmm . . . whatta you think?" Then snap. He couldn't contain himself.

"Listen, I have no intention of holding a conversation with you, so if you don't mind . . ."

"Of course not, Lenny. I just wanted to check out for myself if I was right about you and like, yep . . . I was all the way."

I turned off to what was going on and didn't even notice if Lenny went into the other room or if Dee Bruce split there too. Then John came back.

"We've decided to accept your resignation," he said.

"And you're not going to give me a chance to talk, eh?"

"It's not necessary."

John's calm tone of voice camouflaged any anger he might have. So, too, did his most beautiful benign smile.

"It's okay with me. It wouldn've made any difference probably, or maybe it would. Cause this meeting was your idea." I half laughed and half smiled. And for a short while I stared quietly at John, Dee Bruce, and Lenny.

It was all I could do to keep from pouncing on top of them all. But I held back. It only would've meant good publicity for John and Company.

"Mierdas," I snorted. I quickly turned my back to them and crashed out the door.

Even though I wasn't with the club any more, I kept on finishing commitments I had made with the guys. At the same time, I let them know I had quit.

Lil Man was shaking his head from side to side when I ran it down to him and some of his boys.

"Oh man, Piri. Say it ain't so."

"That's the way it is, papo. No sweat. I'm still tight with you all." I got snatches back that John was putting out the word that I had been fired for incompetence and all the other "break the cat down" maneuvers. I just smiled. I knew where I was at . . .

"Don't let it sweat you, fellers. He's just pulling his coat off more and more. See you around . . . Adelante."

I got home with thoughts of getting back my Fink Bakery job. Or even better, I thought of checking out a job with some other organization working with our kids. But I decided to let things ride for a while.

"Hey, I'm home," I called when I got into the apartment. "Hi, Rachel, como esta?"

"Bien, Piri."

"Where's Nita?"

"In the bedroom."

"Chevere." I smiled.

"There's a phone call for you from the film people," Nita told me as I entered the bedroom. "They left a number." She handed me a paper.

"Oh yeah?" I gave Nita a fast kiss and then dialed the number.

"Hi, it's Piri."

"How's it going?" It was Carl. "We heard you quit. Would you be interested in working for us?"

"Why not?"

I didn't know what they wanted me to do, but it was a job. Carl made some kind of offer. I agreed. "Yeah, I'm ready whenever you all are. Okay, Chevere . . . nine A.M."

"Got a job, Nita." I did a dance with a couple of hops and skips.

"See how things work out."

"You bet." I split to take a shower and had some remembering thoughts of some money offer from the film people and how I accepted and John having gotten up tight about it cause he felt I should have let him negotiate. He hadn't liked my telling him I could negotiate for my own self, like I was no kid, not that I didn't appreciate it. But I was grown up and capable of doing my own thinking.

I gobbled down some good comida, watched some TV and then jumped into bed to get me some chevere sleep so I could wake up beau-coup strong and take care of my brand new job. I couldn't sleep all that good, I felt so great.

"Hey, Nita," I yelled from my bed. "I'll be filming, and it still involves our Barrio and even after the film's done Carl said there'll be other projects. Hey, I may learn how to work one of them cameras. Hey, I may turn out to be one of the world's greatest film makers. Whatta you think?"

I heard Nita's laughter. "Aye, get to sleep, cabezón. I think you're loco in the coco."

I rolled over smiling. "Hey, why not? Maybe even cop an Academy Award or something. Hey, Nita, how would you like a six-foot-tall Academy Award in the middle of our living room?"

"I don't hear you. I don't listen to crazy people talking fantasias."

"You got no faith." And closed my eyes in chevere reverie ignoring Nita and Rachel making jokes at my expense.

I learned a lot making that Barrio film. I learned things like sync-sound, working a Nagra recorder, editing, and on and on. One day Carl came by and watched me work on sinking the sound to the filmstrips.

"How's it going?" His voice was funny.

"Pretty good." I looked up. "How's it with you?"

"Not bad, except John's giving us some flack."

"Like what?"

"Like he wants to put a stop to our filming unless we get rid of you."

"That cat sure knows how to hate." I was starting to heat up. "And what else?"

"And nothing. We told him you're working with us and that's that. But don't worry, if he wants to go into litigation, there's lawyers to take care of that."

I nodded and blinked John out of my thoughts as I went back to trying to sync-sound a kid yelling something.

It was about two weeks later. I got a message that Chinko had gotten busted. It was from his mother. I called her. She began rapid-firing in Spanish in between tears about finding some guns and not wanting them in the house.

"Okay, espera, Señora Torres. I'll be right there."

I turned to Carl, who was checking out the light with his meter. "Wanna come with me? Chinko got busted for something and his mother found some pieces. Uh . . . guns, and doesn't want them around."

"Let's go," Carl said, and like in nada flat we were standing in Señora Torres' kitchen.

"Where are the guns, Señora?"

"I no wan them. I threw out in garbage." Her tears made her talking pretty hard.

Oh Christ, I thought.

"I know where they are."

I looked at Chinko's little brother. "Okay, Pepito, get them for me."

Pepito went out on the fire escape, swung down the ladder and dropped easily into the backyard. He cut around the corner, out of view. I listened to Señora Torres' tears and got cut loose from that when Pepito climbed back into the room and handed me a paper bag. I looked into it and counted six or seven zip guns that were so well made, they looked like the real thing and could off anybody to death just like the real thing. I didn't notice if they were loaded or not. They probably were.

After listening to Señora Torres, I promised to check what Chinko was busted for and Carl and I checked out. I felt mucho uneasy carrying the weapons.

"Uh . . . Carl, would you mind checking these pieces at your office? Like I'm still on parole and I'm carrying a big bad violation in this bag."

"No sweat, Piri."

I left Carl's office after watching him lock up the pieces and took off for home. I came in quiet and phoned the precinct to check Chinko out.

They told me he was picked up with a .22 caliber and was in the Tombs.

I dialed Señora Torres and told her what I had heard.

I sat there for a while, and then it dawned on me. If Pepito had called the club and told them what had happened, then John already knows I've had the guns and might be thinking that I was going around as a representative of the club. Caramba, let me set him straight.

I dialed his home.

"John, this is Piri."

"Oh yes."

"I got some guns."

"Yes, I know all about it."

"Well, I don't want you getting the idea I'm going around like I'm still with the club. A lot of people don't know I've quit yet. I picked those pieces up on my own responsibility and that's where it's at."

"Well, you had no right to. That's why the club's here."

"Diggit, John. I don't want to split short hairs with you. Them pieces were in circulation. They were in a garbage can. Any kid could have found them and any accident could've happened, and even if I had never worked with the club, I would've done the same thing."

"You're not with the club any more, so you don't have our backing. You're violating the law by having those weapons in your possession." His voice had a lot of innuendos in it.

"I don't have them in my possession. Carl from the film crew locked them up in his office."

"Very well." John's voice was ice cold. "I would appreciate it if you brought them to me tonight. They are our responsibility."

"Oh hell, John." I let out a deep sigh of exasperation. "What's the difference? You want them, you got em, just as long as they're out of some kid's hands. They got enough crap killing without their wasting each other too. I'll be up to your place sometime tonight."

"I'll be home. Bring all of them." His voice sounded like some friendly undertaker.

"I said you'll get them." And I hung up gritting my teeth. I dialed Carl at home and ran it down to him. He listened quietly and said, "Okay, I'll meet you at the office and give them to you. See you."

An hour or so later I was driving towards some kind of suburbs watching beautiful homes built on hills whizzing by. I glanced on the floor of the car and listened to the metal of the pieces clanking against each other every time I hit a bump. Like in no time flat, I pulled into the driveway of John's house.

I picked up the bag, got out of the car, and stood for a while looking at his house. I shrugged my shoulders and cut down the distance to it and made some noise on his door. I waited for it to open, wondering what the diablo I was doing here. My eyes took in the shrubbery, his lawn was landscaped with much care.

John opened the door and I nodded to his "You have them." He was holding the door open and I started to enter and he piled a baddo insult on me. He crowded outside, closing the door behind him, like pure and simple letting me know I wasn't worthy of entering his castle. I moved away from him, looked out into the night and found it helped me to clear my throat of something sticking there and spitting it out on the lawn.

"You have the guns?" He didn't bat an eyelash.

I tossed the bag to him, he opened it, looked into it, closed it, tossed it back to me.

"Why are you giving them back to me for? You said it was the club's responsibility and I brought them to you. Where you at, John?"

"I've already notified the state troopers and also the precinct in New York that you're carrying a bag full of weapons. So I would advise you to turn yourself in with them."

I stood there stunned. Checking out my hearing, like I

couldn't believe what was coming out of his mouth. His face had sheer hate on it. And I knew my face had contorted into some mask of hurting rage.

My voice came out between my teeth, "You know I'm on parole. You know I owe over six years to the state."

"You should have thought of that before you picked them up."

"God dammit to hell." I fought my fingers from opening up that paper bag and pulling out one of them pieces, because I knew that there would be no return once my hand would grip a gun. I swear I could hear my heart talking to me. "You're not a killer, Piri . . . you're not a killer, Piri . . ." I took me a most deep and painful breath and let all my energy of how much I despised him drown him. I ripped myself away from his presence and stumbled half out of my mind with rage towards my car.

"You got it your way up to now, John, but it won't always be like that. People will know where you're at someday." My words just bounced off his door closing behind him.

I sat in the car trying to get my body to stop trembling from my far-out anger. I had to get the blood out of my eyes, so I could see to drive. The baddo feeling finally went away and I roared out of his driveway just feeling like the inside of some deep freeze.

Later I pulled over to a gas station and called Carl. I told him what had gone down. I heard Carl's voice let out an angry, "Why that bloody bastard. That man's got to be psychotic or something . . . Listen, I'll meet you at the precinct and we'll get this bloody mess straightened out."

"No sweat, Carl, I'll see you."

By the time I got there, Carl was waiting. We climbed up

to the detectives' office. Carl motioned for me to follow him
and we went into the men's room.

"Listen, Piri, if worse comes to worse, I was the one who
got the guns. I did lock them up in the office safe, and they
weren't on your person except when he asked you to bring
them to him."

"Okay, Carl." I smiled. "Let's see how it goes in there?
Wow, man, like over six years on that sad-ass cat's jive bust."

"I'll perjure myself, so help me God, Piri."

We walked into the office and there were detectives that
I knew.

"Hey, Piri, what's happening?" It was one called Nick. I
shrugged my shoulders.

"Jesus Christ, what's with this John? Man, like he's out
to get you. He swore out this deposition against you, about
carrying dangerous weapons."

"Yeah, I got some guns out of circulation, like I've done a
whole lot of times before."

Nick shook his head. "Something's got to be wrong with
that guy, cause we know you've been working gut-level with
the kids. Whatta you think about that, Bob?"

The detective sergeant nodded his head. "That's where it's
at. What's gone down between you and him?"

"I just quit and he kinda promised he'd see to it I wouldn't
work around the area any more." I felt a little sick in my
guts from just thinking on the possibility of having to make
that prison scene one more time and I fought down some
natural impulse to split from the police station at a hundred
miles an hour.

"What's the next step, Nick?"

"Well, you gotta appear at this court up in the Bronx."
He handed me a paper. I shoved it into my pocket.

Nick called me over to the side. "Look, if there's any way I can help . . ."

I just nodded okay, said something like, "I'll see you around," and walked out. I had forgotten Carl was with me. I hit the streets.

"When is your appearance due, Piri?"

"Oh . . . let's see." I checked the piece of paper. "It's . . . ah . . . for next week."

Carl copied the time, place, and date. "I'll be there as well as the rest of the film crew."

"Yeah, okay, and thanks a lot for everything."

"No sweat." Carl smiled.

"That's right, no sweat." I said it, but I didn't believe it. I was sick with anger about it.

I didn't tell Nita all that went down, and especially the bad thought of maybe having to go back to prison, but like inside me, I spent a bad week waiting till court day. I mean, like no matter how much I tried to put it out of my mind, I'd wake up in a cold sweat dreaming I was back in that damn horror. *"Man, John,"* I screamed out inside my head. *"You got the heart to do what you're doing and still face God and spout the words from that big Bible you own. Oh diggit, may you fry in glorious hell."*

That week went by dragging like it had on a ball and chain and came that morning I dug myself sitting in court.

I thought on how Nita was home thinking I was only going to have to pay a fine. I kept on thinking that I knew I was gonna blow sky high in trying to smash my way out of that court if it sentenced me back for parole violation. *Man,* I thought, *to do time for doing something right, man, that's wrong.*

I looked around and there was Carl and others of the film crew, and like John was nowhere in sight. Finally, I heard my name called.

"John Peter Thomas."

I like Piri Thomas better, I thought. I made my way up to the judge, digging Carl and the others making some thumb-up gesture.

"Are you known as John Peter Thomas, also as Piri Thomas?"

"I am." I looked right into the judge's face. I heard something read and something asked about the guns.

"And I took them out of circulation," I said, or something to that effect, but whatever was said, it was all going down in some kind of records by a court stenographer a mile a moment.

I stood there as comfortable as I could, looking at the judge and, like feeling some kind of funny calm inside me. The judge rustled the paper before him. He read and very matter-of-factly rose up from his bench and leaned over with his outstretched arm to shake my hand. My hand automatically went out to meet his.

I wondered if I was in the wrong court.

"Mr. Thomas, please let the court record note this. This Court wishes to thank you for the fine civic duty you are performing. Carry on the good work."

I swear to the hole in my one shoe, I just nodded and said something like chevere to the judge and walked out of that court, mucho tall and knowing deep inside me that for a short while there, I had hung between walking out of that court with my pride and dignity as a man intact and being sent back to prison for some more years of dehumanization. And I knew that not everybody, except those like me, could ever fully understand the agony of what had gone down for me these last seven days. *"You lost, John, you lost and people will find you out for what you are. Do you understand that? Cause you ain't nada but a BLANK . . . DIGGIT."*

I cut down some streets and ran into some of the young bloods. "Oye, panin. We heard what the motherless faggot tried to put down on you."

"Hey, papo, spare me the anger. I got enough of my own against that Blank."

"Nay, man." I heard a young justified voice. "We'll bomb that cat. Shit, man, like you're our people and he's a lying cocksucker in our land."

"Time, fellers, and spread the word around. You want to make a martyr out of that cat?! Sure, hit on him, and sincere people are gonna idolize him like some kind of second Christ. Later. Let him alone. Till the time comes where he can be shown all over, just where he's at. We don't want to be the cause of putting someone like him up as some kind of object to be worshiped. Hey, we know what good is all about. What love is all about. You cats don't think I feel as bad as you? Let it wait till the time is right. So that not just a couple guys know, like so everybody will know . . . diggit."

"That motherfucker," Lil Man said. "We could throw some kind of gasoline bomba."

I didn't even look at the sound. I only said, "Don't unless you want to create a bullshit martyr."

"Hey, you fellers. You grow straight, entiendes? And get all that good education and wisdom."

"Conyo, Piri, where you going?"

"I'll be around for a while and if I cut out, it's cause I'm trying to do my bit to take care of chevere business. Take care now and walk tall or not at all. Like don't waste your bad-sounding names on him, he ain't even worth that."

"Okay, Piri, see you around, Brother."

"Chevere, dig yourselves, you . . . and you . . . and you
. . . and all of you."

I walked around some kind of corners and found myself
beating my two fists on some wooden fence that had some
kind of Ringling Brothers Circus announcement glued to
it. The pain messed up my knuckles, but cleared my mind to
the thought, *Why make a hero out of a people's enemy? Man,
I'm sorry for all the people all over the country that believe
in that cat.*

I let my feet check me home. I pointed a finger skyward.
"WHEW!!" I said out loud. "Hey, my madre always believed
in somebody up there that was mucho Godlike and divine.
You better check out what's happening down here, Man,
cause some of these people that supposed to represent you
are taking us for all-around poorhouse broke, and like that's
the truth . . . nitty-gritty."

I got home and plopped onto the bed.

"How did everything go?" Nita asked.

"I'm here, ain't I?"

Dammit to hell, John, I thought. *What did Momi say to
me a long tiempo ago about 'Beware of false prophets which
come to you in sheep's clothing, but inwardly they are raven-
ing wolves'?*

"Will there be any more trouble, Piri?"

"I don't think so, Nita. I'm here, ain't I?"

"None?" Her voice was kind of soft.

I didn't answer.

"Piri . . . even if you didn't tell me everything, I know
he tried to send you back to prison. The kids talk to me, too,
you know."

"Nita." I looked at her full-faced. "I wanted to kill him.

When I took the guns to him that night and he pulled that low blow on me, I wanted to kill him."

Nita smiled. "You didn't, negrito, because you are not a savage animal."

"I think it's better that people like him can be seen by everybody in their true darkness."

"Buenas noches, corazón."

"Buenas noches, Nita." I fell asleep with my eyes wide open staring at a wall.

35

You dug slavery, Saint Paul

Por la Cruz (by the cross), I felt mucho angry. Man, like bad thoughts were really eating up my mind even though three weeks had passed since that courtroom scene. Imagine that cat trying to send me back to prison for six or seven years on a jive tip.

I sat in church. One third of me listened to Reverend Hernandez' sermon. Another third watched Nita with Ricky at her side, and the last third observed a middle-aged woman sitting by Ricky. I recognized her as a member of the congregation. She was very fair with straight black shiny hair, something like the picture of ladies of Spain you see on calendars. Her fingers were playing with Ricky's hair and her eyes were intently observing it. She was just checking Ricky's hair texture to see if it were like Nita's or mine.

I leaned over.

"Hermanita?"

She almost blushed at having been caught. Like she had been so obvious.

"It's half and half," I said.

"What do you mean?" she stammered.

"Its texture is half its mother's and half mine."

The hermanita cast her eyes down and pressed her lips in prayer. Nita just smiled and gave me a wink. I gave an exaggerated shrug and gave my wholehearted attention to the sermon. I caught the hermanita looking at me out of the corner of her eye after the service. I smiled most Christian-like and shook her hand in Christian greeting.

"God bless you, Hermanita."

"God bless you, Hermano Piri."

I smiled gently and let my eyes tell her I would rip her apart verbally the next time I caught her checking Ricky's hair like he was some kind of curiosity. Wow, people are something. They even measure your humanity by the quality of your hair.

"Aren't you going to stay for choir practice, Piri?"

I turned around and it was Carmela, Nita's sister.

"Si, but I'm not going to sing. I don't feel like it."

"Sore throat?"

"Naw, just really not in the mood."

"Well, we'll miss your bass voice."

"No kidding." I let my voice drop deep into my socks.

Carmela laughed. "Well, just sit there and memorize your part. Listen to Victor and next choir practice you won't be behind."

"Listen to Victor." I grinned. "If I do, I'm in trouble. Man, Carmela, half the time he's flat off key and the other half he's singing another song."

"Don't be naughty, Piri." Carmela playfully punched me on the arm.

"Only kidding. You know Victor is to the choir what Caruso was to the world."

"Caruso?"

"Si, he used to sing opera."

"Oh." Carmela shrugged as if what I had just said was no big thing.

"I'm taking Ricky home. He's hungry." Nita signaled me from the back. I nodded by-by at them both and sat down to listen to the choir. I felt a tap on my shoulder and it was Victor.

"Como esta, Caruso?" I smiled. "Jesus, but you do sing flat."

"You're just jealous of my talents, dear Brother in Christ." We smiled at each other and shook hands.

The choir began to get together on "El Lirio de Valle," Lily of the Valley, and my mind faded from listening to the choir's valiant efforts to get together on their right keys to the hermanita's intrusion into Ricky's hair. It was a sharp reminder of what had happened in a Christian summer camp where we had taken our club kids to get them out of the city.

. . . My mind continued to take a trip back, again to the Christian camp in the mountains. Some of our kids were involved in Bible discussion with some white kids. They had their Bibles out and it looked like a fierce thing was going down. I walked up close, thinking, *Hey that's chevere. Kids are getting together and checking out the Good-o Book.*

"Hey, Piri, tell these people they're wrong." Lil Man's face was much in anger.

"Que pasa?" I asked.

"They're trying to say that in the Bible it says that it's all right for people to be slaves. Like it's okay to be slaves to your masters if they're Christians."

"Let me check it out," I said to Lil Lena, who handed me her Bible, like I didn't know all the Bible.

I read from I Timothy 6:1–2, from the Revised Standard Version, a letter from Paul to Timothy:

Let all who are under the yoke of slavery regard the master

as worthy of all honor so that the name of God and the teachings may not be defamed.

Those who have believing masters must not be disrespected on the ground that they are brethren. Rather, they must serve all the better since those who benefit by their service are believers and beloved.

I looked at the white kids wondering what part of the country they were from. They were kind of uncomfortable at my looking and one of them said, "We don't believe it. It's, eh . . . just that it's written in the Bible by Paul in a letter to Timothy.

Wow, I yelled inside my head. *Diggit, Paul, you dug slavery. Instead of a real Christian putting slavery down, you're telling people to dig their slavery and like it all the better because their masters are Christians. Paulie, baby, you should have stayed under the name of Saul instead of taking a Christian alias.*

"What do you think about that, Piri?" Lil Man broke in.

"I think that cat was wrong. Damn wrong, and like maybe slavery was accepted two thousand years ago and up to recently but not like now. Not today. At least it's not accepted by us who were subject to that crap in the past."

"But wow," Lil Lena said. "Imagine Paul saying something like that."

Yeah, I thought, *another phony Christian.*

I said, "Like I read that Paul had some kind of thorn in his side. Like something was always bothering him. Maybe it was his conscience on knowing he was for slavery. Or maybe for not believing in slavery and being too chicken to come out and condemn it. Like that's what's wrong with mucho things, cop outs like Paul and others."

"We don't—at least I don't believe in slavery," a girl earnestly cried out. I looked at the young white Christian girl with brown hair and hazel eyes.

"Good for you, kid, cause we don't believe in it either. And like I look at it, not only Christians, but also some of the Scriptures are in mucho need of an overhaul. Like many things that related to two thousand years ago are out of step with today. Like we ain't slaves no more. It doesn't relate to us. Diggit?"

"Better believe it don't," snarled Lil Man.

Christ, I thought as I walked away, *imagine cop out Paul writing that people, if they're slaves, should accept their slavery if their masters are believers and beloved. Caramba, them kind of Christians are believers out of Hell and beloved by the devil himself . . .*

I came back to now time in our Barrio church on 118th Street and Carmela was giving her last flats, A minors, G notes. Everybody started taking off. Soon I split too. Walking home, I thought of how I had stopped my car for a red light a couple of days back and dug John showing some strangers to El Barrio around. I stared at him and his eyes caught mine. I could tell my surprise appearance startled him. I just smiled what I figured was a Christ-like smile to a Judas-like cat.

36

Walk tall or not at all

Nita didn't say anything at first when I began to put up excuses for not going to church as regularly as I had been
going . . . but when I was only going like once or twice a
month and sometimes not even staying for the whole service,
she finally couldn't hold back.

She was getting ready for Saturday night's service, and like
this was one of them special services where four or five
churches got together in a spirit of brotherhood. I dug her
eyes were burning into me as I moved around the kitchen
making a sandwich. I made believe I didn't notice and
walked by her into the living room and sat down in front
of the TV, kicking off my slippers nonchalantly as I clicked
through a couple of channels until I hit an old John Wayne
movie and dug John Wayne just as he shot the hell out of
six or seven Indians. I couldn't help thinking if the West
would've had one more John Wayne there wouldn't have
been a little old Indian left around today.

"Piri," Nita said casual-like.

"Yeah, honey?" I answered without looking up. I knew
what was coming.

"Tonight's a special night at church."

"That's good. Hope it's a great success."

"Aren't you coming?"

"Not tonight. I'm really bushed. Listen, leave Ricky. I'll baby-sit."

"I'd rather you came with me."

I looked up and dug her brushing her hair and went back to clicking channels. I caught a Dracula flick with Bela Lugosi and thought, *Man, that cat's weird.*

"Piri?" she said quietly. "Are you getting cold in the Lord?"

"What do you mean, Nita?" I dug where she was coming from but pretended to be involved with the action on TV.

"I mean you hardly go to church any more and even when you do, you sometimes walk out before the service is over."

I didn't say anything. Nita walked into the bedroom. I could hear her rummaging through the closet looking for a dress to wear. After a while she came out. From the corner of my eye, I dug her and waited for her to say something but she didn't say a word. Calmly she put on her coat, picked up her Bible and started out the door. She looked so alone and sad as she walked out that I couldn't take it any more.

"Okay, Nita honey," I called out. "Let's get it all out."

She had her hand on the door knob.

"Hey, honey, let's talk it out, okay?"

She turned and looked at me with a kind of sadness on her face. She walked back into the living room and sat next to me.

"Honey, I'm not cold with God," I said. "I'm just frozen to death by the hypocrisy. Come here," I said, taking her hand and leading her to the window. Through the nighttime dark below I pointed to the streets.

"Dig, corazón, what's the use of me going to church seven days a week and praying and singing while our Barrio is swinging with all kinds of miseries? No amount of praying and singing is gonna change these ten-thousand-year-old broken-down buildings. God, honey, people can get a hundred pounds of calluses on their knees in going in prayer to the Lord for a way out from all the poverty and exploitation. Diggit, Nita, prayer is good for the soul. Singing to God is good for the spirit. But putting into action the changes that gotta be made is most chevere for the body, and that's where it's at, Nita. We're physical beings also and I personally don't believe in having to go to heaven in order to at last live right."

"John really has messed up your feeling about God, eh, Piri?"

"No, Nita. He's just been instrumental in opening my eyes to where the reality is at. Honey, when we let ourselves be taken over by people like him, we really are helping them to make a worse hell for us."

I looked down at the streets and dug our people intermingling with streetlights and ghetto sounds. At the same time, I heard Nita rustling through the pages of her Bible.

"Can I read you something, negrito?"

"Porque no, honey."

"In I John 4:1 it says, 'Beloved, believe not every spirit, but try the spirits whether they are of God, because many false prophets are gone out into the world.'"

"I've checked that out before, Nita. But like in that same chapter, verse twelve, it's run down like this: 'No man hath seen God at any time. If we love one another, God dwelleth in us, and his love is perfected in us.' Like that's where it's at, Nita. I believe the true salvation of us ghetto people is when we get together in one solid fist and smash down the walls of bullshit hypocrisy. Honey, I've seen more brother- and sisterhood in our nitty-gritty people than in any of those great golden temples. Honey, our people are living in misery and still are kissing a finger with a great diamond ring on it and calling its owner FATHER. We got some missionaries to El Barrio who wheel and deal in souls because they know so many of us want to believe in something other than this hell we're living in."

I felt Nita put her hand on my arm.

"Piri, I understand how you feel. I feel the same as you, but never forget that Dios is with us."

I couldn't help letting out a bitter laugh. "Nita, you say that God is with us? That's what the hell is wrong with so many of us. We cover our eyes with God and become content to live in these damn conditions. I know Christ is great, honey. I just wish he'd come down and walk with us nitty-gritty. Baby, I'm not putting God down. I'm just wondering why the hell we've allowed certain people to put us down. How the hell can I listen to the words of Christ and how He carried the cross? I can't carry no cross and be nailed to it at the same damned time. Wow, honey, don't you dig that to us people of the Barrio the ghetto is our church, and the only way we're gonna make a heaven out of this hell is by getting together. Jesus, honey, ain't I right?"

Nita smiled. I could tell she knew where I was coming from.

"Nita, there ain't no such word as defeat. Diggit. Like them blind churches better get to see where it's really at."

"Porque no, Piri?" Nita said gently. She held my arm tightly with mucho love and corazón. We looked out the window and dug our Barrio below and some kind of light caught Nita and me as we held each other mucho close. The light silhouetted us sharp and clear so that the world couldn't help but see love and dignity. We kissed. Nita moved away from me slowly.

"Where are you going?" I asked softly.

"To church, negrito. I'm late now."

I looked out at the streets below and heard the door quietly close behind me. "We're gonna walk tall or not at all, World," I told myself. Then I smiled and half aloud whispered, "Hey, Jesus Christ, I betcha' there must be a million ghetto crosses out there."

A dialogue with society

No longer can men bend their backs and make a cop out to the
    freedom of dignity.

For all men, and heed me well, bigot, segregationist,
And you hypocritical cop outs who say
"Some of my best friends are Puerto Rican, Blacks, Mexican,
    Asiatics, and our beautiful real American, the American
    Indian."
Don't you know, you pulled your coat long ago.
To say is not to do
But if you do as you are supposed to say
That's the beginning maybe, of an opening of the way.

I speak for myself.
At this moment, my mind rushes back into time,
When I had in my hand a beauty that was truly mine.
I was a little Puerto Rican child running through dark ghetto
    streets,
And capturing the beauty, the right to love that was truly mine.
I let nothing turn my head cause I was too young to know.
I let the sea of hate, of bigotry wash over me
Because Momma, my Momma, had filled my eyes with the
    wondrous city and its pearly gates.

Heed well . . . heed well, World, my America!
Take extra special counsel—

Live by the precepts that this country was supposedly founded
on.
Don't build your golden gardens on the human sufferings of
your fellowman.
Do not give toys to your own children,
Bought at the price of other children that you have sacrificed,
Set not a table spread with good food and comfort
Such as never been seen by the children of your fellow human
being,
Sit not in churches and bend the knee in prayer,
Mouth not the words of Christ, brotherhood, harmony, peace
on earth, good will to all men.
Say not, "I am a good father, I am a good mother, I am a good
husband, I am a good wife, I am a good Christian,"
If you know truly in your heart that you are lying . . . lying.

While you are smiling and living well,
Indian children, Puerto Rican children, Black children, Brown
children, multi-colored children, white children, yellow children . . . children . . . children . . . because of your hypocrisy are dying
Physically, mentally, morally, spiritually, and
Worst of all, secretly . . .

Wow, America!
Wow, America!

You must understand, you, who for many years have named
us a minority,
And have finally found out for yourselves
(And I can understand the fear in your hearts)
The stark reality, the blinding flash of awareness,
The truth as it pours in overwhelming waves,
My God! We are really the minority,
They are together now, there is a unity.

If I could have the power—
I'd wipe out all past memories,
But since I don't, I'll give you a piece of advice,
Cool breeze, cut like a piece of ice, warm as the sun
High as the moon, bright as the stars, deep as the ocean, wide
    as the earth, as unlimited as the universe,
Share, let our children share.
Stop teaching them the petty stinking hates.
Children know love from the git-go, from the very beginning,
And you, you all who are without love, have taught them to hate.
Up to the very ending.

It's now in our hands, bigots, segregationists, power structure,
Multi-multi, multimillion-dollar murderers,
It's now in our hands
Cause we're on our way.
You want to hate? I said, do you want to hate?
We'll put you all together so you can hate yourselves.
Want to make war?
We'll put you all together so you can waste yourselves.

We're tired of you demi-gods, of you tyrants,
We're tired of any human being bred by a mother and father
That leaves his mark on earth a death chant
A mountain of sufferings, a dirge.

It is time for a new bell to toll.
It is time for new trumpets to blare.
It is time for a new language to be heard.
It is time for new friendships to be formed.
For from the very beginning of time unto this time
We should have learned by now, we should have learned how,
We should have learned to love.

My world

My world is a world of creativeness, name it whatever you want,
For my world is our world, and our world is my world
Of no more poverty or human indignity,
No more hot and cold running cockroaches and king-sized rats,
Or horror, hunger, and pain running free.

My world is all the warmth that always comes through free,
My world is no more promises that never come to be,
My world is never scorn, hatred, beatings, and bigotry,
My world is human beings, wailing, feeling freedom and dignity.
My world is really loving.

My eyes have beholden poor peoples march
Whose only hopes have been dashed.
My eyes have beholden humanity smashed
Whose only want was to be free.

But always will my eyes refuse to see,
As long as life lives in me,
The hopes of my people crushed under all the world's adversity.

I do not wish destruction to be our course,
But I do not believe that all my brothers and sisters
Among all the cities and all the mountains
And all the valleys and by the sea,
Can stop short of anything but dignity
No matter what their color may be.

GLOSSARY

adelante	onward
albañil	bricklayer
alma	soul
amigo	friend
amor	love
arroz con gandules	rice with peas
arroz con pollo	rice with chicken
aye, bendito	oh, blessed
bandido	bandit
basura	garbage
bate	bat
bien linda	very pretty
blanco hombre	white man
bodega	store (also used against Puerto Ricans as a derogatory term)
bodeguero	grocery store man
bolos	dollars (slang)
bomba	bomb, bad happening (slang)
borrachon	a drunk
brazos	arms
breaking night	staying up all night (slang)
buena suerte	good luck
buenas noches	good night
bueno	good
buenos dias	good day

cabeza	head
cabeza dura	hardhead
cabezón	stubborn
calle	street
calmete	calm yourself
carajo	hell
caramba	dammit
cara palo	deadpan expression
carcel	jail
chamacos	youngsters
chevere	great, swinging (slang)
comida	food
como con amor	like with love
como esta?	how are you?
concho	dammit
con cuidado	with care
conyo	alluding to a woman's vagina (slang)
contento	content, pleased
corazón	heart
coro	chorus
cosa	thing
cuchifritos	dish made of pig's ears, tongue, blood sausage, green bananas
cuerdas	small rear end
cuerpos bonitos	acres
culito	pretty bodies, coquettes
dinero	money
Dios es amor	God is love
Dios te bendiga	God bless you
dulce	candy

entiende?	do you understand?
el bien Dios	the good God
es un mundo de pecado	in a world of sin
escuchame	listen to me
Escuela Biblica	Sunday School
este Sabado	this Saturday
estufa	stove
exacto	exactly
familia	family
game time	it's over, finished (slang)
garganta	throat
gato	cat
gracias	thank you
gray	a white man (slang)
hasta luego	until later
heba	chick, girl friend (slang)
hermanas y hermanos en Christo	sisters and brothers in Christ
hijo	son
hombre	man
iglesia	church
igual	the same
infierno	hell
inteligente	intelligent
jalumbo	great big kiss (slang)
lo mas	the most
lo mismo	the same

macho	man
madre	mother
mal suerte	bad luck
malo	bad
mañana	tomorrow
mas nunca	never
mavi	herb drink
memorias	memories
mente	mind
mierda	shit
mira	look
muchacha	young woman
muchacho	young man
mucho	much
muerto	dead
mundo	world
muy bien	very good
narizon	big nose
negrito	dark one
novios	sweethearts
nunca	never
ojos	eyes
oye	listen
palabras	words
panin, panita	buddy, partner
payaso	clown
pecalungel	up your ass (Italian)
peito	little fart
pensamiento	thought
pero	but
pistola	gun

pobrecito	poor little one
poco	little
por Dios	for God's sake
por favor	please
porque no?	why not?
presidio	prison
proposito	purpose
punto	point
que chevere	how great
que cosa	such a thing
que dices?	what did you say?
que Dios te bendiga, negrito	may God bless you, little dark one
que pasa?	what's happening?
que te pasa?	what's the matter with you?
quemalo	burn him
queridos	dearest
quien es?	who is it?
quien sabe?	who knows?
racismo	racism
razon	reason
resentimiento	resentment
sangre	blood
short	car (slang)
son hermosa	they are very pretty
tecata	drugs, heroin (slang)
teta	breast
tia	aunt
tiempo	time
tienes hambre?	are you hungry?

togged out	dressed up (slang)
tu sabes	you know
venganza	vengeance
verdad?	is it not so, true?
vieja	old woman
yerba	pot, grass, marijuana
yo tambien	me too
yo te amo	I love you